IMPROVING TEACHING THROUGH OBSERVATION AND FEEDBACK

In response to Race to the Top (RttT), schools nationwide are rapidly overhauling their teacher evaluation processes. Often forced to develop and implement these programs without adequate extra-institutional support or relevant experience, already taxed administrators need accessible and practical resources. *Improving Teaching through Observation and Feedback* brings cutting-edge research and years of practical experience directly to those who need them. In five concise chapters, Alyson L. Lavigne and Thomas L. Good briefly outline the history of RttT and then move quickly and authoritatively to a discussion of best practices. This book is a perfect resource for administrators reworking their processes for new evaluation guidelines.

Alyson L. Lavigne is an Assistant Professor of Curriculum Studies at Roosevelt University in Chicago, Illinois, USA.

Thomas L. Good is a Professor Emeritus of Educational Psychology at the University of Arizona, USA.

IMPROVING TEACHING THROUGH OBSERVATION AND FEEDBACK

Beyond State and Federal Mandates

Alyson L. Lavigne and Thomas L. Good

NEW YORK AND LONDON

First published 2015
by Routledge
711 Third Avenue, New York, NY 10017

and by Routledge
2 Park Square, Milton Park, Abingdon, Oxon, OX14 4RN

Routledge is an imprint of the Taylor & Francis Group, an informa business

© 2015 Taylor & Francis

The right of Alyson L. Lavigne and Thomas L. Good to be identified as authors of this work has been asserted by them in accordance with sections 77 and 78 of the Copyright, Designs and Patents Act 1988.

All rights reserved. No part of this book may be reprinted or reproduced or utilised in any form or by any electronic, mechanical, or other means, now known or hereafter invented, including photocopying and recording, or in any information storage or retrieval system, without permission in writing from the publishers.

Trademark notice: Product or corporate names may be trademarks or registered trademarks, and are used only for identification and explanation without intent to infringe.

Library of Congress Cataloging-in-Publication Data

Lavigne, Alyson Leah.
  Improving teaching through observation and feedback : beyond state and federal mandates / by Alyson L. Lavigne and Thomas L. Good.
      pages cm
  Includes bibliographical references and index.
  1. Observation (Educational method) 2. Teaching.   3. Interaction analysis in education.   I. Good, Thomas L., 1943–   II. Title.
   LB1027.28.L38 2015
   371.102—dc23
   2014034868

ISBN: 978-1-138-02251-5 (hbk)
ISBN: 978-1-138-02253-9 (pbk)
ISBN: 978-1-315-77703-0 (ebk)

Typeset in Bembo
by Apex CoVantage, LLC

CONTENTS

Preface   *vii*
Acknowledgments   *xi*

1. Being a Principal in an Era of High-Stakes Teacher Evaluation   1

2. Race to the Top and Beyond: The Demand for More Classroom Observation   31

3. What Do We Know About Good Teaching?   63

4. Research on Improving Teaching and Student Achievement: The Role of the Principal   103

5. Considerations for Principals When Working with Teachers to Improve Practice   125

Appendices   *145*
Index   *155*

PREFACE

As we write this book, Race to the Top (RttT) is on a race to nowhere. Parts of it are seriously flawed—the overemphasis on value-added models, in particular. And even the potential value of evaluative feedback based on classroom observations is severely limited by a lack of understanding of the complexity of teaching and learning in today's classrooms. We believe that the move towards high-stakes teacher evaluation as inspired by RttT will do little to improve America's schools and in some cases will even be harmful. We believe that a focus on supervisory (as opposed to evaluative) aspects of RttT, including observing and helping teachers, holds the greatest potential for improving teaching and learning. However, even here much work needs to be done to improve principals' understanding of the teacher effectiveness literature, observational instruments, and how to provide effective feedback to teachers.

With those beliefs in mind, one goal of our book is to help administrators and other evaluators understand that the expectations placed upon them for immediate and large achievement are unrealistic. This is not because administrators cannot do the task of teacher evaluation well, but because change is a complex and slow process and one that needs a level of support not possible with the funds provided by RttT. Thus, we provide considerations and advice for principals coping with difficult decisions, including: How should contradictory evidence of effective teaching (e.g., student achievement data, observation data) be interpreted? Which teachers should be observed first? We approach these questions by keeping in mind the practices that may yield the largest gains for teaching and learning.

The rationale for our book emerged in conjunction with a series of events. Our story begins during the summer of 2012, when the authors of this book began writing *Teacher and Student Evaluation: Moving beyond the Failure of School Reform*. We embarked on this book to address the increasing demand that schools, teachers, and students be held accountable on the basis of high-stakes achievement test scores. We, like others, were concerned that these trends were pushing forward despite protests from researchers and teachers. In our first book, we provided a foundation for understanding the instructional nature of reforms and provided knowledge about good teaching that might guide classroom observation.

A few months later, and in collaboration with Ron Marx, Dean of the College of Education (University of Arizona), we began planning a conference held in Tucson, Arizona, in October 2012. Fueled by similar concerns, it was entitled "High-Stakes Teacher Evaluation: High Cost—Big Losses." As RttT was rolling out fast and with still no brake lights in sight, several scholars from the field brought to the forefront a number of concerns related to the use of teacher evaluations for consequential decision making. Particular attention focused on the use, or misuse, of value-added data. The expanded conference papers were later published in a special issue of *Teachers College Record* (Lavigne, Good, & Marx, 2014).

The first conference allowed us the opportunity to hear about practical issues of those grappling with what these new changes would mean for their roles as superintendents, principals, and teachers. The mission of RttT was to create more "rigorous" teacher evaluation models quickly without regard to evidence or implementation. To better understand and respond to the practical issues that were voiced in the first conference, new data were collected (see Lavigne & Chamberlain, 2014) and a second conference was planned. "Using Observational and Student Achievement Data to Improve Teaching" was held in Tucson, Arizona, in January 2014. The intent of the conference was to empower school leaders, who now faced the responsibility of a new teacher evaluation model under RttT, and others with strategies and resources. As materials from the conference became available, more data collection was planned, and we realized (and will illustrate in this book) that many principal preparation programs were not designed to help principals cope with changes that would require them to devote endless hours to teacher supervision and evaluation. Actually, in most cases, principals were spending less than 10% of their time on such tasks.

Both authors have extensive experience in classroom observation research, and across a period of 3 years, our understandings were enhanced by the opportunity to listen to teachers, principals, and superintendents. In particular we came to understand better both what they were trying to do and their frustrations with RttT mandates. We wrote this text out of our concern for those doing evaluations and in our disappointment as professional educators over policy makers' simplistic conception of the problem—a flawed system for evaluating teachers. Our own backgrounds, coupled with an awareness of these concerns, led us to conduct a review of the literature to understand how the process was working (or not). We identify strategies administrators can use to survive and manage modern-day teacher evaluation. We hope these strategies sustain principals in their important work despite RttT.

In Chapter 1, we illustrate that principals take on many roles and tasks in a given day and across a school year. Many administrators feel that their work is becoming more challenging and complex, and many are considering leaving the profession in the near future. We also demonstrate that the push for leaders to spend large amounts of time on observation under RttT is a significant change from practice. And we provide considerations for helping principals if they choose to spend more time in classrooms. We briefly discuss the limits of currently used observation systems and note that principals will have to supplement them.

In Chapter 2, we explain in detail what "more rigorous teacher evaluation" means under RttT. We reveal that the emphasis is primarily on evaluation, giving principals little guidance on providing teachers with feedback that improves instruction. We also take the opportunity to help identify the flaws of RttT while simultaneously emphasizing the value in focusing on instruction—a void that is not currently filled by RttT.

In Chapter 3, we demonstrate that knowledge about teacher expectations and students as social beings can help principals provide teachers with feedback that goes above and beyond current standard observation instruments that purport to capture effective teaching. Here we provide a comprehensive summary of what is known about teaching that influences students' achievement positively.

In Chapter 4, we focus more closely on the principal's task at hand—observing teachers and providing feedback. We discuss what is known about principal effects, particularly how instructional leadership explains student achievement outcomes. We then discuss one aspect of instructional leadership—teacher observation and feedback. We provide readers with a thorough review of what is known about teacher change and feedback to supplement the fledgling literature that describes characteristics of effective principal feedback.

In Chapter 5, we step into the shoes of administrators and consider the practical issues that school leaders face. We tackle questions principals may be asking themselves, such as: How do I provide effective feedback? What is the best way to help low-performing teachers improve? Should I evaluate some teachers (e.g., special education teachers, English Language Learner specialists) differently? How can I best utilize multiple observers? How can I measure/understand teachers' interactions with particular kinds of students?

In reflecting on our text, our perspective on education reform runs parallel to that expressed by Daniel Duane (2014) about the fitness craze. In his recent *New York Times* op-ed piece, Duane describes his journey for fitness, trying every new idea from Bosu balls to P90X, each method with a different, new, and improved hypothesis about how to achieve top fitness. In education, like in fitness, many hold the false belief that a magic bullet exists that does a better or faster job at reaching the intended results. But, after trying a number of these new and groundbreaking methods that purported to strengthen his core or create muscle confusion, Duane went back to the basics: Barbell training—that is, doing the same set of strength exercises (three sets, five reps)—on alternating days, followed by a glass of milk. He gradually added more weight over time, repeating the method for an entire year. Would something so simple, so basic work? Indeed, it did. Essentially, what works, works. And, change, when it does happen, is gradual. With those two messages in mind, we carry one final reflection into the writing of this text: It turns out that just as in fitness, in education old methods aren't necessarily ineffective methods, and we'll show that the same holds true for research—some of what we know about good teaching has been known for some time. However, as in exercise, faddism abounds in education and separating what is known (and how to appropriately apply it) from what is advocated is no simple task.

References

Duane, D. (2014, May 24). Fitness crazed. *New York Times*. Retrieved from www.nytimes.com/2014/05/25/opinion/sunday/fitness-crazed.html?emc=eta1&_r=0

Lavigne, A.L., & Chamberlain, R. (2014, January). *Coping with increased demands for teacher evaluation: School leaders' perceptions of problems and possibility*. Invited paper presented at Using Observational and Student Achievement Data to Improve Teaching. Tucson, AZ.

Lavigne, A.L., Good, T.L., & Marx, R.M. (Eds.) (2014). High-stakes teacher evaluation: High cost—big losses [Special Issue]. *Teachers College Record, 116*(1).

Conference Resources

High-Stakes Teacher Evaluation: High Cost—Big Losses (2012) www.coe.arizona.edu/highstakes

Using Observational and Student Achievement Data to Improve Teaching (2014) www.coe.arizona.edu/usingdata

ACKNOWLEDGMENTS

Alyson Lavigne and Tom Good acknowledge the helpful and extensive work by Toni Sollars, who typed numerous drafts of manuscript chapters, and Amy Olson, who skillfully prepared several tables. We also thank Mary McCaslin and Francesca López, who read and provided thoughtful and helpful feedback on selected chapters. Finally, we would like to thank Rebecca Novack, our tireless and dedicated editor, who was with us every step of the way.

1
BEING A PRINCIPAL IN AN ERA OF HIGH-STAKES TEACHER EVALUATION

We will illustrate (and most of our readers know) principals work long hours and have difficult jobs. Yet policy makers now call for principals to spend more time supervising teachers. This advocacy is done without any advice about how principals can find time to do this or any evidence that increasing the amount of time principals spend in classrooms will increase student achievement. Principals today are under increased pressure to improve their schools, and advice about how they should do this abounds.

With this context in mind, this chapter describes certain characteristics of today's school principal. We look at factors such as salary, years of experience, and other demographic variables. Some information is presented as an average across the U.S. Some information is reported at the state level to show that context is often important and that there is considerable variation in principals' beliefs and job situations.

Next, we report on principals' beliefs about their job. Although conceptions of the "good" principal continue to evolve, consensus is that the job is very demanding. It is useful to consider issues where principals believe they have more or less influence and to consider the levels of job satisfaction and stress that principals experience. Then, we turn to a description of what principals are expected to do based on considerations from theory, professional societies, and those who study school leadership. We describe the many roles that principals are expected to and do play. Lee Sherman (2000) provides the perfect advance organizer:

> Research tells us that principals are the linchpins in the enormously complex workings, both physical and human, of a school. The job calls for a staggering range of roles: psychologist, teacher, facilities manager, philosopher, police officer, diplomat, social worker, mentor, PR director, coach, cheerleader.

> The principalship is both lowly and lofty. In one morning, you might deal with a broken window and a broken home. A bruised knee and a bruised ego. A rusty pipe and a rusty teacher.
>
> (p. 2)

After describing the roles noted by Sherman, we illustrate that expectations for what good principals "should do" are varied and complex, and often change without any evidence to suggest that the recommended changes will work. Thus, it is not surprising that the research base on effective principals is undeveloped as definitions of what constitutes good practice vary over time.

We examine principals' tasks and see that they respond to an overwhelming set of duties replete with frequent interruptions. Sometimes they must do two or more things simultaneously. Principals face many demands, but they have limited time available to complete duties. We explore how principals use their time, and we summarize the results across several studies. One major finding is that principals generally do not spend much time observing/evaluating teachers. And, despite policy makers' (and state and federal mandates') push for principals to spend more time supervising teachers, those who have studied and who have reported this finding have *not* recommended that principals necessarily spend more time on this activity.

We end this chapter considering modern-day issues that characterize the work and lives of school leaders. We revisit what is known about what principals do and within the context of new reform demands. The fact that principals spend little time on supervision and evaluation creates tension with the state and federal mandates that call for increased time spent on these tasks. We ask: Where would principals find the time to do this? Do they have this knowledge? We address these questions in Chapter 2.

The Face and Voice of School Principals

Table 1.1 shows (based upon data from the U.S. Department of Education 2011–2012) how principals vary in terms of gender, race/ethnicity, highest degree earned, average age, experience, annual salary, and average hours spent on the job per week. For example, 51.6% of principals are female. The average number of years of experience of principals is 7.2; the average salary for principals for fewer than 3 years is $83,500, and for those with 10 or more years of experience, $96,000. The average age of principals is 48, and the average hours spent per week on all school-related activities is 58.1.

Table 1.1 also reports these same data during 2007–2008. We see that principal characteristics are fairly stable during this time period. For example, the percentage of teachers who are female, male, and white remains essentially the same. One exception is that principal salaries at all levels increased notably (given the economy) from 2007 to 2012. And this is especially true for principals with 10 or more

TABLE 1.1 Principal Characteristics: 2011–2012 and 2007–2008

Principal Characteristics	2011–2012	2007–2008
Gender		
Female	51.6	51.0
Male	48.4	49.0
Race/ethnicity		
White	80.3	80.9
Black	10.1	10.6
Hispanic	6.8	6.5
Other	2.8	2.0
Highest degree earned		
Bachelor's degree or less	2.2	1.5
Master's degree	61.7	61.1
Education specialist or professional diploma	26.2	29.0
Doctorate or professional degree	9.9	8.4
Average age	48	49
Experience		
Average years of total experience	7.2	8.1
Average years at current school	4.2	4.8
Average annual salary, by years of experience		
Fewer than 3 years	$83,500	$73,500
3–9 years	$90,900	$80,200
10+ years	$96,000	$82,700
Average days in contract year	230	227
Percent of principals newly hired	8.6	9.3
Average hours spent per week on		
All school-related activities	58.1	58.4
Interacting with students	22.5	20.8
Percentage of principals who thought they had a major influence on:		
Evaluating teachers at their school	96.2	94.2
Hiring new full-time teachers at their school	85.1	90.4

years of experience (whose salary rose by $14,000). We have presented averages for principals across the U.S., but describing principals is much more complicated than averages suggest. For example, Table 1.2 illustrates the variability in principal salary in five randomly chosen states.

Compensation for principals in Pennsylvania is considerably higher, at all levels of experience, than in Montana. The level of absolute compensation for principals needs to be studied in relation to the fact that the principal contract year is roughly 230 days. Principals' salaries also need to be considered in terms of principals' job satisfaction, the extent to which they can control work conditions, and the amount of stress they experience. Not only do principals' salaries vary, but also their beliefs about the extent to which they can influence their job conditions vary (see Table 1.3).

TABLE 1.2 Average Annual Salary for Public School Principals in Five Randomly Selected States by Years of Experience

State	Average annual salary	Less than 3 years	3 to 9 years	10 years or more
United States	90,500	83,500	90,900	96,000
Louisiana	74,800	71,300	74,200	79,600
Montana	65,800	53,200	68,900	75,700
Pennsylvania	98,100	92,100	96,600	105,500
Utah	82,100	72,700	83,900	84,500
Wyoming	92,500	80,700	90,100	99,900

Source: U.S. Department of Education (2013).

TABLE 1.3 Percentage of Public School Principals in Five Randomly Selected States Who Thought They Had a Major Influence on Decisions Concerning Various Activities at Their School

Decisions	Region					
	United States	Michigan	New Hampshire	Ohio	Oregon	Utah
Setting performance standards for students	73.6	75.3	71.5	70.5	79.9	71.7
Establishing curriculum	43.2	46.5	50.2	37.3	41.3	37.0
Determining the content of in-service professional development programs for teachers	69.8	72.3	73.2	59.8	71.8	76.3
Evaluating teachers	96.2	95.9	96.4	95.8	93.6	98.5
Hiring new full-time teachers	85.1	81.8	92.2	84.5	90.7	97.2
Setting discipline policy	79.8	82.3	86.4	79.0	78.2	84.9
Deciding how their school budget will be spent	64.1	55.3	71.5	60.9	70.9	86.1

Source: U.S. Department of Education (2013).

The context in which the principal operates is important. Although virtually all principals believe they have a dominant voice in evaluating teachers, principals clearly believe that they have considerably less influence on the curriculum. This is the case in all selected states but especially so in Ohio and Utah. The fact that principals are accountable for student achievement growth—yet have little control over curriculum—must be frustrating to some. Readers interested in states other than those reported can consult the National Center for Education Statistics, Schools and Staffing Survey website (https://nces.ed.gov/surveys/sass/).

School Principals: Role Conceptualizations and Expectations

Society, various organizations, and those who study the work of principals hold various beliefs about what principals should do—what roles and responsibilities fall under their job functions. The list is always expanding. Table 1.4 describes some of the work supported by the Wallace Foundation partnership with one school district to broaden the conceptualization of how principals should behave. For additional examples see the Wallace Foundation (www.wallacefoundation.org).

TABLE 1.4 Leadership Standards at One School District

	Strategic	Instructional, culture and equity, planning and assessment	Micropolitical, organizational	Human resource	Cultural, school climate	Community
School Leadership Framework—Denver Public Schools—Colorado						
Leads for equity toward college and career readiness		X				
Leads for culture of empowerment, continuous improvement, and celebration		X				
Leads for high-quality, data-driven instruction by building the capacity of teachers to lead and perfect their craft		X				
Leads for the academic and social-emotional success of *all* students		X				
Identifies, develops, retains, and dismisses staff in alignment with high expectations for performance				X		

(Continued)

TABLE 1.4 (Continued)

	Strategic	Instructional, culture and equity, planning and assessment	Micropolitical, organizational	Human resource	Cultural, school climate	Community
Applies teacher and staff performance management systems in a way that ensures a culture of continuous improvement and accountability				X		
Leads the school's vision, mission, and strategic goals to support college readiness for all students	X					
Distributes leadership to inspire change in support of an empowered school culture	X					
Aligns people, time, and money to drive student achievement			X			
Ensures effective communications with and between all staff and stakeholders			X			
Advocates for members of the school community and effectively engages family and community						X
Demonstrates professionalism and continuous professional growth						X

Source: Adapted from Wallace Foundation (2013).

Further, federal and state agencies are not shy about prescribing activities for principals and teachers. These prescribed activities sometimes change abruptly and often radically. For example, in the 1980s it was commonly advocated that principals were instructional leaders (with an emphasis on improving instruction and student learning) and that effective schools were differentiated from less effective schools because of principals' instructional leadership. Ron Edmonds' (1982) characterization of effective schools was widely cited. Edmonds' correlates follow:

- The leadership of the principal characterized by substantial attention to the quality of instruction.
- A pervasive and broadly understood instructional focus and orderly, safe climate conducive to teaching and learning.
- Teacher behaviors that convey the expectation that all students are to obtain at least minimum mastery.
- The use of measures of pupil achievement as the basis for program evaluation.

Although these beliefs were widely shared and advocated, the supporting research base was never firmly established. Further, this conception of principal as instructional leader was relatively short-lived. In the 1990s principals were seen as encouraging teachers (and sometimes community members, such as parents) and expected to assume an important role in making program and budget decisions in the school. This form of leadership has been called various things, but one dominant form of literature speaks to the distributive aspects of leadership—broadly delegating important decisions to others and assuming a support role for helping to implement school policies. Thus, professional beliefs about what principals should *do* changed dramatically within a period of 10 years. Changing conceptions of the principal's role in establishing and maintaining effective schools were not based upon any definitive research. For a review of the research on conceptions of effective schools and principals in the 1980s, see Good and Brophy (1986) and Purkey and Smith (1983), and for conceptions of distributed leadership, see Firestone and Martinez (2007).

Furthermore, federal and state mandates have also shaped what constitutes effective practice. As an example of federal prescriptions, consider the 2001 Comprehensive School Reform (CSR) Act. This legislation amended the previous CSR funding (which was designed to encourage innovative practice). Now research evidence, not innovative practice, is required to receive federal funding. Here are a few of the CSR components:

- Uses proven strategies and methods for learning, teaching, and school management based upon scientifically based research and effective practices successfully in multiple schools.

- Integrates a comprehensive design with aligned components focused on helping students meet standards and addressing needs identified in a school needs assessment.
- Provides high-quality, ongoing professional development.
- Includes measureable goals and benchmarks for student academic achievement.
- Has the support of staff within the school.
- Provides for parental and community support and involvement.
- Has been found through scientifically based research to significantly improve student academic achievement, or has shown strong evidence that it will.

Despite the strong pronouncements urging principals to use scientifically validated research, in most areas there was limited research and in other areas the research was inconsistent. These illusionary beliefs about the abundance of research evidence continue today. Race to the Top (RttT) assumes that student achievement can be increased substantially, and policy makers have again recommended how federal funds can be used to improve achievement. Now, the conception of what principals should do is changing substantially under the pressure of high-stakes teacher evaluation. The view of the principal as an instructional leader has returned to center stage. History suggests that many of the things that policy makers believe that principals should do will change again. Being a successful principal at times requires an ability to withstand unwarranted advocacy.

Frameworks for Organizing Principals' Activities

Beyond arguments about what principals should do, we know that principals have a very complex and demanding job. Principals are often interrupted in the middle of tasks, must overlap different activities at the same time, and deal with different types of people who present varied opportunities and challenges. Sometimes principals have to delay more important problems to deal with minor ones because an immediate task cannot be avoided (e.g., an irate parent shows up unexpectedly).

Amid this endless list of tasks, principals must decide which tasks to do first and which tasks to delay. Arguably how they distribute their time to these tasks, including delegating these roles to other individuals, allows some principals to be more effective than others. Obviously, effectiveness can be defined in many different ways, including the percentage of students who come to school on time, the percentage of students who attend school regularly, student achievement scores, student graduation rates, and student suspensions. Some principals might be better at student discipline and others more able in helping teachers to raise student achievement scores. As the reader can imagine, research documenting the extent to which principals influence these outcomes is sparse, and most of the research describing the behavior and characteristics of effective principals deals with student achievement outcomes. We will describe this research in Chapter 3. Given that most advocacy for what effective principals should do is derived from anecdotes and small case studies, in Chapter 3 we focus on principals as instructional leaders and, hence, describe research that links teaching with increases in student achievement.

There are numerous attempts to categorize the seemingly unending list of individual activities that principals do into more organized frameworks. Ebmeier and Crawford (2008) suggest that Parsons' (1960) representation and conception of school organization continue to be a powerful way for examining the work of principals. Parsons maintained that schools have four major functions: maintenance activities, adaption activities, goal attainment, and integration. Table 1.5 presents specific tasks that fall within these four generic school organizational processes.

Maintenance includes building school culture, maintaining staff morale, and supporting school events, such as musical performances, school plays, school sports, and so forth. Adaptation activities are those that build community support, such as joining clubs in the community, surveying parents and citizens about their expectations for what schools should be doing, and keeping the curriculum up to date and aligned with community support. Goal attainment is the school's ability to define its goals and to obtain resources for achieving them. Integration includes maintaining curricular coherence across grade levels, scheduling courses, and providing various services, including school transportation, lunches, and so forth.

Later in this chapter we report that principals believe their jobs are becoming more stressful due to changes in societal expectations and in state and federal regulations that affect their jobs. And we agree. Still we suggest that these generic school organizational processes that Parsons articulated remain a viable way for organizing how principals navigate their professional duties. For example, in terms of maintenance activities it may be that in 1900 school principals spent more time worrying about heating the school, while principals in 2015 worry more about accommodating the demands for student achievement and related activities. The principal role has evolved but within that, the Parsons framework is still relevant—at the core successful principals must deal with *all* of these aspects of school organization well.

We have seen that principals are expected to do many things, and various professional societies and foundations have advanced plans and standards for what principals need to do (e.g., Wallace Foundation, 2013; Council of Chief State School Officers, 1996). As seen in Table 1.4, the Wallace Foundation has been doing much work in building principals' capacity for enhancing their effectiveness as school leaders. Additional examples can be found on its website.

TABLE 1.5 Specific Tasks Conducted within Four Generic School Organizational Processes

Specific task	Adaptation	Integration	Maintenance	Goal attainment
Planning	Establishing communication links to the external environment; organizing new ideas and suggestions received from the outside; generating alternative implementation strategies	Identifying and establishing key coordination points and linkages; pinpointing areas where coordination within the organization is inadequate; establishing change strategies	Establishing strategies to build common school culture	Identifying student and teacher outcomes objectives consistent with school and district goals
Decision making	Focused on establishing priorities for the use of new procedures and methods of implementation	Focused on improving internal efficiency and communications between school's subunits	Focused on involving individuals as a means of gaining commitment and developing a common culture	Focused on identifying and promoting practices that result in improving classroom instruction and student learning
Evaluating	Examination of the extent to which the school's programs and clients' expectations are consistent	Examination of the extent of work duplication, work flow, and efficiency of the school	Examination of the extent to which employees believe in school-sanctioned customs and values	Examination of student outcomes, including the frequent monitoring of classroom instruction and the provision of feedback
Approaching conflict	Client preferences and improvement of practice are the driving forces	Conflict between work subunits or teachers is bad because it leads to inefficiency; typically dealt with by structural or rule changes	Conflict over values is divisive because it results in loss of school focus; dealt with by indoctrination and removal of employees not sharing the majority's values and beliefs	Conflict over goals is divisive; thus, schools must take steps to reduce the variance from specific outcome goals through removal, reassignment, retraining, recruitment, and evaluation of instruction

Goal setting	Focused on establishing feedback links to clients, including parents, and implementation of new practice based on that feedback	Focused on increasing internal efficiency	Focused on building and maintaining a common culture and belief system	Focused on careful articulation of student outcome goals, instructional methods, materials, and procedures
Communication	Increasing the flow of information between the school and external agencies	Increasing the flow within the school to reduce redundancy	Increasing the opportunity to share common experiences and demonstrate system values, thus building a sense of unity	Increasing the opportunity to convey information about intended student outcomes and desirable teaching processes

Source: Adapted from Ebmeier and Crawford (2008).

How Principals Spend Their Time

Advice abounds for what principals should do. We now turn to examine what is known about how principals actually allocate their time and what they *actually* do. To start, consider just a few of the tasks most principals address:

- Attend meetings; coordinate requests from the central office and the state department of education.
- Plan, implement, and evaluate school curriculum.
- Plan professional development for teachers and school staff.
- Write or oversee grant writing and other activities to garner resources.
- Plan school schedules.
- Hire and evaluate teachers.
- Assign teachers and students to classrooms.
- Deal with parents, teachers, and student issues about classroom assignments.
- Order supplies, including computer software.
- Oversee textbook selection.
- Prepare reports needed by the central office or by state and federal agencies.
- Supervise or oversee lunch room, recess, and after-school programs.
- Supervise, hire, and evaluate staff.
- Coordinate school and community public safety, buses, field trips, and after-school programs.
- Develop or maintain school policies (e.g., attendance, extended absences).
- Organize bond campaigns or drives to purchase equipment.
- Attend and plan various school events (e.g., school nights, award ceremonies).
- Discipline students.
- Communicate with parents face-to-face and through website and newsletter.
- Deal with teacher-teacher conflicts.
- Deal with parent conflicts with teachers, coaches, or other staff.
- Assign substitutes for absent teachers.
- Handle social media issues honestly but tactfully.

Observational Studies of What Principals Do

So how much time do principals spend on these and other tasks? Some researchers have studied how principals allocate their time. We will see that over 30 years how principals spend their time has remained fairly *stable* despite changing popular demands for principals to play different roles. Nearly 30 years ago, Martin and Willower (1981) noted that although high school principals were among the most familiar community leaders, there was very little data to describe what they actually did. And most available information was indirect and came through self-report surveys and questionnaires. They lamented that what they felt was a better strategy, to observe principal behavior directly, had surprisingly been ignored by most educational researchers.

Drawing upon Mintzberg's 1973 framework, Martin and Willower (1981) developed a structured observation system to describe how principals allocated their time. Five school principals were selected, representing a variety of school types and community settings. The sample included rural, small town, middle-sized city, suburban, and urban schools. The sizes of schools ranged from 400 to 1,000 students. Principals were observed for 25 instructional days. Ahead we will describe how these secondary principals allocated their time to particular tasks when we compare their time allocations with results from a study of elementary principals. General findings included the fact that principals often performed several activities simultaneously (e.g., outlining an agenda for a staff meeting, while signing a form handed to them by the secretary and talking on the phone to a concerned parent). Martin and Willower called these simultaneous activities polychronics; however, more recently this type of behavior is referred to as overlapping.

Principals were often interrupted and their task behavior was often fragmented. Martin and Willower (1981) report, "Some idea of the magnitude of interruptions can be gained from the fact that 50% of all observed activities were either interrupted or were interruptions" (p. 74). Principal tasks were also very *brief*, as 81.4% of the activities principals engaged in ranged from 1 to 4 minutes. The modal duration time for any task observed during the 25 days of observation was 1 minute. Clearly principals move from task to task very quickly.

Martin and Willower (1981) provided an important caveat for future researchers: "Structured observation does not lend itself to qualitative analysis, and therefore, infrequently performed but vitally important tasks can be lost in a sea of empirical appraisal" (p. 87). Unfortunately, this good advice has seldom been followed in subsequent research.

Kmetz and Willower (1982) studied how elementary school principals allocated their work time. Five principals in different and diverse districts were observed (rural, inner city, suburban) and in schools of varying size (250–1,000 students) and of varying student demographics. Each principal was observed for an entire week. The authors also compared their findings to the study of secondary principals (Martin & Willower, 1981) that we just described. Kmetz and Willower found that elementary school principals averaged 41.7 hours at work and spent an additional 8 hours at home per week, yielding an average of 49.7 (as compared to the 53.2 hours for secondary principals). Today, principals' workweeks are about 10% longer (58.1 hours per week; see Table 1.1).

Elementary principals participated in 3,058 activities across all observations, averaging 611.6 each per week and 122.3 each day. Breaking down elementary school principals' activities by type, we see that they spend an average of 522.2 minutes per week or 18.6% of their time on desk work. In terms of scheduled meetings, principals averaged 8.4 each week, and these meetings tended to be long; they averaged 34.6 minutes in length and used 10.3% of the principals' time. Attempts to have focused discussions were problematic as scheduled meetings were often interrupted to address other issues. Hastily arranged contacts (i.e., unscheduled meetings), which typically occurred spontaneously, consumed 32.5% of principals' time, more than any other activity. Forty unscheduled meetings occurred per day, and they were all reasonably short, on average lasting 4.4% of their time. Understandably, there was some variation across principals, and the mean number of daily activities ranged from a low of 87.6 to a high of 148 activities per day.

Importantly (at least in terms of today's policy mandates requiring principals to spend more time in classrooms), elementary school principals spent only 2.5% of their total time observing teachers. In contrast, organizational maintenance took 38.6% of their time and accounted for 53.7% of the elementary school principals' activities.

As shown in Table 1.6, the distribution of time and activity for elementary school principals compared generally well with the secondary school findings obtained by Martin and Willower (1981).

Table 1.6 shows that the main differences between elementary and secondary principals were that they engaged in fewer activities, had fewer interruptions, and less correspondence. Elementary school principals spent more time on the school's instructional program and less on extracurricular activities.

Kmetz and Willower (1982) concluded that

> events ordinarily controlled the principals rather than the other way around. In other words, the principals had not worked out means for deliberately

TABLE 1.6 The Chronological Record for the Elementary and Secondary Principals

Activity	Number of activities		Total time (in minutes)		Mean percentage of time	
	Elementary	Secondary	Elementary	Secondary	Elementary	Secondary
Desk work	267	254	2611	2394	18.6	16.0
Phone calls	424	393	1117	868	8.0	5.8
Scheduled meetings	42	117	1453	2601	10.3	17.3
Unscheduled meetings	1027	1221	4565	4122	32.5	27.5
Exchanges	842	1355	842	1355	6.0	9.0
Monitoring	92	82	613	828	4.4	5.5
Tours	146	88	583	1158	4.2	7.7
Trips	37	11	754	327	5.4	2.2
Observing	9	8	357	363	2.5	2.4
Personal	67	133	501	767	3.6	5.1
Announcing	49	61	101	103	0.7	0.7
Teaching	7	2	271	18	1.9	0.1
Support chores	49	5	264	103	1.9	0.7

Source: Adapted from Kmetz & Willower (1982).

> allocating their attention. They seemed to spend little time thinking about the activities in which they were engaged or attempting to anticipate and give meaning to future ones.
>
> (p. 77)

They recommended that principals needed to save time for their most valued goals while handling the continuous demands of administrative tasks. Kmetz and Willower also provided a strong caveat suggesting more attention needed be placed on the quality of principals' efforts.

> The tendency to gauge principals' effectiveness in school program matters in terms of the amount of time they spend in classrooms is simplistic. The quality of their work with instruction and curriculum is more likely to be reflected in their efforts to motivate faculty and in planning that facilitates good teaching.
>
> (Ibid., p. 74)

Interestingly these researchers, while reporting that principals spent little time in classrooms, noted that they *did not* necessarily believe that this time allocation was problematic nor that increasing their classroom observations would necessarily improve teaching and learning. Fundamentally these researchers prefigured the question that dominates *today's* literature, a question we revisit in Chapter 3: Is principals' influence on teacher and student performance through direct or indirect means?

Roughly 30 years later, Horng, Klasik, and Loeb (2010) contended (as Kmetz and Willower had) that observational studies describing how principals spend their time were limited and those that had been conducted (e.g., Martin & Willower, 1981; Wolcott, 1973) were ethnographic studies of only a few principals, making the generalizability of findings to other settings unknown. They acknowledged the availability of survey and self-reported data, but they stressed the limitations of this research (accuracy, depth).

To address deficiencies of previous research, Horng et al. (2010) conducted a study in Dade County, Florida, involving 65 principals (41 high school, 12 elementary, and 12 middle school principals). Principals were shadowed by a researcher for 1 instructional day. Every 5 minutes the researcher coded the primary principal activity that had occurred during the preceding 5 minutes. The list of 43 tasks that researchers used to describe principal behavior was largely drawn from work by Spillane, Camburn, and Pareja (2007). These tasks were aggregated into six categories: administration, organizational management, day-to-day instruction, instructional program, internal relations, and external relations. Appendix A describes some of the individual tasks coded within these broader categories. As can be seen in Appendix A, tasks associated with observing teachers and evaluating them were included in the day-to-day instruction category, not the instructional program category.

So how did school principals spend their time? Horng et al. (2010) reported (as did Martin and Willower [1981] and Kmetz and Willower [1982]) that the bulk of principals' time was spent on administration and organizational management (see Table 1.7).

These data are broken down by school type in Table 1.8. Principals in elementary, middle, and high schools allocated their time similarly. Principals spent most time on administration and organization management. Less time was spent on internal relations, and considerably less time was spent on day-to-day instruction, the instructional program, and external relations. *All* principals spent roughly one-half of their time on administration and organization management. Given the current advocacy that principals should spend more time in classrooms, it is instructive to see that principals spent little time on day-to-day instructional tasks. Elementary school principals did more work here than other principals, but still they spent only 9.26% of their time on daily instructional tasks.

Horng et al. (2010) also studied principals' time allocation as a function of principal variables (e.g., gender, years of experience) and school context

TABLE 1.7 Principals' Percentage of Time Use

Activity	M (SD)	Range*
Administration	27.46 (10.19)	17.27–37.65
Organization management	20.95 (7.42)	13.53–28.37
Day-to-day instruction	5.88 (8.29)	0–14.17
Instructional program	6.73 (7.60)	0–14.33
Internal relations	14.64 (7.60)	7.04–22.24
External relations	4.69 (7.09)	0–11.78
Other tasks	18.68 (7.67)	11.01–26.35

Source: Adapted from Horng et al. (2010).
Note: Ranges represent the mean +/− one standard deviation.
*In cases where subtracting one standard deviation would result in a negative number, zero has been entered.

TABLE 1.8 Comparing Principals' Time Use across School Level

School type	Administration	Organization management	Day-to-day instruction	Instructional program	Internal relations	External relations
Elementary	25.31 (3.50)	20.86 (3.76)	9.26 (2.83)	6.97 (2.40)	17.23 (3.39)	4.61 (1.87)
Middle	22.48 (3.68)	23.76 (3.73)	8.38 (2.42)	8.63 (2.92)	11.01 (1.63)	4.39 (1.79)
High	27.43 (1.63)	20.95 (1.19)	5.88 (1.33)	6.73 (1.22)	14.64 (1.22)	7.70 (1.13)

Source: Adapted from Horng et al. (2010).

(percentage of minority students, degree of poverty), but these characteristics generally did not influence how principals spent their time. For whatever reason (principals' conceptions of their job, work constraints) principals allocate their time similarly.

Grissom, Loeb, and Master (2013) studied 125 principals' allocated time. Data comparing elementary, middle, and high school principals were collected in 3 different years (2008, 2011, and 2012), using a similar protocol as used by Horng et al. (2010). The observers shadowed principals from the Miami-Dade County School District for 1 day in 2008, 2011, and 2012. Principals' major activity was rated every 5 minutes with the selection of one category from the roughly 50 activities. After selecting the best description of how time was used, the rater coded other information, such as the location of the activity. Data were collected initially in all 41 high schools and in 12 randomly selected elementary and 12 middle schools. The district enrolled roughly 350,000 students, of whom 62% were Hispanic and 75% were eligible for subsidized lunches.

Table 1.9 presents the data reported by the researchers in 2008 and in 2012. In 2008 middle school principals spent more time on instructional tasks than did peers in other school settings. In 2012, elementary principals spent more time here than did their peers. In both years, high school principals spent the least amount of time on instructional activities. Principals across two time periods spent little time on instructional activities, as the percentage of time ranged from 10.1% to 17%.

Table 1.9 shows that in 2012 the elementary school principal on average spent 16.5% of his or her time on instructional activities. However, it is important to consider that an average can be more or less descriptive. Table 1.9 also provides the standard deviation (SD), describing how scores vary around the mean. Elementary principals spent on average 16.5% of their total workweek on instructional activities; however, the standard deviation of 11.8 is fairly large (in comparison to the mean of 16.5) and a SD of 11.8 indicates that two-thirds of the principals in the study spent 16.5% plus or minus 11.8 percentage points of time on instructional activities. Table 1.9 also provides the range (the spread from lowest score to highest score). The range across all elementary principals in 2012 was from 4.7% to 28.3%. Considering the average along with SD and range provides a more complete picture than by looking only at the average. The variation in elementary principals' allocation of time shown in Table 1.9 is such that we can conclude that some elementary principals spent much time on this activity, but others very little. Also, note that the range shows that some principals did not engage in a particular activity at all. For example, an examination of the coaching teachers category in 2008 and 2012 shows some principals at all school levels spent *no* time coaching their teachers.

TABLE 1.9 Observed Percentage of Principal Instruction Time Use by School Type and Year

Instructional time use		2008			2012		
		High school	Middle school	Elementary school	High school	Middle school	Elementary school
Total instructional time use	M (SD)	11.7 (10.6)	17.0 (8.7)	16.4 (13.9)	10.1 (10.0)	12.0 (10.8)	16.5 (11.8)
	Range	1.1–22.3	8.3–25.7	2.5–30.3	0.1–20.1	1.2–22.8	4.7–28.3
Coaching teachers	M (SD)	0.8 (1.4)	0.8 (1.2)	0.7 (1.3)	0.1 (0.5)	0.5 (1.3)	0.0 (0.3)
	Range*	0–2.2	0–2.2	0–2.0	0–0.6	0–1.8	0–0.3
Developing the educational program	M (SD)	0.9 (2.1)	2.6 (4.8)	1.7 (3.7)	2.5 (6.5)	2.1 (4.2)	4.1 (7.5)
	Range*	0–3.0	0–7.4	0–5.4	0–9.0	0–6.3	0–11.6
Evaluating teachers	M (SD)	1.0 (2.9)	1.2 (2.7)	2.7 (6.6)	0.9 (3.0)	2.1 (5.1)	2.2 (4.9)
	Range*	0–3.9	0–3.9	0–9.3	0–3.9	0–7.2	0–7.1
Classroom walk-throughs	M (SD)	5.2 (8.4)	5.9 (4.4)	6.3 (7.9)	4.1 (6.1)	4.8 (4.8)	7.0 (7.2)
	Range*	0–13.6	1.5–10.3	0–14.2	0–10.2	0–9.6	0–14.2
Required or non-required teacher PD	M (SD)	0.9 (2.2)	3.7 (6.4)	2.0 (2.2)	0.1 (0.5)	0.3 (1.0)	0.3 (0.7)
	Range*	0–3.1	0–10.1	0–4.2	0–0.6	0–1.3	0–1.0
Other instructional time use	M (SD)	2.9 (4.5)	2.8 (5.6)	2.9 (4.0)	2.3 (4.5)	2.1 (3.6)	3.0 (3.6)
	Range*	0–7.4	0–8.4	0–6.9	0–6.8	0–5.7	0–6.6
n of schools		37	11	12	44	32	29

Source: Adapted from Grissom, Loeb, and Master (2013).
Note: Ranges represent the mean +/- one standard deviation.
* In cases where subtracting one standard deviation would result in a negative number, zero has been entered.

Overall, the authors report that principals spend 12.7% of their time on instructional-related activities. Within the instructional activities, we see that principals spend most of their time in walk-throughs.

- 5.4% walk-throughs
- 1.8% formal evaluation of teaching
- 5.0% informal coaching
- 2.1% evaluating school educational programs
- 2.4% nine other ways

Table 1.9 shows that in general the 2008 time allocations are similar to those in 2012. This is instructive, as given the increased interest in high-stakes teacher evaluations during this time span, principals might have increased the time they spent on instructional tasks. This did not occur in this school district. We see that principals at all levels in the 2008–2012 comparison years spent most of their time on classroom walk-throughs, but it is also the case that some principals across all levels spent no time on walk-throughs.

How Principals Spend Their Time 1981–2013

Studies using different methodologies and samples have shown consistently that principals allocate very little of their time to observing and evaluating teachers. The two more modern studies have collected data on more principals, but their results are restricted by the fact that all of the observations were collected in a single day. Grissom, Loeb, and Master (2013) are correct in noting the weaknesses of previous research using small samples because of the limited or unknown generalizability of the results. However, we believe Kmetz and Willower (1982) and Martin and Willower (1981) have certain advantages that are important to consider. The samples were small. But the samples included diversity (more than one school district) and had much more observational information on individual principals. In one study, principals were observed on 25 different occasions, and in the other study principals were observed for a full week. Further, we see that Grissom et al. (2013) have not addressed the concerns addressed by Martin and Willower and Kmetz and Willower that it is important to move beyond accounts of time and speak more directly to considerations of context and quality. Clearly, Grissom et al. (2013) have made an important contribution to the literature, but as we try to consolidate and improve research over time, what is needed now is more research on how time (and its quality) is used and how it impacts outcomes like teacher satisfaction and student achievement. For example, we will suggest in Chapter 5 that quality of principal feedback is critical if teachers are to improve practice.

Issues that Characterize the Modern-Day Principalship

We have described who principals are and what they do. We have established that there is little knowledge about how principals' use of time to supervise teachers relates to improved practice. Yet, as noted, policy makers want principals to spend more time in classrooms and working with teachers. Kafka (2009), in a history of the principalship, argues that the role of principals has not radically changed—their position within the educational hierarchy has remained stable, as have the fundamentals of schooling—and that school leadership has always required school leaders to possess multiple roles (e.g., manager, administrator, supervisor, instructional leader, politician) simultaneously. Other researchers have indicated otherwise—that school leaders now face an increased emphasis on accountability, use of technology, fiscal changes, and changing student demographics (Matthews & Crow, 2003). It has been argued that the role of a school leader is more difficult and time-consuming today than in the past (Goodwin, Cunningham, & Eagle, 2005), and we hinted at this and other trends. Here, we extend our analysis to consider other changes that are particularly relevant to today's principals.

The Principalship Is Becoming More Complex and More Stressful

Rich information about the context in which principals work has been provided by the MetLife Foundation's (2013) comprehensive report entitled *Survey of American Teachers: Challenges for School Leadership*. The report provides details of teachers' and principals' beliefs concerning the problems they face and the satisfactions they derive from their employment. In general, principals in high-need schools responded in similar ways to principals in more advantaged schools. That is, the general directions of the responses were similar, but the magnitude differed as a function of school context. For example, principals in high-need schools reported less satisfaction than did other principals.

Teachers and principals agreed that the principal is ultimately responsible for everything that happens to students in the schools. Interestingly, teachers more strongly believe this than they did 25 years ago. Thus, principals, both because of public expectations and teacher expectations, are placed in a position of high accountability, which likely causes stress and lowers job satisfaction for some principals. In the recent MetLife survey (2013), 75% of principals reported that the job has become too complex and roughly 50% of principals report feeling under great stress several times a week or more:

- 20% almost every day
- 28% several days a week
- 37% once or twice a week
- 15% less often than once a week

Part of the stress is because principals feel that they have very little control in making decisions about school finances. Although the economy has improved recently, many principals surveyed were in schools where state budgets declined over several consecutive years. Furthermore, although principals feel that they have considerable control in hiring teachers, many reported that they have little control over the curriculum or removing low-performing teachers.

These data showing that principals report little control over certain key aspects of their jobs are similar to data presented earlier in the chapter from the Schools and Staffing Survey (U.S. Department of Education, 2013). These stresses are likely to increase. For example, many states have adopted a common curriculum (Common Core State Standards)—standards that have been imposed with little or no sensitivity to the varied conditions of American schools. What is proposed to be standard material in schools serving high-income students in fourth-grade math maybe more problematic in fourth-grade classes populated by diverse students who come from low-income homes. Problems in these schools are exacerbated by the fact that many children are not fluent in English (nor are their parents) and these homes typically have few resources for enriching the non-school lives of their children. Yet the common curriculum places emphasis upon normative standards where improvement is strangely but largely ignored. Thus, principals are expected to exert leadership in ways that influence student achievement, but they have little freedom in choosing the curriculum and removing teachers and have few resources for investing in new programs to meet the needs of struggling students. As we write this, several states are reconsidering their commitment to the Common Core and others are challenging Common Core rationale (Gamson, Lu, & Eckert, 2013); nevertheless, principals and teachers must continue their training for a "common core" that may or not be implemented. These ambiguous conditions create considerable tension.

Job Satisfaction

The MetLife survey showed that 45% of teachers rated principals as excellent and 40% as pretty good. These strikingly supportive data from 85% of teachers are *higher* than in 1986, when 73% of teachers rated their principals as excellent or pretty good. Yet, despite these high approval ratings by teachers, the MetLife Foundation (2013) survey found only 59% of principals being very satisfied with their job. One-third of principals reported that they are very or fairly likely to leave their job as a school principal for a different occupation. Principals who are less than very satisfied with their job are more likely than others to say they are more likely to leave the profession. Clearly a number of principals are considering leaving the field, and although some might argue that these are low-performing principals, there are no data to link the quality of principals (e.g., those who successfully improve performance) to attrition. Still, when we couple this information with the fact that teacher job satisfaction is lower than it ever has been (according to the MetLife survey, 39% of teachers reported that they were very satisfied with their jobs, a 23-percentage-point decline since 2008), it seems plausible to reason that as accountability increasingly focuses on principals, principals' job satisfaction may further decrease in the near future (e.g., if principals do not feel effective by allocating more time to classroom observation).

Diversity of Students

Principals (83%) and teachers (78%) in the MetLife survey reported that their biggest challenge is accommodating individual student needs. Interestingly, the current policy debates imposed by RttT resulted in the use of student achievement scores and observational measures of teachers' classroom performance, and most, if not all, classroom observation systems that are used *ignore* individual differences in students. Teachers are given a score based upon the classroom mean, and the diversity of student performance on this measure (e.g., student is highly engaged, students are asked higher-order questions) is rarely examined. When an observation instrument does address individual differences, it does so on the basis of groups of students (e.g., students with special needs) or in the context of differentiation, but still fails to capture rich and authentic ways that teachers address the needs of individual students. Furthermore, these components usually represent one or two items in an instrument that may be nearly 60 items long (Lavigne & Oberg De La Garza, forthcoming). This inattention to individual students is perhaps one of the reasons teachers feel that feedback about their performance is not helping them to improve student learning. It is disappointing that federal and state policies are implementing a measure of classroom performance that is insensitive to what individual students do. There is an abundance of data to suggest that when interactions of teachers with different types of students are measured, students in the same classroom frequently experience notably different classroom environments (e.g., Good & Brophy, 2008; Jones, Dindia, & Tye, 2006). Yet another possible source of stress for some if not many principals is that the time they spend in observing classroom instruction does not provide them with student-level data or strategies for helping students who struggle.

Principals as Observers

In Chapter 2 we will review how principals are trained on instruments picked for them by the state or school districts. However, having mentioned one problem with these instruments, we thought it useful to provide a summary of common problems with the intent of suggesting to principals that they will need to supplement common instruments if they want to improve teaching.

Common problems of observational instruments. Popular observation instruments have some value when they provide scores that are above average, as they indicate that teachers have exhibited behaviors that are consistent with measures believed to reflect normative practice. However, these observational instruments have little value when teachers score low, as they do not provide useful information about how teachers can improve. Here we summarize some of the common problems that reduce the effectiveness of these instruments for improving teaching. And we do this because principals need to understand the weaknesses of instruments that they are often required to use and to equip themselves with skills that go beyond knowing an observation instrument.

The instrument measures a limited amount of teaching. Current use provides for the collection of data from 10 minutes to a full lesson. What precedes and what follows the observed segment are often unknown. And this limits our ability to define good teaching, as appropriate teaching involves a sequence of lessons that build upon each other in logical manner.

Class averages are often misleading. Commonly used instruments provide a description of how the teacher interacts with the class as a whole. This provides some information, but average descriptions are often incomplete, misleading, or wrong. For example, if an observation instrument tells us that students are engaged 92% of the time, how do we use this information? If it is accurate, it suggests that students appear to be engaged in the lesson (but we likely would want to know who the uninvolved 8% are and why). Further, we must realize that engagement rates are inferences that the observer makes (students appear to be writing or listening), but in actuality some students might be writing but about an assignment for the class that follows. Measures of engagement are often artificially high.

Much interaction is with individual students. There is variation from classroom to classroom, but in many classrooms most of the interaction is with individual students and some students receive more or fewer interactional opportunities than do others. Considerable literature suggests that interaction patterns differ in terms of teachers' perceptions of student ability (are they more or less capable), gender, ethnicity, and social class. Information about the class as a whole may be misrepresentative.

The instrument provides limited information about students who are performing least well. It seems that given the goal of improving student achievement, observational measures would be more useful if they provided information about what students with low achievement do and how their interactions with teachers and peers might be improved.

Teachers look alike. In addition to the fact that instruments yield an average record of classroom interactions that may or may not be accurate, most teachers are given an average score. Ruzek et al. (2014), using a large sample from the Measures of Effective Teaching study, found that the Classroom Assessment Scoring System (CLASS; Pianta, La Paro, & Hamre, 2008) identified most teachers as average. Yes, some teachers score high and low, but consistently classroom observations place the vast majority of teachers in the average category. And as we noted, they provide little information for how to improve. Thus, what does one do with the obtained information?

Instruments see selectively. Research consistently shows that when observational measures of teaching correlate with student achievement typically only a few of the instruments scales correlate with achievement (Polikoff, 2014). Thus, if our intent is to identify teaching that predicts student achievement, very little of the obtained data is helpful. Or, to put it another way, one might be better off using only the two scales that related to achievement and to use observational time for measuring other aspects of classroom interactions.

Although classroom instruments have some limited utility for evaluation, they have little if any value for improving instruction. Accordingly we recommend that you supplement required instruments with other data collection tools.

Being a Principal in Schools Serving Students from Poverty

We have noted that as we begin to move into a more precise examination of principals' impact, whether direct or indirect, on teachers and students (more on this in Chapter 4), it is important to consider context. One especially important context is leadership in low-income schools. We just reported that principals are under stress, but this is true especially for principals working in disadvantaged schools. Principals and teachers rate one another lower in these schools than principals and teachers in more advantaged schools. The MetLife report found that "Teachers and principals in schools with more than two-thirds low-income students are less likely than those in schools with one-third or fewer low-income students to give teachers an excellent rating (48% versus 73% for teachers; and 51% versus 75% for principals)" (2012, p. 7).

What appears to us is systemically a self-fulfilling prophecy of perceived mediocrity induced by the failure to measure and to celebrate *progress* and small wins improvements for teachers, students, or schools. This is a disturbing analysis, but participants in high-need schools seem to be more oriented toward failure than progress; this is perhaps due to the fact that since tests emphasize normative comparisons, the individual progress of students (which is sometimes considerable) is not recognized. Note that principals in low-performing schools grade teachers more harshly than do principals in high-performing schools. Similarly, teachers in low-performing schools assign lower marks to their principals than in higher-performing schools (MetLife Foundation, 2013). Although these could

TABLE 1.10 Ratings of Teachers' and Principals' Performances as a Function of School Level, Location, and Student Characteristics

	Rated teachers' performance as excellent	
	Principals	Teachers
Total	63%	58%
School level		
Elementary	67%	65%
Middle/high school	55%	51%
School location		
Urban	56%	51%
Suburban	67%	66%
Rural	66%	56%
Percentage of students from low-income families		
0–33%	75%	73%
34–66%	67%	55%
67+ %	51%	48%
Percentage of students from minority families		
0–33%	72%	68%
34–66%	57%	56%
67+ %	50%	43%
Students at/above grade level in English language arts and math		
All/most	74%	70%
Some/very few/none	44%	43%

Source: Adapted from the MetLife Survey of the American Teacher: Challenges for School Leadership (Metlife, 2013).

be veridical reports that accurately describe performance, it seems equally possible that the general societal conception of low-income schools and the constant bombardment in media sources and government policy reports that these schools are deficient lead to participants not fully recognizing the difficulties that they collectively face in these schools (Berliner & Glass, 2014; Good, 2014; Marx, 2014).

There are many reasons why principals and teachers rate one another more harshly in low-performing schools than in high-performing schools. The simplest explanation is that these principals and teachers are less effective than their peers, and indeed, research has shown that bottom teachers in higher-poverty schools are less effective than bottom teachers in lower-poverty schools (Sass, Hannaway, Xu, Figlio, & Feng, 2010). Although this may be part of the explanation, we do not think it is the fundamental truth. Sass et al. (2010) found that the best teachers were equally effective, regardless of poverty context. Furthermore, we base our reasoning on our experience in studying schools enrolling primarily low-income students (Lavigne & McCaslin, 2008; McCaslin & Good, 2008; Wiley, Good, & McCaslin, 2008). Our research team studied 21 schools that had been awarded CSR awards, and the research included measures of student achievement, student motivational reports, classroom observations, and in-depth interviews with school principals.

The sample was representative of CSR schools in Arizona. Data were collected in 21 of the 23 schools that were awarded in that time period. The 21 participating schools served students with concentrations of poverty ranging from 41% to 100% ($M = 73\%$). Schools varied notably in size (range 43–1131 students, $M = 600$; most schools enrolled between 400 and 700 students), and were located in urban areas, small cities, and rural communities. The study included schools where the dominant student population was African American, Anglo, Hispanic, or Native American (although the dominant population across the entire sample was Hispanic). Observational data were collected in an unannounced fashion, strengthening our belief that the obtained data were reasonably representative. Observational measures described instructional practices, opportunities for learning, classroom management strategies, and teacher-student relationships, and data were collected in both reading and math (see Wiley et al., 2008, for more detail).

The data provided strong evidence for meaningful student activities, good teacher-student relationships, effective instructional practices, and principal support. Principals were consistently supportive of their teachers during extensive interview sessions (Good, 2008). "Some principals reported reservations about the ability or motivation of a few teachers, but as a group the principals we met were adamant in their beliefs that most teachers worked hard, that classroom environments were positive, and that students were learning . . ." (Good, 2008, p. 2483). Wiley, Good, and McCaslin (2008) concluded, "Consistent with principals' beliefs about the classroom environments in their schools, our observational data from the present study show that students were actively and productively engaged in assigned tasks in classrooms in which teachers were pleasant and supportive" (p. 2385). Students in some classes were given little opportunity for choice in academic or social activities and their assigned work, particularly in math, which primarily involved basic skills and facts. Thus, we thought that aspects of the instructional program could be improved, but in general, we felt that the teaching in these settings was generally effective and responsive to the school context and classroom learning. Furthermore, principals' beliefs support our working hypothesis that in schools with high numbers of students failing to achieve grade level the performance of teachers and principals is underevaluated.

We realize that there have been documented cases of incredibly poor teaching in some circumstances; however, we suspect that in most schools that serve high proportions of low-income students, the absence of normative achievement is likely to be at least, if not more, of a comment on the conditions of poverty than on the quality of teaching (Berliner, 2014). Still, to the extent that a culture of defeat exists in these schools, it is likely that practice will continue to be evaluated lower than perhaps it objectively is. The consequences of a culture of mediocrity are, of course, more teacher and principal stress, less job satisfaction, higher turnover, and more fragile school environments.

We hypothesize that the lower ratings in schools—with objectively the hardest teaching circumstances—arise in part from a culture of defeat. This is possible because these schools' constituencies primarily hear about the school in terms of normative standards that compare them with other schools, many of whom have more resources. Public reports of their failures are frequent and highly visible to all. Furthermore, participants in low-performing schools see more teacher and student mobility and the cues of starting over are constant and potentially demoralizing. Even more concerning is a recent finding that all teacher turnover hurts student achievement (Ronfeldt, Loeb, & Wyckoff, 2012).

In Chapter 5 we present suggestions for how principals can work with teachers in all school settings to improve student achievement. In high-poverty schools principals need to focus primarily on instructional goals. Given the low community expectations for struggling schools, it is particularly important for these principals to provide evidence that students are making progress. As we noted earlier, in CSR schools we felt that principals could be more effective advocates of what they were doing well. Furthermore, principals should realize that they cannot do everything at once, and they should focus on the most critical tasks and work with teachers who are ready to improve. Furthermore, as we noted earlier and as others have found elsewhere (Bryk, 2010), some schools are functioning comparatively well in difficult circumstances.

The "Greening" of the Teacher Workforce

In the U.S., principals are working with a changing teacher population. Ingersoll and Merrill (2012) have noted that in the 1987–1988 school year 65,000 new teachers began teaching, but in 2007–2008 200,000 new teachers entered the field. Marx (2014), commenting upon the "greening" of the teaching force, wrote, "Along with the well-known phenomenon that we lose about half of the new teachers within 5 years of their entry to the field (Ingersoll & Perda, 2012), the rate of first-year teacher attrition is actually going up (Ingersoll & Merrill, 2012)" (p. 12). These patterns assure that many principals will be working with inexperienced teachers. While new teachers often bring new ideas and energy, they also have less knowledge about how schools work and often less knowledge about dealing with problematic colleagues, parents, and students. We will discuss the implications of principals working with less experienced teachers in Chapter 5. However, it is worth considering who will replace departing teachers. Lavigne (2014) noted that teaching morale is at an all-time low and that the current high-stakes evaluation practices may discourage some, if not many, from entering teaching.

Conclusion

In this chapter, we provided a voice and a face for principals who are implementing high-stakes teacher evaluation. We discussed who principals are and what they do. We have seen that principals have complex and busy jobs, and research spanning over 30 years shows that principals are busy, have little time for reflection, and often multitask. Although the types of tasks a principal deals with over the course of the year may be somewhat predictable, the timing of those tasks often is not, resulting in frequent interruptions and unplanned activities.

This chapter shows that principals (like teachers) work long weeks and have stressful lives. Roughly half of principals, in a national report, indicated that they feel great stress several times a week. Even more concerning is that overworked and overstressed principals are now being asked to spend more time in classrooms evaluating teachers than ever before. To further complicate matters, teacher job dissatisfaction is at an all-time high, and this too adds to the frustration of principals as they cope and help teachers who are also under stress, especially in the context of high-stakes evaluations. Given that teachers and principals are judged on their ability to improve student achievement scores, it must be stressful for many principals when they know they have but little influence in removing teachers and have little control over other aspects of their jobs, such as curriculum.

We have also discussed two emerging aspects that some principals must cope with. Some principals face deteriorating climates in schools that enroll high numbers of low-income students and minority students; in schools that have fewer students performing at grade level, principals are rated lower than principals in schools with more high-income students. Perhaps, not surprisingly, these principals reciprocally rate their teachers' effectiveness lower than principals rate teachers in schools populated with more higher-income students. We have argued that perceptions and lower ratings in these schools may be more about the culture of defeat than the actual abilities of teachers and principals. Another issue is the changing teaching force, and it is clear that principals in most school settings will have to deal with what some have referred to as a "greening" of today's teachers. Teachers, even relatively new teachers, are leaving teaching more quickly than in the past, resulting in the fact that some schools will be populated with teachers who have very limited experience. New teachers generally need considerable support as they deal with instructional challenges inherent in the first years of teaching. Principals of schools that enroll high numbers of low-income students also experience high teacher attrition, and as such may be differentially impacted by the "greening" of the teacher workforce.

We have reviewed research describing what principals have been observed to do during their workday spanning 40 years. Principals spend little time observing and evaluating teachers. Principals are very busy and under great stress, yet they are being asked to spend more time in classrooms. In Chapter 2, we will describe RttT—what it means for teachers and principals and specifically how putatively it will change how principals use time. But many questions beg for answers: How will principals find the time to accommodate the increase in required observations? How will they achieve these tasks in ways that allow them to have extended (and uninterrupted) time in observing and conferencing with teachers?

References

Berliner, D. C. (2014). Exogenous variables and value-added assessments: A fatal flaw. *Teachers College Record, 116*(1). Retrieved from www.tcrecord.org/content.asp?content id=17293

Berliner, D. C., & Glass, G.V. (2014). *Myths and lies that threaten America's public schools: The real crisis in education.* New York: Teachers College Press.

Bryk, A.S. (2010). Organizing schools for improvement. *Phi Delta Kappan, 91*(7), 23–30.

Council of Chief State School Officers. (1996). *Interstate school leaders licensure consortium: Standards for school leaders.* Washington, DC: Author.

Ebmeier, H., & Crawford, G. (2008). Principals. In T. L. Good (Ed.), *21st century education: A reference handbook* (pp. 31–41). Thousand Oaks, CA: SAGE.

Edmonds, R. (1982). Effective schools for the urban poor. *Educational Leadership, 40,* 12–15.

Firestone, W., & Martinez, C. (2007). Districts, teacher leaders, and distributed leadership: Changing instructional practice. *Leadership and Policy in Schools, 6,* 3–35.

Gamson, D.A., Lu, X., & Eckert, S.A. (2013). Challenging the research base of the Common Core State Standards: A historical reanalysis of text complexity. *Educational Researcher, 42*(7), 381–391.

Good, T. (2008). In the midst of Comprehensive School Reform: Principals' perspectives. *Teachers College Record, 110*(11), 2341–2360.

Good, T.L. (2014). What do we know about how teachers influence student performance on standardized tests: And why do we know so little about other student outcomes? *Teachers College Record, 116*(1). Retrieved from www.tcrecord.org/content.asp?contentid=17289

Good, T., & Brophy, J. (1986). School effects. In M. Whitrock (Ed.), *Handbook of research on teaching* (3rd ed., pp. 570–602). New York: Macmillan.

Good, T., & Brophy, J. (2008). *Looking in classrooms* (10th ed.). Boston, MA: Allyn and Bacon.

Goodwin, R., Cunningham, M., & Eagle, T. (2005). The changing role of the secondary principal in the United States: An historical perspective. *Journal of Educational Administration and History, 37*(1), 1–17.

Grissom, J.A., Loeb, S., & Master, B. (2013). Effective instructional time use for school leaders: Longitudinal evidence from observations of principals. *Educational Researcher, 42*, 433–444.

Horng, E., Klasik, D., & Loeb, S. (2010). Principal's time use and school effectiveness. *American Journal of Education, 116*(4), 491–523.

Ingersoll, R., & Merrill, L. (2012). *Seven trends: The transformation of the teaching force.* Philadelphia: Consortium for Policy Research in Education, University of Pennsylvania.

Ingersoll, R., & Perda, D. (2012). *How high is teacher turnover and is it a problem?* Philadelphia: Consortium for Policy Research in Education, University of Pennsylvania.

Jones, S.M., Dindia, K., & Tye, S. (2006). Sex equity in the classroom: Do female students lose the battle for teacher attention? In B.M. Gayle, R.W. Preiss, N. Burrell, & M. Allen (Eds.), *Classroom communication and instructional processes: Advances through meta-analysis* (pp. 185–215). Mahwah, NJ: Erlbaum.

Kafka, J. (2009). The principalship in historical perspective. *Peabody Journal of Education, 84*, 318–330.

Kmetz, J., & Willower, D. (1982). Elementary school principals' work behavior. *Educational Administration Quarterly, 18*(4), 62–78.

Lavigne, A. (2014). Exploring the implications of high-stakes teacher evaluation on schools, teachers, and students. *Teachers College Record, 116*(1).

Lavigne, A., & McCaslin, M. (2008). Student perceptions of teacher support. *Teachers College Record, 110*(11), 2423–2437.

Lavigne, A., & Oberg De La Garza, T. (forthcoming). The practice and evaluation of culturally responsive literacy for English language learners in the 21st century. In R. Gabriel & D. Allington (Eds.), *Evaluating literacy research: Principles and promising practices.*

Martin, W.J., & Willower, D.J. (1981). The managerial behavior of high school principals. *Educational Administration Quarterly, 17*(1), 69–60.

Marx, R. (2014). Reforming again: Now teachers. In A. Lavigne, T. Good, & R. Marx (Eds.), High-stakes teacher evaluation: High cost-big losses [Special Issue]. *Teachers College Record, 116*(1). Retrieved from www.tcrecord.org/Content.asp?ContentId=17296

Matthews, J., & Crow, G.M. (2003). *Being and becoming a principal: Role conceptualizations of contemporary principals and assistant principals.* New York: Pearson.

McCaslin, M., & Good, T. (2008). A study of Comprehensive School Reform programs in Arizona. *Teachers College Record, 110*(11), 2319–2340.

MetLife Foundation. (2013). *The MetLife survey of the American teacher: Challenges for school leadership.* Retrieved from www.metlife.com/metlife-foundation/about/survey-american-teacher.html?WT.mc_id=vu1101

Mintzberg, H. (1973). *The nature of managerial work.* New York: Harper & Row.

Parsons, T. (1960). *Structure and process in modern society.* Glencoe, IL: Free Press.

Pianta, R. C., La Paro, K., & Hamre, B. K. (2008). Classroom Assessment Scoring System (CLASS). Baltimore, MD: Paul H. Brookes.

Polikoff, M. S. (2014). Does the test matter? Evaluating teachers when tests differ in their sensitivity to instruction. In T. Kane, K. Kerr, & R. Pianta (Eds.), *Designing teacher evaluation systems: New guidance from the Measures of Effective Teaching Project* (pp. 278–302). San Francisco: Jossey-Bass.

Purkey, S. C., & Smith, M. S. (1983). Effective schools: A review. *Elementary School Journal, 83*(4), 427–452.

Ronfeldt, M., Loeb, S., & Wyckoff, J. (2012). How teacher turnover harms student achievement. *American Educational Research Journal, 50*(1), 4–36.

Ruzek, E. A., Hafen, C. A., Hamre, B. K., & Pianta, R. C. (2014). Value added for the evaluation and professional development of teachers. In T. Kane, K. Kerr, & R. Pianta (Eds.), *Designing teacher evaluation systems: New guidance from the Measures of Effective Teaching Project* (pp. 205–233). San Francisco, CA: Jossey-Bass.

Sass, T., Hannaway, J., Xu, Z., Figlio, D., & Feng, L. (2010). *Value added of teachers in high-poverty schools and lower-poverty schools*. Urban Institute. Retrieved from http://files.eric.ed.gov/fulltext/ED513819.pdf

Sherman, L. (2000, Spring). The new principal. *NW Education Magazine, 5*(3), 2.

Spillane, J. P., Camburn, E. M., & Pareja, A. S. (2007). Taking a distributed perspective to the school principal's workday. *Leadership and Policy in Schools, 6*(1), 103–125.

U.S. Department of Education. (2013). *Characteristics of public and private elementary and secondary principals in the United States: Results from the 2011–2012 Schools and Staffing Survey*. Retrieved from http://nces.ed.gov/pubs2013/201

Wallace Foundation. (2013). *Recent leader standards: From the six principal pipeline districts*. Retrieved from www.wallacefoundation.org/knowledge-center/school-leadership/principal-training/Documents/Recent-Leader-Standards.pdf

Wiley, C. R. H., Good, T., & McCaslin, M. (2008). Comprehensive School Reform instructional practices throughout a school year: The role of subject matter, grade level, and time of year. *Teachers College Record, 110*(11), 2316–2388.

Wolcott, H. F. (1973). *The man in the principal's office: An ethnography*. San Francisco, CA: Holt, Rinehart & Winston.

2
RACE TO THE TOP AND BEYOND
The Demand for More Classroom Observation

Chapter 1 described the difficult and complex roles of principals. Many principals report heavy stress and reduced job satisfaction, and some are considering leaving the profession in the very near future as job expectations expand and principals are being held more accountable for teaching and learning. Thus, the principal's job is becoming even busier.

Before moving forward with the principal's immediate task, we take a step back. Here, we present a brief history of education reform, demonstrate its circular nature, and identify Race to the Top (RttT) as its latest cycle. We describe the timing of RttT in the context of criticism over teacher evaluation and recent advances and interest in teacher effects, and show how these trends have informed RttT requirements. Subsequently, we report on how states are responding. The chapter ends with a summary of what we have learned to date and a description of RttT push-back.

Around and Around We Go: Sit

Many reviews exist on education reform over the past 70 years (Cuban, 2013; Good & Braden, 2000; Ravitch, 2010; Tyack & Cuban, 1997) and in the context of student motivation and the learner (McCaslin, 1996, 2006; McCaslin & Lavigne, 2010). It is important to note that problems with American education are not new. Over 40 years ago, Tyler (1969) found that 15% of children in the U.S. did not possess literacy levels necessary for employment, and 40–60% of urban sixth graders functioned academically at the level of second graders (cited in Brophy & Good, 1974). In reflecting on how the American government has responded these "problems," we argued that education reform in the U.S. is cyclical, ineffective, and not informed by research (Lavigne & Good, 2013). From our previous writing, we narrow our account to four significant reform efforts occurring prior to RttT.

We identified the first notable reform as a response to a math-science crisis that resulted from America's apparent loss in the race to space. When the Soviets launched Sputnik in 1957, Americans were shell-shocked—what went wrong? There was a quick and "easy" answer. American students were inadequately prepared in mathematics and science. The solution was new math. New math was proposed as a more rigorous and more abstract mathematics program that introduced junior high math concepts in the elementary grades. The reform came, large amounts of money were spent, teachers invested considerable time in learning new math, and then it quickly disappeared.

The second reform was a response to *A Nation at Risk*, a scathing review of American education issued by the National Commission on Excellence in Education in 1983. The problem now was that American schooling was abysmal, leaving the country vulnerable to military and economic threats. The "solution"? More is better. Longer school years, longer school days, and more homework. Students and teachers needed to work harder. These recommendations had little impact on student achievement.

The third crisis/reform was caused by a report from the National Education Commission on Time and Learning, *Prisoners of Time* (1994). It said that American schools were still failing, but rather than more schooling, the new solution was structural changes—students needed more time to think more deeply (e.g., inquiry, exploration, discussion). So, now schools were encouraged to use time efficiently and on core subjects (because other "successful" countries spent time on core subjects). Like other reforms, its narrow problem conceptualization (ignoring systematic factors, such as poverty and inadequate funding) did little to improve student outcomes.

The fourth reform, No Child Left Behind (NCLB), became law in 2001. This reform asserted that the problem was that American education was leaving too many children behind. Previous reforms (merely responses to reports) paled in comparison to this reform, which held the potential for much more systematic change because it was law. In this bold law, the solution to the alleged problem was greater accountability, challenging state standards (as measured by standardized tests), and a better understanding of important variables, such as race and English proficiency, by requiring states to report test results by groups. The possible costs were real: unsuccessful schools would be required to restructure or close—no carrots, only sanctions. NCLB's theme was "improve or else." Unfortunately this reform did not narrow the achievement gap between rich and poor or black and white (see McKown, 2013).

The history of education reform in the United States has common similarities (Lavigne & Good, 2013). First, the "problem" driving reform bounces from one problem or victim to another without any evidence that the "problem" characterization is valid. The asserted problem was curriculum in the math-science crisis. In *A Nation at Risk*, it was students. In *Prisoners of Time*, the problem was that core subjects were neglected, and in NCLB, it was schools. Other trends that characterize education reform in the U.S. include the following:

- Each crisis is a concern for poor achievement on standardized tests.
- Each crisis is based on international comparisons of student performance, not on goals set by the educational community.
- The general solution is based on a rejection of the status quo and a call for something sharply new and that has not been piloted.
- In time, data suggest that the new reform has not resolved the problem.
- The professional community has not been active in speaking against problematic reform in a timely fashion.
- American policy makers embark on costly new endeavors without even defining what the movement means. (Lavigne & Good, 2014, p. 39)

RttT is no different. We suggest that evaluators responding to RttT requirements do so carefully, as many actions called for today will pass in time because much of what is now recommended lacks a research base and will not improve practice. Consider that there is limited evidence that new teacher evaluation models will improve teaching and learning. Further, several have described the difficulties in using value-added (VA) scores in evaluating teachers (see Amrein-Beardsley, 2014; Berliner & Glass, 2014; Lavigne, Good, & Marx, 2014; Loeb, 2013; Raudenbush, 2014; Raudenbush & Jean, 2012), particularly because they are weakly related to observational data. Later, we will present more arguments for and against VA to allow readers to determine if our logic about the limitations of VA is valid. This chapter also discusses what we do and do not know about how observation and feedback can meet one mission of RttT—improve teacher effectiveness.

Race to the Top: An Overview

As of 2014, over $6 billion has been allocated to RttT (U.S. Department of Education [USDOE], 2013b), a competitive grant program designed to encourage and reward states to pursue innovative and systematic reform to improve learning in America's schools. Race to the Top emphasizes four major improvement areas:

- standards and assessments,
- data systems that capture and distribute information about student progress,
- teacher and school leader effectiveness, development, recruitment, and retention, and
- interventions for the lowest-performing schools

(USDOE, 2013a)

Three RttT application and granting phases occurred from March 2010 to December 2011 (not including Early Learning grant winners), awarding funds to

18 states and the District of Columbia (USDOE, 2010a, 2010b, 2011). In 2012, RttT-District was launched, investing nearly $400 million in schools to create models that offer personalized learning for students (USDOE, 2013c). Even states and districts that were not awarded RttT dollars have been reforming teacher evaluation as part of the RttT application submission process. We now focus on one branch of RttT: support for teacher and school leader effectiveness, development, recruitment, and retention (also known as Great Teachers and Leaders).

Why Race to the Top

Nationally we are radically changing how teachers are evaluated. As we argued earlier, reforms emerge out of perceived problems. And, in RttT the "problem" with American education is now seen as ineffective teachers and poor evaluation systems.

The problem conceptualization of teacher evaluation: an overview. Teacher evaluation has been plagued by inadequate definitions (what constitutes effective teaching) and inadequate research. One highly publicized critique comes from *The Widget Effect*, a report summarizing findings from a study of 15,000 teachers and 1,300 administrators (Weisberg, Sexton, Mulhern, & Keeling, 2009). The finding, that nearly 99% of teachers in some districts receive proficient or highly proficient ratings, generated considerable *concern* because skewed distributions offer limited opportunity to differentiate between teachers. In a July 2009 speech, U.S. secretary of education Arne Duncan responded to the report's findings, with "Who in their right mind really believes that?" Like Duncan, for policy makers, ratings are not believable because historically student test scores have been perceived as atrocious, especially in comparison to South Korea, Taiwan, Singapore, and Japan (Rich, 2012). Further, those who have illustrated this rationale as flawed (Berliner & Biddle, 1995; Berliner & Glass, 2014; Good & Braden, 2000) have not been successful in quieting the critics. Thus, the belief that American education is a system in crisis continues to be perpetuated. These negative beliefs about U.S. schools, exacerbated by other problematic elements of teacher evaluation, such as limited observations per teacher and the infrequent use of evaluation data to inform personnel decisions (Weisberg et al., 2009), provide the perfect storm, one that points to the inability to evaluate teachers well as a crucial lever in the "underachievement of U.S. public schools."

Two complementary trends help fuel this perfect storm. In the past decade, "new" research has emerged, challenging traditional measures of teacher quality and establishing a new definition of teacher quality. Concurrently, researchers have been attempting to identify and refine methods that are proposed to be more effective at capturing teacher effects. We now discuss these two trends.

Redefining teacher quality. Historically, teacher quality has been defined by what teachers *are*, not by what teachers *do*. Thus, policy makers measured teacher quality by the degrees a teacher held, years of experience, scores on certification exams, and so forth. These variables have been used for some time to inform salary increases, despite the fact that they have little explanatory power in predicting student outcomes and do not capture variations in teacher effectiveness (Buddin & Zamarro, 2009; Goldhaber & Brewer, 1997; Kane, Rockoff, & Staiger, 2008; Monk, 1994). This may be due to the imprecise nature of these measures and an inherent inability to capture what teachers actually do that makes them effective. Susan Rosenholtz (1989) captures the conceptual problems with such measures, like experience, by insightfully noting that ten years of experience is sometimes associated with an image of teachers gaining new skills, but in some cases it may mean only that a teacher has had the same experience ten times. To present another case, we consider a study attempting to relate teachers' knowledge of math to effective teaching. Hill, Umland, Litke, and Kapitula (2012) administered mathematics assessments to 34 elementary and middle school teachers and observed and rated their instruction. Although poor performance on the written mathematics assessment predicted poor performance in classroom instruction, teachers who scored in the middle of the written assessment distribution varied considerably in their classroom practice. For example, two teachers who had scored in the *middle* of the distribution on a written assessment of mathematics knowledge and skills had *strong* instruction. And several teachers who scored *moderately well* had *weak* instruction. Essentially, assessments of teachers' mathematical knowledge and skills may not accurately identify teacher effectiveness. These findings contribute to the general consensus that traditional, albeit indirect, indicators of teacher effectiveness (e.g., degree, certification exams) are not good measures of a teacher's instruction or the student achievement gains a teacher produces. Naturally, direct measures of effective teaching and the intended outcome of good teaching—student learning—are now the preferred measures.

Proposed advances in capturing teacher effects. In addition to using more direct measures of teaching practice, a second trend has emerged, calling for greater accuracy in capturing teacher effects—more precisely *a* teacher's effect on student achievement. Innovative methods of analysis, such as value-added (VA), have allowed researchers to measure teacher effects in ways argued to be better (more accurate and appropriate) for making personnel decisions. Proponents of VA argue that scores are reasonably valid, touting evidence that VA reliability is higher (on average between .3 and .5) than that of a single observation, as found in the well-known Measures of Effective Teaching (MET) project (Harris, 2012).

Ironically, VA procedures were stimulated by "new" information on the strong effects of teachers on student achievement. Over a decade ago, it was established that teachers explain 7.5–21% of the variance in student achievement outcomes (Goldhaber & Brewer, 1999; Hanushek, Kain, & Rivkin, 1998). And these data were quickly confirmed by others (Aaronson, Barrow, & Sanders, 2007). But this was not a new understanding. More than 30 years ago, it was established that teachers matter (Brophy & Good, 1986; Good & Grouws, 1979; Good, Grouws, & Ebmeier, 1983). Statistical models like VA may be new and improved, but we have long known that teachers have strong and direct effects on student learning. What *is* new is research that examines the variability of teacher effects. Konstantopoulos and colleagues, using data from a Project STAR, a study of randomly assigned students to teachers, have considered differential teacher effects—do teacher effects vary across grades, across students? Konstantopoulos (2011) found that teacher effects are smaller in earlier than later elementary grades, and are more pronounced in reading than math. Students who are taught by teachers at the 85th percentile of the teacher effectiveness distribution for kindergarten, first, and second grades experience achievement increases of about one-third of a standard deviation in reading—equivalent to nearly one-third of a year's growth in reading achievement. Konstantopoulos and Sun (2012) found that teacher effects in one grade predict student achievement in following grades. Essentially, teacher effects persist. The most recent iteration of teacher effects is VA modeling. Value-added has extended the conversation on teacher effects from "How much do *teachers* matter?" or "How do *teachers* matter?" to "How much does *a* teacher matter?"—the goal being to quantify how a given teacher "has contributed to student learning in a particular subject in a particular year" (Raudenbush & Jean, 2012, p. 2). Value-added caught the attention of policy makers after Chetty, Friedman, and Rockoff (2013) released their findings from a study examining the long-term impact of teachers on students. In their research, one standard deviation increase in teacher VA was associated with an increase in lifetime earnings (about $350 more per year by age 28), reduction in teenage pregnancy, increase in neighborhood SES, and savings (as measured by the presence of a 401k). The study was frequently cited and gave policy makers a platform to promote VA.

In short, these two trends have created the "solutions" to the "problem" of teacher evaluation under RttT. There is a greater emphasis on direct measures of a teacher's instruction by allocating substantial weight to observational measures and promoting *more* observations of a teacher's instruction. Simultaneously, proposed advances in measuring teacher effects have translated to states' greater use of student achievement growth measures, like VA. This practice is supported by the premise that VA measures are better at capturing the unique contributions teachers make toward their students' achievement and thus are more appropriate for evaluation purposes. Later we challenge these premises, but for now we continue describing RttT.

Great Teachers and Leaders

One RttT goal is to develop evaluation systems that identify teacher and leader effectiveness so that those who excel can be rewarded and acknowledged and those who do not can be supported in their improvement or removed. It is argued that these intended outcomes can be met through:

- Recruiting, preparing, developing, and rewarding effective teachers and leaders.
- Focusing on teacher and leader effectiveness in improving student outcomes.
- Supporting states and districts in bold actions to increase the number of effective teachers and leaders where they are needed most.
- Strengthening pathways into teaching and school leadership positions in high-need schools.

(USDOE, n.d., p. 1)

With these goals in mind, there are five guiding mechanisms. See Table 2.1.

As seen in Table 2.1, the proposed mechanisms by which RttT winners can improve the quality of teaching seem to rest on *evaluation* rather than *supervision*. And, although most models include supervisory aspects, we have seen little evidence of providing meaningful feedback on teaching (and monitoring subsequent improvement) as part of this venture. In this book, we hope to make modest gains in addressing this gap.

TABLE 2.1 Guiding Principles in the Blueprint for Great Teachers and Leaders

Principle	*Description*
Flexibility with Results	Flexible grant funding
Rigorous and Valid Evaluation Systems	Improved state-approved teacher evaluation plan that uses multiple categories, student achievement data, and provides meaningful feedback for the improvement of instructional practices
Strengthen the Profession	Improve the professionalization of teachers through supporting collaboration, implementing pay-for performance models, and professional development that is closely aligned with teacher evaluation
Equity	More equitable distribution of effective teachers using data-driven decisions with those LEAs not meeting or struggling to meet performance targets
Data Transparency & Decision-Making	Using data to assess program performance, human-capital report cards, and assessment of the effectiveness of both professional development and teacher preparation programs

Source: Adapted from *Great Teachers and Leaders* (USDOE, n.d.).

Measuring Effective Teaching under Race to the Top

One way RttT has interpreted "rigor" is by requiring multiple measures of teacher effectiveness in teacher evaluation, including: observations of teacher performance, student achievement data, teacher self-reports, student and parent teacher evaluations, and other classroom artifacts. The major catch is that student growth must be one significant measure of teacher effectiveness (USDOE, 2010c). Some states have student growth accounting for 50% of a teachers' score (when data are available), and the remaining composed of observational data or other artifacts. Each RttT state calculates a teacher's final teacher evaluation score differently. Typically scores are composites—measures are weighted and teachers receive a rating for each measure that contributes to a final score that falls into one of four or five categories.

An Example: Tucson Unified School District

To provide a concrete illustration, we describe how one district, the Tucson Unified School District (TUSD), in an RttT state, Arizona, constructed its teacher evaluation model (Scott, 2014). Under Arizona's Framework for Evaluating Teachers, TUSD is required to use student achievement growth and classroom observation data. Student achievement data must account for 33–50% of a teacher's evaluation, and classroom observation data 50–67% of a teacher's evaluation. Teachers are divided into two groups—those with classroom-level achievement data (Group A) and those without (Group B). Observations must be based on multiple classroom observations. See Figure 2.1.

The district uses a four-category rating scale designated by three cut-points: Ineffective (0–39 points), Developing (40–55 points), Effective (56–73 points), and Highly Effective (74–100 points). Cut-points for the rating categories are not equal and were based on the prior year's data, the normal distribution, and natural breaks in teacher effectiveness distributions, considering both consequential and face validity. The model is designed so that teachers scoring in the lowest growth group for achievement data can still be rated as highly effective—thus, student growth data does not exclude teachers from any rating category. Final data from the first year of model implementation (2013–2014) revealed the following distribution: Ineffective: .5%, Developing: 2.9%, Effective: 48.5%, and Highly Effective: 48.1%.

Tucson Unified School District's preliminary data mirror historic distributions of teacher effectiveness (e.g., *The Widget Effect*) and those found in other states (as illustrated later in this chapter). Regardless of whether districts and states use different composite models or choose different methods of determining cut scores, to date, distributions of teacher effectiveness have remained fairly stable. Most systems are works in progress and attempt to respond to stakeholder needs as the evaluation systems move forward. Furthermore, there is flexibility and variation, such as locally developed (with state approval) observation instruments, and other

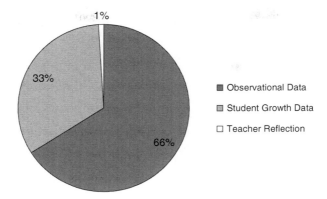

FIGURE 2.1 Tucson Unified School District's Teacher Evaluation Model

possibilities within a set of state-approved guidelines, such as the weight allocated to model components (as illustrated by TUSD). Next, we provide a brief summary of classroom observations and student achievement. These measures were chosen because they are the most frequently used in RttT teacher evaluations and are assigned the greatest weight.

Measures of Teacher Effectiveness

Classroom observation. All RttT winners are using classroom observations as one measure of teacher effectiveness. It is difficult to summarize to what extent states and districts are implementing various observation protocols; however, most use some modification of the following rubrics: Framework for Teaching (FfT; Danielson Group, 2013), Causal Teacher Evaluation Model (Marzano, 2011), or the Classroom Assessment Scoring System (CLASS; Pianta, La Paro, & Hamre, 2008). Marzano's Causal Teacher Evaluation and the FfT are most similar in the dimensions of teaching addressed, as they both cover classroom environment/instruction, planning, and reflection. The CLASS provides a greater emphasis on what happens in the classroom—instruction and climate.

Patterns in teacher evaluation across states reveal that most states are moving toward models in which teachers are observed at least annually. Number of observations may vary based on tenure status or prior effectiveness rating. For example, in Tennessee, apprentice teachers were initially required to have six observations for a minimum of 90 minutes total. All other teachers received a minimum of four observations for a total of minimum of 60 minutes (Tennessee State Board of Education [TSBE], 2011). In Year 2, modifications were made to reduce the number of observations, and make required observations dependent on prior individual value-added or overall evaluation score (TSBE, 2012b).

Usually states require some combination of announced and unannounced observations and formal and informal observations (TSBE, 2011). Walk-throughs are one common informal observation method used by evaluators (Ohio

Department of Education [ODE], 2013). Visits are usually brief (3 to 5 minutes) followed by a conversation with the teacher (Downey, Steffy, Poston, & English, 2010). Formal observations typically last a class period or anywhere from 20 to 45 minutes and are completed using an observation rubric (North Carolina State Board of Education [NCSBE], 2012; ODE, 2013; TSBE, 2011). Formal observations often consist of pre- and postconferences. In North Carolina, a pre-observation conference consists of a review of the teacher's self-reflection from the start of the school year, the teacher's most recent professional development (PD) plan, and the lesson that will be observed, including a written lesson plan from the teacher. Postobservation conferences are often conducted within a given window—anywhere from a week to two weeks following the observation—and are expected to consist of a review of how the teacher was scored on the observation rubric, emphasizing the teacher's strengths and weaknesses (NCSBE, 2012).

An example of the observation cycle: Marana Unified School District. In another district in Arizona, Marana Unified School District (MUSD), teachers and their supervisors participate in an evaluation process specifically designed to emphasize instructional improvement (Dumler, Reidy, Cadigan, & Clem, 2014). The process is composed of five steps: (1) Formative Reflection Conference, (2) Informal Observations (at least two), (3) First Formal Observation Cycle (Planning Conference, Observation, Reflection Conference), (4) Second Formal Observation Cycle (or two additional Informal Observations), and (5) Summative Reflection Conference. The goal of the Formative Reflection Conference is to discuss a teacher's self-reported strengths and weaknesses, describe the evaluation process, and set any expectations and goals for the teacher's professional growth. Schools are recommended to conduct an informal observation prior to the First Formal Evaluation Cycle in order to build communication and set expectations, but informal observations do happen throughout the year. In the First Formal Evaluation Cycle, a pre-observation conference (Planning Conference) occurs in which the teacher is asked to describe what the evaluator will be observing (e.g., "Briefly describe your lesson from beginning to end. How will you engage students in the learning? What will you do? What will your students do?"). The evaluator then completes the formal observation, using Danielson's Framework for Teaching, and follows with a Reflection Conference (or postobservation conference). In the Reflection Conference, the teacher is asked to rate his or her own lesson and respond to a number of prompts (e.g., "Did all the students achieve the content goal for this lesson? What is your evidence?").

With instructional improvement in mind, the major cornerstones of MUSD's teacher evaluation include: trusting relationships, evaluator-teacher dialogue centered on progress and reflection, and an emphasis on the formative (rather than summative) nature of teacher evaluation. According to Dumler et al. (2014), clarity and explicit evidence of what was observed are crucial to effective teacher evaluation. The district's approach provides an excellent beginning point for other districts as they consider how to implement observational components of teacher evaluation. We provide information related to postobservation conference feedback later, including specific prompts, structure, and feedback processes that help support teacher growth and development.

Student achievement and growth. The second and most hotly debated component of teacher evaluation is the use of student achievement data, in part because it is often allocated substantial weight and many challenge whether standardized achievement tests are a valid measure of instruction and student learning. States typically use multiple ways to measure student growth—end-of-year scores, student gain scores from fall to spring, and other measures, such as VA. In Tennessee, student achievement represents 50% of a teacher's evaluation; growth (as measured by VA data) accounts for 35% of a teacher's evaluation score, and an additional 15% is represented by other student achievement measures (percentages are different for teachers of non-tested subjects)(Tennessee Department of Education, n.d.). In most cases, though, RttT winners require that student achievement data account for anywhere from 30% (Illinois) to as high as 50% of a teacher's evaluation score. Across and within states, there is some leeway. In Arizona, as noted, TUSD bases 33% of a teacher's evaluation score on student achievement growth data, whereas an adjacent district could utilize the maximum, 50%. These decisions have important implications as the chosen measures (and associated weights) included in any model can significantly change which teachers are identified as effective and ineffective (Rothstein & Mathis, 2013).

Some states stagger the implementation of new teacher evaluation models, adding student achievement last, given its complexity. This component is challenging because many subject areas are *not* tested, so states often need to develop new measures for non-tested subjects and grades. This can delay teacher evaluation implementation for states.

Value-added models. Another reason why student achievement is difficult to implement is because some analyses require multiple years of data, such as VA. Multiple years of data have been shown to help identify performance differences among teachers (Goldhaber & Hansen, 2008; Lipscomb, Teh, Gill, Chiang, & Owens, 2010) and decrease the effects of outliers (McCaffrey, Sass, Lockwood, & Mihaly, 2009). Two years of data are significantly better than one, but additional years (beyond two and up to six) have shown only modest gains in predictive power (Loeb & Candelaria, 2012). Unfortunately, for many teachers, especially new teachers and those who teach in non-tested subject areas or grades, these data are not readily available. For example, in Tennessee's Year 1 of RttT, only 36% of teachers were teaching in tested grades and subject areas and received an individual value-added score, leaving a whopping 64% of teachers without data related to the students they actually taught during the 2011–2012 school year (TDOE First to the Top, 2012). In another study of four districts, only 22% of teachers were evaluated using VA data (Whitehurst, Chingos, & Lindquist, 2014). When individual VA data are not available, sometimes school-level VA data are used. This is problematic because teachers may be held accountable on the basis of what *other* teachers do.

Despite these challenges, supporters assert that VA is better than other statistical techniques (end-of-year scores or pre- and postgrowth) in capturing student background variables and can, with certain assumptions met, provide unbiased measures of teacher effectiveness (Harris, 2008; Harris & Sass, 2006). Value-added scores seek to capture a teacher's contribution to student learning in a given year and subject. Let's take Teacher A. Teacher A's VA score is based on all students in Teacher A's classroom. Students' end-of-year achievement test scores from the prior year are compared to the current year, capturing only the "growth" that could have been achieved under Teacher A's instruction. In some models, important variables such as socioeconomic status are controlled for. Because VA scores are derived by comparing the average *expected* achievement gains of students in a given teacher's class to the average *actual* achievement gains of a teacher's students (Raudenbush & Jean, 2012), Teacher A's VA is determined by understanding the growth that similar students make under the instruction of *other* teachers. But because students are not randomly assigned to teachers, there is significant doubt that such models can capture only the effect of a single teacher without capturing other variables as well. Furthermore, the effects of high student mobility on VA scores are unclear. Imagine that in the following year Teacher A has 10 of her 22 students remaining at the end of the school year, whereas her colleague down the hall, Teacher B, has all 22 of his students remaining. For Teacher A, how representative are those ten students of the instruction she has offered throughout the year? Such questions make the debate over VA a heated one.

Teacher Evaluators and Observers

Those designing and making decisions about teacher evaluation models also need to be keenly aware of *who* evaluates teachers. Evaluators are typically responsible for determining a teacher's final summative evaluation score. Evaluators may also observe teachers in their own building or another building in the district. Observations require considerable time, and most new teacher evaluation plans require multiple observations and sometimes multiple observers (see Hillsborough County Schools [HCS], 2011). States cope with this in many ways. States may have separate certification processes for observation and evaluation, allowing the opportunity for more individuals to be certified to observe. In the District of Columbia Public Schools (DCPS), peer review and assistance (PAR) is used to reduce case loads. Master evaluators outside of the district assist in observing teachers; most evaluators have a case load of 80–100 teachers (Headden & Silva, 2011). Peer observers are trained on evaluation systems, but can also serve as mentor teachers. Some benefits of PAR, beyond sharing the burden of observations, are that peer observers can be selected to best suit the teacher being observed (e.g., matched on grade level or content area). But peer observers aren't free—they need release time from classroom teaching, training, and recalibration. In DCPS, peer observers cost $1,500 per teacher being evaluated. If observers serve as mentors, the cost increases substantially. In Florida (Hillsborough County Schools), peer observers cost $1,125 per evaluated teacher, but cost $4,250 if mentoring is included (Jacques, 2013). And costs are higher for teachers who qualify for intervention—ranging from $6,000 to $10,000 per teacher. The greatest expense related to PAR is hiring replacement teachers for teachers who become consulting teachers and are released half-time or full-time, which accounts for 75% of all expenditures. A second expense is the consulting teacher's stipend, which costs districts $5,000 to $10,000 per stipend (Papay & Johnson, 2011). Clearly, peer review is no small expense, but it may be worth it (or necessary) in districts that require several observations annually (HCS, 2011). Furthermore, although no causal effect has been found, urban districts using PAR have demonstrated high teacher retention rates for first-year teachers—an average of 90%, offsetting some of the costs of PAR (Papay & Johnson, 2011) by saving districts nearly $10,000 to $20,000 per first-year teacher retained (Barnes, Crowe, & Schafer, 2007). Historically, principals and assistant principals have been responsible for supervision and evaluation, but the demands of new evaluation models require states to find other individuals who have the capacity to provide important feedback to teachers.

Evaluator and observer training. How do individuals become qualified to evaluate teachers? Most states require evaluators to pass a training that covers state laws and legislation, establishes reliability on an observation instrument, and provides guidance in gathering evidence and using student growth components (see Massachusetts Department of Elementary & Secondary Education [MDESE], n.d.). In some states, refresher trainings happen throughout the year (e.g., Tennessee). And in some districts (e.g., TUSD), evaluators need to be recertified to evaluate every year. It is unclear, however, if these trainings are required and if evaluators who are unable to recalibrate to an appropriate level of reliability are required to seek additional support. It is important to note that the number of individuals passing reliability training can be easily adjusted by modifying the passing score. Videos of classroom instruction vary in their coding difficulty—those on the margin and in the middle of a scoring rubric (average teachers) prove to be particularly difficult. The lack of stringent standards for pass rates and reliability on teacher evaluator training is concerning, particularly if teacher evaluations are used in high-stakes ways.

What We Have Learned So Far

As of September 2013, five RttT recipients had fully implemented their teacher and principal evaluation systems—Delaware, the District of Columbia, Florida, North Carolina, and Tennessee. Six other states—Hawaii, Maryland, New York, Ohio, Massachusetts, and Georgia—were in either the pilot or the partial implementation phase of new evaluation systems (U.S. Government Accountability Office, 2013). Given this progress, we note and extend comment on related issues or lessons that have arisen or in some cases reemerged in the context of RttT from pilot and/or early years of implementation reports, and concurrent research.

Problems of the Past Persist

Earlier in the chapter we noted a number of problems that have undermined education reform. We turn now to discuss three characteristics of past failed reforms that continue to haunt education reform.

Poor problem conceptualization. Perhaps the most debilitating issue facing education reform is unclear or misguided problem conceptualization. The push for more rigorous models of teacher evaluation was driven, in part, by the problem that all teachers were rated as effective. Some argue that traditional dichotomous classifications of teachers (e.g., effective/ineffective) cause principals to rate teachers higher than normal, resulting in few ineffective teachers and making it difficult to determine how teachers differ in effectiveness (Weisberg et al., 2009). The "evidence" that this was indeed a problem was the achievement of U.S. students as compared to international peers, a comparison that we believe to be problematic. So it comes as no surprise that these criticisms, nor the multiple rating categories and data-driven components of the revamped teacher evaluation models, have not significantly changed principals' perceptions of teachers. The evidence is overwhelming. Nearly 98% of principals rate teachers in their school as doing a good or very good job (MetLife, 2013). Following the 2012–2013 school year in New York City, 97% of teachers were rated as satisfactory (Fleisher, 2013), and in Rhode Island, 95% of teachers were rated as effective or highly effective (Rhode Island Department of Education [RIDOE], 2013). And in Georgia's pilot year, 93.85% of teachers were rated as proficient or exemplary (Georgia Department of Education [GDOE], 2012). Furthermore, Lavigne and Chamberlain (2014) asked Illinois school leaders ($N = 606$) to report the intended distribution of teacher ratings in the 2013–2014 year. On average, school leaders expected 92.29% of teachers to be rated as excelling or proficient. Some expected 100% of their teachers would be rated as excelling or proficient.

Principals continue to come under fire for these skewed distributions. Georgia's Department of Education (2012) had a few possible explanations. One was that principals needed more training, but as we will show ahead, more training may not alleviate these issues. A second explanation was that principals did not take the evaluation seriously. And, indeed, in another state (Rhode Island) 66% of principals admitted to giving higher ratings than they believed teachers should have received (RIDOE, 2013). This second argument could benefit from more research to understand what mechanisms may be related (e.g., district money and resources available to support ineffective teachers). Finally, it was argued that the skewed distribution was evidence of an unbalanced implementation process and that "principals and teachers must recognize that every teacher can improve in some capacity and truly exemplary teachers represent only a very small percentage of most faculties" (GDOE, 2012, p. 29). Clearly, there is some intended distribution in mind, but evidence supporting such a distribution is not obvious. Likewise, distributions should vary across districts and schools if the standard is absolute and not relative. Most importantly, these responses illustrate a disjointed solution, something that might be attributed to conceptual flaws that exist in the problem representation driving RttT.

Another concern about the skewed distribution of teacher effectiveness (other than its possible inaccuracy) is that rating teachers as effective gives teachers no incentive to improve. It also reduces the number of teachers who get support that may aid in improving their practices. In response to the skewed ratings, DCPS changed the cutoff scores for the rating categories in its IMPACT teacher evaluation system in the 2012–2013 year, making it harder for teachers to earn an "Effective" rating, and added a fifth category, "Developing." Teachers are evaluated on a 100–400-point scale, and under the new change, teachers are rated based on the following categories: Ineffective (100–199), Minimally Effective (200–249), Developing (250–299), Effective (300–349), and Highly Effective (350–400). This decision was guided by evidence that in the 2011–2012 school year, teachers in the lower end of the "Effective" category produced 8 fewer months of learning in math and 6 fewer months of learning in reading than teachers in the upper end. Adding a fifth category, "Developing," meant that more teachers would have access to PD and coaching, but also that they would be at risk of being fired if they did not improve in three years (DCPS, 2012). Given that moving from a dichotomous to a multiple category rating system did not alter teachers' effectiveness distributions, it is unclear how moving from four to five categories will improve anything. And if distributions do change, there are additional challenges. For example, we know little about the feedback that principals give to more effective and less effective teachers—will having more teachers rated as ineffective offer them access to better-quality feedback on their instruction? And PD has been criticized for failing to change teachers' practices significantly (Loucks-Horsley, Hewson, Love, & Stiles, 1998). Are resources and PD offered to struggling teachers under RttT better than those of the past? These are complex issues, but readers need to understand that these findings demonstrate that an ill-defined problem may have failed RttT at the starting line.

Higher stakes? Better results? In recent education reform, there has been the underlying belief that higher stakes would force schools and teachers to change in ways that improved student achievement. We have learned through NCLB that high stakes come with many negative and unintended consequences (see Nichols & Berliner, 2007). Despite this and in ahistorical fashion, many RttT states are using teacher evaluation data to make high-stakes decisions. Beyond decisions of dismissal and tenure, RttT is also pushing pay-for-performance methods, although such methods are ineffective (see Lavigne, 2014; Lavigne & Good, 2013). In a special issue of *Teachers College Record* focused on high-stakes teacher evaluation, many scholars warned against the use of teacher evaluation data in making high-stakes decisions, particularly when using VA data (Lavigne et al., 2014). And new warnings continue to emerge. New evidence begs for assessing whether warnings about VA are warranted.

The limited and recent results on the effectiveness of tying high stakes to teacher performance have been mixed. In one study, Dee and Wyckoff (2013) examined DCPS' IMPACT teacher-evaluation system, a high-stakes teacher evaluation system that results in dismissals for ineffective teachers and substantial bonuses for highly effective teachers. The system is based on three components: student achievement, observation, and commitment to school community. Student achievement includes individual or school value-added scores and/or a student learning measure selected by the teacher and principal. The observation instrument is based on the district's Teaching and Learning Framework, with most teachers receiving five formal observations, four of which are unannounced. Commitment to school community assesses teachers' professionalism, including support for school initiatives and collaboration with others. Teachers receive a composite score derived from their group assignment, which depends on the availability of individual value-added data. Group 1 teachers' final composite score consists of: 50% individual value-added score, 35% observation, 10% commitment to school community, and 5% school value-added score, whereas Group 2 teachers' score includes: 75% observation, 10% teacher-assessed student achievement data, 10% commitment to school community, and 5% school value-added score.

Dee and Wyckoff (2013) examined the first three years of implementation (the four-category rating system) and found that IMPACT improved the overall effectiveness of the teacher workforce through differential attrition of low-performing teachers and performance gains of those teachers who remained, as measured by IMPACT scores. The effect size was small—.24. Performance gains (approximately 10 percentage points) were observed for teachers who received a "Highly Effective" rating and would qualify for a significant bonus if they received the same rating the following year. Similar gains were seen for teachers who received a "Minimally Effective" rating in one year and were under the threat of dismissal if they received the same rating the following year. Findings indicated uniquely high performance effects for teachers whose initial scores were on the *threshold* of an effective rating—these teachers were also under the threat of dismissal if they received a second "Minimally Effective" rating, but had fairly promising prospects of avoiding this.

One concern about high-stakes teacher evaluation is that firing ineffective teachers will only put schools at risk of hiring new, inexperienced, and equally if not less effective teachers. Dee and Wyckoff found this not to be the case. Replacement teachers had an average IMPACT score of 281, 26 points higher than the teachers they replaced ($M = 255$)—a difference of half a standard deviation. The authors note that this finding is heavily based on the supply. It is well known that schools that struggle the most with student achievement serve a larger percentage of minority and low-income students, and also struggle to retain and recruit highly effective teachers (Lavigne, 2014). Although DCPS is a district that generally serves a similar student population, we do not know if any within-district variation existed that would suggest the impact of teacher evaluation operates differently across school conditions. Without this knowledge, it is still possible that high-stakes teacher evaluation, then, may sustain or increase the persistent academic disparities between groups of students—low-income students and their more affluent peers, minority and majority students, and English Language Learners (ELL) and non-ELL students. Only time will tell. Another issue related to supply is the trend we described in Chapter 1—the "greening" of the teacher workforce (Ingersoll & Merrill, 2012). This is particularly important, because Dee and Wyckoff found that teachers in their first two years of teaching had an average IMPACT score 17 points lower than teachers with 3+ years of experience. Linking improvement to an evaluation system may become quickly complicated if all replacement teachers are new teachers.

In conclusion, Dee and Wyckoff's (2013) study provided the possibility that high incentives might encourage low-scoring teachers to leave teaching and that teaching performance can be improved through evaluation. These are promising findings. However, these results must be qualified by the consideration that most studies of teacher incentives have not showed the value of incentives for changing teacher behavior or improving student achievement. The authors suggest that this may be because previous efforts have provided too little positive incentive or too few negative consequences. Yet these high-stakes incentives and the highly politicized context of the district in which the study was conducted place strong constraints on the exportability of these findings to other school settings.

Others suggest that high stakes are not necessary for improvement. Taylor and Tyler (2012) found that evaluation improved teacher performance, even when stakes were fairly low (study participants were tenured teachers). In a quasi-experimental study, fourth- through eighth-grade teachers in Cincinnati Public Schools ($N = 105$) were randomly assigned to an evaluation year across a 6-year period. Student achievement gains in classrooms of teachers prior, during, and after a year of evaluation were assessed. An "evaluation" year consisted of a practice-based evaluation based on observation. Teachers were observed four times—once by the supervising principal, and three times by an experienced peer—and rated using Danielson's Framework for Teaching. Postobservation, teachers were provided with written feedback and observers met with teachers at least once. Only the final observation score was recorded as the evaluation outcome. Like in RttT states, 90% of study teachers were rated in the top two rating categories (in a four-category system). Taylor and Tyler found students of teachers who were in their evaluation year scored .05 higher on end-of-year math exams, and these achievement gains persisted. A student taught by a teacher following the teacher's evaluation year scored 10% of a standard deviation higher than a student taught in a year prior to when the teacher was evaluated. No improvement was seen in reading achievement. Contrary to Dee and Wyckoff's (2013) findings, teachers who made the *largest* postevaluation gains were those who were the *weakest* prior to evaluation, suggesting that districts that immediately dismiss teachers for low performance may be shooting themselves in the foot. These findings also illustrate that more experienced teachers can demonstrate improvement in student achievement, contrary to research indicating that teachers' student achievement gains eventually plateau (Henry, Bastian, & Fortner, 2011; Rivkin, Hanushek, & Kain, 2005).

Noteworthy is that Taylor and Tyler's (2012) work was conducted in a school district where teacher unions and school administrators have agreed to work together to improve evaluation practices. The study was conducted with a very experienced set of principals and teachers. And the authors report and we agreed that there is no understanding of what mechanisms actually drive improvement. Hence, the external generalizability of these data is limited by both the sample used and an inability to link feedback to classroom process and student outcomes. Still, the study provides evidence that evaluation has positive influence in some contexts.

Taken together, these preliminary studies offer some interesting findings, and support the notion that teacher evaluation efforts can improve student achievement in some situations. But these studies largely inform policy. *How* teacher evaluation improves teaching remains largely unknown, leaving those who do the evaluation with few tools in their toolbox. One might ask, are the results a function of the *presence* of evaluation or the *actual feedback* that administrators provide during evaluation? Consider placebo effects, Hawthorne effects, and expectancy effects (Roethlisberger & Dickson, 1939). Most readers are aware that when drugs are marketed in the U.S. they have to pass clinical trials that show the drug has effects on health beyond those of a placebo (a pill known to have no medical value). This is required because for various and complex reasons our *belief* that we will get better has effects in ways (e.g., more exercise, less anxiety, more laughter, positive affect) that show positive results in the short run. Just as with drug trials, it might be valuable to demonstrate that the processes of evaluation (e.g., feedback on instruction) yield changes in teachers' practices and student achievement outcomes in ways beyond the effects of just being observed and evaluated.

Capacity. Many past reforms have failed because they were wrong or misguided, but some reforms may have failed because there was not enough time, resources, or money to implement the reform well, making any measureable change improbable. This knowledge is not new, but is particularly relevant to RttT. Doing teacher evaluation well is expensive, and issues of capacity arose quickly in the first years of RttT. For example, one New York district used $63,000 of its own money in addition to the $23,000 it received from RttT (U.S. Government Accountability Office, 2013). And it is not just money—time is also in short supply. We established that even prior to RttT, principals have long workweeks. Revamped teacher evaluation models add time demands, but offer little guidance about how to balance time and tasks. In Tennessee, principals and assistant principals conduct the bulk of teaching evaluations—75% of principals and 66% of assistant principals conducted 41 or more teacher observations in 2013 and spent approximately 7 hours a week on teacher evaluations (Ehlert, Pepper, Parsons, Burns, & Springer, 2013). In Illinois, school leaders report spending, on average, 7.78 hours evaluating a single teacher during the 2012–2013 school year. Some reported having as many as 30 teachers to evaluate, equating to nearly 210 hours in a given year spent evaluating teachers, or 5.5 40-hour workweeks. Many school leaders (85%) report the new teacher evaluation limits the time they have for other duties (Lavigne & Chamberlain, 2014). Some states (like Tennessee) have acknowledged these challenges by reducing the number of required observations (TSBE, 2012a), but in other states it is unclear what other activities principals are putting on the back burner and how this may undermine improvement. While it is important to understand capacity, states also need to continually assess the minimum requirements needed for evaluation components to be reliable and valid. Simply put, it makes no sense to cut required observations from four to one, if one observation does not produce reliable findings.

New Reform, New Lessons?

Many problems of the past persist. Yet we find that there are some important lessons specific to RttT. We perceive that the observation of teachers will continue despite RttT's success (or not). Next, we comment on two concerns that need to be addressed before observation and feedback can be used to improve teaching and learning.

Can observers identify teachers who have more or less influence on student achievement? Principals historically have spent little time observing and evaluating teachers, but are now asked to spend considerable time in this capacity. A critic might wonder if principals can do this task well given that their preparation programs have not emphasized this aspect of principalship. Furthermore, trainings under new evaluation models may hold minimal expectations, or, worse, be conducted online, offering limited opportunities for observers to develop a thorough consensus of disagreements and agreements on observation rubrics with others using the same rubric (or a master rater)—a minimal expectation for implementing observation rubrics well. Yet policy makers (if they have even considered it) are not deterred by this consideration.

Requirements under RttT reflect a belief that it is easy to separate more and less successful teachers. Thus, even if principals have not been trained to observe and provide effective feedback, it should be easy to do so. Although more and less effective teachers have been identified in previous work (Brophy & Good, 1986), it was exceedingly difficult to identify the relationships between teaching and student learning. Yet many believe that good teaching is so obvious that one can separate good from poor teachers by quickly observing teachers for a few minutes. Strong's (2011) work dispels this myth. Strong identified teachers who were consistently higher or lower in influencing students' math achievement over three consecutive years. Two-minute segments were selected from whole-class fraction lessons of teachers who were randomly chosen from high- and low-effective groups. These segments were then viewed by 100 judges, who varied in experience (school administrators, math educators, elementary school students, and adults who had no educational role). Lavigne and Good (2013) noted that the belief that observers could identify effective teaching on the basis of 2 minutes seems to strongly reflect a belief that *it is* easy to evaluate teachers. And the results provided clear evidence that separating good and less effective teachers was *not* easy. Across all judges, the agreement was .24 and there was no relationship between type of judge and accuracy of judgment. Actually, the most accurate judges were elementary school students!

Following the "failed" experiment, Strong (2011) provided six explanations in the attempt to understand why observers could not identify effective teaching. These included too small of a contrast in student achievement between more or less capable teachers, inadequately trained judges, and non-representative segments. A second experiment was conducted with a new sample of teachers and a more experienced and larger group of judges. For those who believe that teaching is easy to judge, the results were highly similar to those obtained in Experiment 1. Now with more experienced and better-trained judges, the correlation between observational ratings and student achievement was only .03 higher at .27. Clearly additional training and more experienced judges were no better than a larger, diverse set of raters in Experiment 1. These findings may also inform why, generally speaking, distributions of teacher effectiveness remain fairly unchanged by new evaluation models that are justified by required training for teacher evaluators (or more training, when distributions are less than ideal).

Experiment 3 varied other aspects of the research design in the attempt to obtain better results. Judges were given additional training time and used an established observation protocol (CLASS; Pianta et al., 2008). Unfortunately, trained observers using an established observation instrument and who viewed an *entire* lesson produced results no different than those of the first two experiments. The classification of teachers as more or less effective was no better than chance.

After Experiment 3 Strong used a subset of observational items to reanalyze the data. The subset of items consistently predicted more effective teachers and was from the instructional support scale of the CLASS. Items from the CLASS organization and emotional support scales did *not* predict effective teaching. We return to this finding in Chapter 3 as it differs notably from some studies that we review there.

In short, identifying good from poor teaching is no simple task. Obviously, if principals cannot consistently identify less effective teachers (as determined by student achievement scores), how can they provide teachers with meaningful feedback to improve their performance? Indeed, they may be trying to improve good teachers and ignoring less effective ones!

These issues are intricately tied to a poor problem conceptualization, but are particularly relevant to RttT as teacher evaluation is the new magic bullet that will improve instruction and student achievement. But, even so, relating measures of teaching to student achievement, even when done by highly trained experts, is exceedingly difficult to do. Hill et al. (2014) studied the relationship between teachers' VA scores and their mathematics instruction as observed by expert observers. Data were drawn from a pool of 250 fifth-grade mathematics teachers in different school districts. Teachers in each district were ranked on the basis of their VA scores, and then three teachers in the top, middle, and lowest quintiles were selected and rated on six videotaped lessons. The congruence between VA and observational measures varied across districts (−.47, .02, and .66). The researchers reported, "This is highly variable across districts, and, on average, lower than most correlations found in prior studies, suggesting that under the current study's protocol, at least, raters could not accurately predict value-added rank from viewing instruction" (Hill et al., 2014, p. 20). Finally, Hill et al. noted that 7 of the 27 teachers changed categories from high to low or from low to high. Such variation in rating the quality of teaching challenges the use of these measures in high-stakes evaluation.

Principals are being trained to use observational systems that are examples of what it is *believed* that effective teachers should be doing, but the foregoing findings raise some serious concerns. First and foremost, before we attempt to improve ineffective teachers' instruction, we need to be certain we can accurately identify which teachers *are* ineffective and to understand how their practices differ from their more effective peers. In Chapter 4, we present a deeper analysis of principal preparation and the ability of trained principals to identify effective teaching. Given what we have just reported, it will not be surprising to see there is substantial opportunity for improvement.

Alignment between measures of effective teaching. Observers' inability to differentiate between more or less effective teachers has also been packaged as a problem of alignment between multiple measures of effective teaching. Again, this is an issue tied to problem conceptualization, but relevant to RttT. Early findings from Tennessee's First to the Top implementation of teacher evaluation revealed significant misalignment between teachers' individual VA scores and observation scores. In response, Tennessee issued a document suggesting that there was an appropriate level of alignment (TSBE, 2012a). For example, if a teacher were to score a "3" on VA, the appropriate observation scores would be 2, 3, or 4 (on a 5-point scale). There was also a suggestion that observers need more training—something that we already know may do little to improve one's ability to observe "well." One would hope that if a teacher were indeed an effective teacher, all arrows would point the same direction. However, it is important to consider that no measure of effective teaching is precise and most of the measures are weakly correlated. MET Project results indicate correlations between observation scores using the Danielson Framework and VA scores range from +0.12 to +0.34 (Bill & Melinda Gates Foundation, 2012). Other researchers (Polikoff & Porter, 2014) using a subsample of the MET Project data ($N = 300$) found mostly non-significant and weak correlations between other measures of instructional quality (instruction-standards alignment) and VA measures. Correlations ranged from +.35 to −.029. Alignment, to some extent, is important to establish validity, but to what extent these measures should and ultimately can be aligned is less clear. It is equally important to establish if misalignment varies across a distribution of teachers, what the subsequent impact is on error classifications when such data are used in high-stakes ways.

In conclusion, we highlight five important points.

- Poor problem conceptualization has led to recommendations that offer little help in achieving the goal of improving teaching and learning.
- Some preliminary findings on high-stakes teacher evaluation are promising, but we caution that the potential unintended consequences to teachers, students, and schools have been poorly considered and may do more harm than good.
- It appears exceedingly difficult for observers to identify more or less effective teachers as measured by student achievement, through observation.
- There is limited evidence that principals are receiving the necessary support and resources to accommodate the new demands on their time.
- There exists weak alignment between student achievement measures and those that measure instructional practice or quality.

Much remains to be learned, but initial findings raise significant concerns about using teacher evaluation data to make high-stakes decisions to meet RttT goals.

Race to the Top Push-Back

Earlier, we noted that too often in the past ill-advised reforms have been implemented in part because the professional community has not systematically spoken out against reform until it is too late. Although not consistent across communities, we believe there has been a stronger, earlier voice of opposition in RttT than in past reforms. Most of the opposition toward RttT is about the use of achievement data, specifically VA measures.

Two years ago, in *Teacher and Student Evaluation: Moving beyond the Failure of School Reform*, we described how various organizations were responding to the rollout of high-stakes teacher evaluation. We noted teacher protests that had occurred across the United States, the National Education Association's position to reduce an emphasis on standardized testing, and the American Federation of Teachers' (AFT) stand for higher-quality preparation programs. At that time, we made a fairly grim forecast for the ability of push-back to make significant progress. And despite more timely responses (see Rothstein, 2014) to related issues, like the elimination of tenure laws, we anticipate that push-back will slightly alter how teacher evaluation is implemented but will not derail the RttT train anytime soon. As legal issues continue to emerge, the cost of RttT may clearly begin to outweigh any benefit (whether it is real or only perceived).

In 2010, the AFT advocated for the use of VA data as one measure in what Randi Weingarten, the president of the AFT, termed "constructive evaluation" (Weingarten, 2010). More recently, Weingarten has receded in her position, embarking on an anti-value-added measures (VAM) campaign, led by the phrase

"VAM is a sham," targeting the error-laden and inconsistent nature of VA scores (Sawchuk, 2014a).

Tensions have also risen in courthouses. The National Education Association's Florida affiliate filed a lawsuit (Cook v. Stewart) in 2013, challenging the VA component of Florida's teacher evaluation model, asserting that some teachers were being judged on students or subjects they did not teach. In April 2014, a federal judge dismissed some allegations, but ruled the lawsuit valid (Pudlow, 2014). In Tennessee, the teachers union filed a federal lawsuit arguing that the student achievement component of the teacher evaluation model is flawed and in violation of constitutional rights. The lawsuit challenges the high-stakes use of the evaluation model. The plaintiff, Mark Taylor, teaches eighth-grade science. His VA score was based on one class or 22 students, fewer than 16% of the total number of students he teaches (Sawchuk, 2014b). In his other courses, students are not required to take the standardized state exam. Unfortunately, situations like this are far too common, as many teachers do not have test scores for all of the students whom they instruct, or in some cases, none.

Other organizations have jumped on the bandwagon. In April 2014, the American Statistical Association (ASA) released a statement warning against the use of value-added models (VAMs). They make three points that support our own positions.

- Research on VAMs contends that educational effectiveness that is measurable and within teacher control represents a small part of the total variation in student achievement. Variation in student achievement is attributable to factors outside of the teacher's control, such as student and family background, poverty, curriculum, and unmeasured influences.
- VAM scores have large standard errors, even when using several years of data. Combining VAMs across multiple years decreases the standard error of VAM scores, but does not help problems caused when a model systematically undervalues teachers who work in specific contexts or with specific types of students. The systematic undervaluation would be present in every year of data.
- VAM scores may provide teachers and administrators with information on their students' performance and identify areas for improvement, but scores do not provide information on how to improve teaching.

(American Statistical Association, 2014, p. 7)

Simultaneously, a slew of research has brought to light countless concerns, including misclassification. In one study 4–15% of teachers switched from the top fifth of the distribution of teacher effectiveness to the bottom fifth (McCaffrey et al., 2009). How can districts decide if these teachers should receive bonuses? Others have questioned the sustainability of VA effects. For example, Raudenbush (2014) notes that VA scores have been shown to "fade out" over time—with limited evidence that students who have teachers with high VA scores will perform better on *achievement tests* the following years (p. 2). Furthermore, Konstantopoulos (2014) notes the following:

- Value-added models (VAMs) are hypothesized to provide more accurate estimates of teacher effectiveness than studies that do not take into account information about student background and previous achievement.
- But not all VAMs control for student background (e.g., SES), and sometimes controlling for student background in VAMs may overadjust teacher effects estimates.
- It is unclear that VAMs eliminate possible confounding effects completely and warrant causal interpretation of teacher effects.
- When students and teachers are randomly sorted into classes, causal inferences are valid; but if not, causal interpretations can be misleading.

(p. 9)

Given the rarity of true random student assignment to teachers, these warnings hold real value. And, for many teachers, the confidence intervals of their VA scores overlap substantially with other teachers, making it difficult to distinguish between teachers (Raudenbush & Jean, 2012). It is important to note that VA scores are estimates, and with any measure there is error. A 95% confidence interval essentially indicates we know with 95% confidence that a teacher's true VA score falls within the designated confidence interval (CI). Imagine that we have three teachers:

- Teacher A: VA score estimate of −0.18 and a CI of −0.29 to −0.08.
- Teacher B: VA score estimate of +0.11 and a CI of −0.02 to +0.42.
- Teacher C: VA score estimate of +0.30 and a CI of +0.10 to +0.50.

Ranking these three teachers on VA score estimates from most effective to least is simple: Teacher C, Teacher B, Teacher A. However, upon closer examination we can see that the confidence intervals of Teacher B and Teacher C overlap significantly—by nearly 0.32. Thus, we cannot conclude with much confidence that Teacher B and Teacher C are different in their effectiveness, because their true scores could place them in a different rank order. Patterns such as the one we described are not rare and make it very difficult for administrators to use these data to make high-stakes decisions.

Taken together, these findings have challenged RttT and have helped increase the number of skeptics of VA who question its value for "actionable practice" (Loeb, 2013, p. 2), especially when scores are not meaningfully associated with the content or quality of instruction (Polikoff & Porter, 2014). From a broader perspective, we also wonder: What value do value-added models add to teacher evaluation? And, do proposed advances in capturing teacher effects actually tell us less than we already know about effective teaching? We could continue noting limitations of VA scores, but we suspect that our accounting of VA weaknesses have justified why we place but little emphasis on this technique. For those seeking more, we direct readers to material provided by the Carnegie Foundation for the Advancement of Teaching (Carnegie-KnowledgeNetwork.org).

Keeping an Eye on the Prize: Measuring Teacher Improvement

In light of various negative responses to RttT, we ask: Is there any possibility of a silver lining? One goal of teacher evaluation is to improve instruction. Unfortunately, because of RttT pressures many states are focused on compliance and implementation and have lost sight of this prize. We believe that RttT offers school leaders an excellent opportunity to reflect more on how to use observational data and feedback to improve instruction. According to an independent study conducted on Tennessee's First to the Top program, nearly half of the teachers reported that their evaluator never followed up with them after their observation about areas in need of improvement (Ehlert et al., 2013). Limited follow-up increases the perception that observations are for evaluation rather than improvement, and it makes it nearly impossible to measure the effectiveness of evaluations in improving teaching practices and, subsequently, student learning. Rarely do RttT reports indicate how observation scores vary across a single year or multiple years, and to what extent change is related to factors such as teaching assignment. There is limited systematic data collection of the pre- and postconversations, the professional development resources that teachers access postobservation, and how this relates to improved classroom practices. In short, despite how these new teacher evaluation models now function, there is opportunity for improvement.

As with RttT, no one would argue against high expectations and standards for teachers. However, we suggest that poor problem conceptualization, limited capacity, losing sight of the prize with high stakes, and unresolved issues related to observations and alignment of measures have limited successful implementation of RttT so that intended goals go unmet. We argue that although student learning should be a by-product of instructional practices, we understand that these measures will rarely be perfectly correlated because of the "noise" inherent in these measures and because these measures are conceptually different—one assesses output and the other process. We contend that if teacher evaluation is to be effective, the primary emphasis needs to be placed on the process (how to use evaluations to improve teachers' instructional practices and student learning in measurable ways). To that end, in the chapters that follow we will continue to focus on what we believe holds the most potential for improving teachers' practices—well-conducted observations and meaningful feedback.

Conclusion

We have argued that RttT is the most recent of a series of largely failed reforms. Like its predecessors, it can be characterized on several dimensions, including the following:

- International comparisons drive the concern for poor student achievement on standardized tests compared to those in other countries.
- The status quo is largely rejected in favor of a new reform without evidence that new reforms will improve practice.
- The American government (both federal and state) invests in sweeping reform without any evidence that the costly reform will work.

We have described RttT's guidelines and its intended goals. Although there is variation from state to state in terms of how teachers' effectiveness is classified, the criteria imposed by states substantially define teacher effectiveness in terms of observed classroom performance and student achievement.

Moving beyond reform, we have looked at a variety of practical and technical issues. These include criteria for who should be evaluators and the training necessary for these evaluators to code classroom behavior reliably. We have considered the various arguments for using student achievement data to evaluate teachers, and we have noted the problematic assumptions in using VA data; considerable time was used to look at issues concerning the use observation systems and feedback to teachers. We have reviewed some of the initial findings from RttT, and although there are some positive aspects, the evidence on the whole shows that these initial efforts have been unimpressive. Concerns we reviewed include the following:

- There is little correspondence between the two core measures of teacher effectiveness. Observation scores are weakly correlated with student achievement.
- The focus to this date has been on the *principal's role as evaluator*, and little attention has been paid to the *principal's role as supervisor*.

Like other reforms, this reform has suffered from an inadequate conception of the problem, and the attempt to do too much too quickly without evidence.

In Chapter 3, we review findings on classroom teaching as it relates to student achievement gains, and how principals and others can use this knowledge base to improve instruction. Understanding and using this knowledge base are fundamentally important if teaching and learning are to be improved.

References

Aaronson, D.L., Barrow, L., & Sander, W. (2007). Teachers and student achievement in the Chicago Public Schools. *Journal of Labor Economics, 25*(1), 95–135. http://dx.doi.org/10.1086/508733

American Statistical Association. (2014, April 8). *ASA statement on the use of value-added models for educational assessment.* Retrieved from www.amstat.org/policy/pdfs/ASA_VAM_Statement.pdf

Amrein-Beardsley, A. (2014). *Rethinking value-added models in education: Critical perspectives on tests and assessment-based accountability.* New York: Routledge.

Barnes, G., Crowe, E., & Schaefer, B. (2007). *The cost of teacher turnover in five school districts: A pilot study.* Washington, DC: National Commission on Teaching and America's Future. Retrieved from www.nctaf.org/resources/demonstration_projects/turnover/documents/CTTFullReportfinal.pdf

Berliner, D. C., & Biddle, B. J. (1995). *The manufactured crisis: Myths, frauds, and the attack on American's public schools.* Reading, MA: Addison Wesley.

Berliner, D. C., & Glass, G.V. (2014). *50 myths and lies that threaten America's public schools: The real crisis in education.* New York: Teachers College Press.

Bill & Melinda Gates Foundation. (2012). *Gathering feedback for teaching: Combining high-quality observations with student surveys and achievement gains.* Retrieved from www.metproject.org/downloads/MET_Gathering_Feedback_Practioner_Brief.pdf

Brophy, J., & Good, T. (1974). *Teacher-student relationships: Causes and consequences.* New York: Holt, Rinehart and Winston.

Brophy, J., & Good T. (1986). Teacher behavior and student achievement. In M. Wittrock (Ed.), *Handbook on research in teaching* (3rd ed., pp. 328–375). New York: Macmillan.

Buddin, R., & Zamarro, G. (2009). Teacher qualifications and student achievement in urban elementary schools. *Journal of Urban Economics, 66*(2), 103–115. http://dx.doi.org/10.1016/j.jue.2009.05.001

Chetty, R., Friedman, J.N., & Rockoff, J.E. (2013). Measuring the impacts of teachers II: Teacher value-added and student outcomes. NBER Working Paper Series, No. 19424. Retrieved from www.nber.org/w19424

Cuban, L. (2013). *Inside the black box of classroom practice: Change without reform in American education.* Cambridge, MA: Harvard Education Press.

Danielson Group. (2013). *The framework for teaching evaluation instrument.* Retrieved from www.danielsongroup.org/userfiles/files/downloads/2013EvaluationInstrument.pdf

Dee, T., & Wyckoff, J. (2013). Incentives, selection, and teacher performance: Evidence from IMPACT. National Bureau of Economic Research. Working Paper No. 19529. Retrieved from www.nber.org/papers/w19529

District of Columbia Public Schools. (2012). *Key changes to IMPACT for 2012–2013 year.* Retrieved from http://dcps.dc.gov/DCPS/Files/downloads/ABOUT%20DCPS/Human%20Resources/Downloadables/IMPACT%202012–2013%20Key%20Changes.pdf

Downey, C.J., Steffy, B.E., Poston, W.K., Jr., & English, F.W. (2010). *Advancing the three-minute walk-through: Mastering reflective practice.* Thousand Oaks, CA: Corwin Press.

Dumler, C., Reidy, K., Cadigan, P., & Clem, S. (2014, January). *Providing teachers with observational feedback intended to improve teaching performance: Opportunities and challenges.* Paper presented at Using Observational and Student Achievement Data to Improve Teaching. Tucson, AZ.

Duncan, A. (2009, June 14). States will lead the way to reform: Secretary Arne Duncan's remarks at the 2009 Governors education symposium. Retrieved from www2.ed.gov/news/speeches/2009/06/06142009.html

Ehlert, M., Pepper, M., Parsons, E., Burns, S., & Springer, M. (2013). *Educator evaluation in Tennessee: Initial findings from the 2013 First to the Top survey.* Tennessee Consortium on Research, Evaluation, and Development. Retrieved from www.tnconsortium.org/data/

files/gallery/ContentGallery/Educator_Evaluation_in_Tennessee_Initial_Findings_from_the_2013_First_to_the_Top_Survey6.pdf

Fleisher, L. (2013, July 26). Evaluation law may provide protection for teachers. *Wall Street Journal*. Retrieved from http://online.wsj.com/news/articles/SB10001424127887324564704578630272100661716

Georgia Department of Education. (2012). *Teacher keys and leader keys effectiveness systems 2012 pilot evaluation report*. Retrieved from www.gadoe.org/School-Improvement/Teacher-and-Leader-Effectiveness/Documents/Pilot%20Report%2012-13-2012%20FINAL%20Clean.pdf

Goldhaber, D., & Brewer, D. (1997). Why don't schools and teachers seem to matter? Assessing the impact of unobservables on educational productivity. *Journal of Human Resources, 42*(4), 765–794.

Goldhaber, D., & Brewer, D. (1999). Teacher licensing and student achievement. In C. Finn & M. Kanstoroom (Eds.), *Better teachers, better schools* (pp. 83–102). Washington, DC: Thomas B. Fordham Institute.

Goldhaber, D., & Hansen, M. (2008). *Assessing the potential of using value-added estimates of teacher job performance for making tenure decisions*. Center on Reinventing Public Education. Retrieved from www.cedr.us/papers/assessing_the_potential.pdf

Good, T.L., & Braden, J.S. (2000). *The great school debate: Choice, vouchers, and charters*. Mahwah, NJ: Erlbaum.

Good, T.L., & Grouws, D. (1979). The Missouri mathematics effectiveness project: An experimental study in fourth-grade classrooms. *Journal of Educational Psychology, 71*(3), 355–362. doi:10.1037/0022-0663.71.3.355

Good, T.L., & Grouws, D.A., & Ebmeier, M. (1983). *Active mathematics teaching*. New York: Longman.

Hanushek, E.A., Kain, J.F., & Rivkin, S.G. (1998). *Teachers, schools, and academic achievement*. National Bureau of Economic Research. Working Paper No. 6691.

Harris, D.N. (2008). The policy uses and policy validity of value-added and other teacher quality measures. In D.H. Gitomer (Ed.), *Measurement issues and assessment for teacher quality* (pp. 99–130). Thousand Oaks, CA: SAGE.

Harris, D.N. (2012, October 15). How do value-added indicators compare to other measures of teacher effectiveness? Carnegie Knowledge Network. Retrieved from www.carnegieknowledgenetwork.org/briefs/value-added/value-added-other-measures/#respond

Harris, D.N., & Sass, T.R. (2006). *Value-added models and the measurement of teacher quality*. Retrieved from http://myweb.fsu.edu/tsass/Papers/IES%20Harris%20Sass%20EPF%20Value-added%2014.pdf

Headden, S., & Silva, E. (2011). Lessons from D.C.'s evaluation system. *Journal of Staff Development, 32*(6), 40–44.

Henry, G.T., Bastian, K.C., & Fortner, C.K. (2011). Stayers and leavers: Early-career teacher effectiveness and attrition. *Educational Researcher, 40*(6), 271–280.

Hill, H.C., Blazar, D., Humez, A., Litke, E., Beisiegel, M., Barmore, J., … Rabinowicz, S. (2014). *Examining high and low value-added mathematics instruction: Can observers tell the difference?* Retrieved from http://cepr.harvard.edu/cepr-resources/files/news-events/ncte-examining-high-low-vam-hill-et-al.pdf

Hill, H.C., Umland, K., Litke, E., & Kapitula, L.R. (2012). Teacher quality and quality teaching: Examining the relationship of a teacher assessment to practice. *American Journal of Education, 118*, 489–519.

Hillsborough County Schools. (2011). *Teacher evaluation handbook: Empowering effective teachers.* Retrieved from www.fldoe.org/profdev/pdf/pa/Hillsborough.pdf

Ingersoll, R., & Merrill, L. (2012). *Seven trends: The transformation of the teaching force.* Philadelphia: Consortium for Policy Research in Education, University of Pennsylvania.

Jacques, C. (2013). *Leveraging teacher talent: Peer observation in educator evaluation.* Center on Great Teachers & Leaders: American Institutes for Research. Retrieved from www.gtlcenter.org/sites/default/files/docs/GTL_AskTeam_LeveragingTeacherTalent.pdf

Kane, T., Rockoff, J.E., & Staiger, D. (2008). What does certification tell us about teacher effectiveness? Evidence from New York City. *Economics of Education Review, 27*(6), 615–631.

Konstantopoulos, S. (2011). Teacher effects in early grades? Evidence from a randomized experiment. *Teachers College Record, 113*, 1541–1565.

Konstantopoulos, S. (2014). Teacher effects, value-added models, and accountability. In A.L. Lavigne, T.L. Good, & R.M. Marx (Eds.), High-stakes teacher evaluation: High cost—big losses [Special Issue]. *Teachers College Record, 116*(1).

Konstantopoulos, S., & Sun, M. (2012). Is the persistence of teacher effects in early grades larger for lower-performing students? *American Journal of Education, 118*, 309–339.

Lavigne, A.L. (2014). Exploring the implications of high-stakes teacher evaluation on schools, teachers, and students. In A.L. Lavigne, T.L. Good, & R.M. Marx (Eds.), High-stakes teacher evaluation: High cost—big losses [Special Issue]. *Teachers College Record, 116*(1).

Lavigne, A.L., & Chamberlain, R. (2014). *Coping with increased demands for teacher evaluation: School leaders' perceptions of problems and possibility.* Invited paper presented at Using Observational and Student Achievement Data to Improve Teaching. Tucson, AZ.

Lavigne, A.L., & Good, T.L. (2014). *Teacher and student evaluation: Moving beyond the failure of school reform.* New York: Routledge.

Lavigne, A.L., Good, T.L., & Marx, R.M. (Eds.) (2014). High-stakes teacher evaluation: High cost—big losses [Special Issue]. *Teachers College Record, 116*(1).

Lipscomb, S., Teh, B., Gill, B., Chiang, H., & Owens, A. (2010). *Teacher and principal value-added: Research findings and implementation practices.* Retrieved from http://files.eric.ed.gov/fulltext/ED531785.pdf

Loeb, S. (2013, December 19). How can value-added measures be used for teacher improvement? Carnegie Knowledge Network. Retrieved from www.carnegieknowledgenetwork.org/briefs/teacher_improvement/

Loeb, S., & Candelaria, C.A. (2012, October 15). How stable are value-added estimates across years, subjects, and student groups? Carnegie Knowledge Network. Retrieved from www.carnegieknowledgenetwork.org/briefs/value-added/value-added-stability/

Loucks-Horsley, S., Hewson, P.W., Love, N., & Stiles, K.E. (1998). *Designing professional development for teachers of science and mathematics.* Thousand Oaks, CA: Corwin Press.

Marzano, R. (2011). *The art and science of teaching causal teacher evaluation model.* Blairsville, PA: Learning Sciences International.

Massachusetts Department of Elementary and Secondary Education. (n.d.). *Quick reference guide: Educator evaluation training.* Retrieved from www.doe.mass.edu/edeval/resources/QRG-TrainingReqs.pdf

McCaffrey, D.F., Sass, T.R., Lockwood, J.R., & Mihaly, K. (2009). The variability of teacher effect estimate. *Education Finance and Policy, 4*, 572.

McCaslin, M. (1996). The problem of problem representation: The Summits' conception of student. *Educational Researcher, 25*(8), 13–15.

McCaslin, M. (2006). Student motivation dynamics in the era of school reform. *Elementary School Journal, 106*(5), 479–490.

McCaslin, M., & Lavigne, A.L. (2010). Co-regulation approach to research on student motivation. In T.C. Urdan & S.A. Karabenick (Eds.), *The decade ahead: Applications and context of motivation and achievement* (pp. 211–249). Bingley, UK: EmeraldBooks.

McKown, C. (2013). Social equity theory and the racial-ethnic achievement gaps. *Child Development, 84*(4), 1120–1136.

MetLife. (2013). *The MetLife survey of the American teacher.* Retrieved from www.metlife.com/assets/cao/foundation/MetLife-Teacher-Survey-2012.pdf

Monk, D.H. (1994). Subject area preparation of secondary math and science teachers and student achievement. *Economics of Education Review, 13*(2), 125–145.

National Commission on Excellence in Education. (1983). *A nation at risk: The imperative for education reform.* Washington, DC: U.S. Department of Education.

National Education Commission on Time and Learning. (1994). *Prisoners of time.* Washington, DC: U.S. Government Printing Office.

Nichols, S.L., & Berliner, D. C. (2007). *Collateral damage: How high-stakes testing corrupts America's schools.* Cambridge, MA: Harvard Education Press.

No Child Left Behind Act of 2001, Pub L. 107–110, 20 U.S.C. § 6301 et. Seq.

North Carolina State Board of Education. (2012). *North Carolina teacher evaluation process.* Retrieved from www.ncpublicschools.org/docs/effectiveness-model/ncees/instruments/teach-eval-manual.pdf

Ohio Department of Education. (2013). Teacher evaluations. Retrieved from http://education.ohio.gov/Topics/Teaching/Educator-Evaluation-System/Ohio-s-Teacher-Evaluation-System

Papay, J.P., & Johnson, S.M. (2011). *Is PAR a good investment? Understanding the costs and benefits of teacher peer assistance and review programs.* Retrieved from www.gse.harvard.edu/~ngt/par/resources/PAR%20Costs%20and%20Benefits%20-%20January%202011.pdf

Pianta, R. C., La Paro, K., & Hamre, B. K. (2008). Classroom Assessment Scoring System (CLASS). Baltimore, MD: Paul H. Brookes.

Polikoff, M.S., & Porter, A.C. (2014). Instructional alignment as a measure of teaching quality. *Educational Evaluation and Policy Analysis.* Retrieved from http://epa.sagepub.com/content/early/2014/04/11/0162373714531851.full.pdf+html

Pudlow, M. (2014, April 28). FEA lawsuit on state evaluation procedures can move forward. Florida Education Association. Retrieved from http://feaweb.org/fea-lawsuit-on-state-evaluation-procedures-can-move-forward

Raudenbush, S. (2014). *What do we know about the long-term impacts of teacher value-added?* Retrieved from www.carnegieknowledgenetwork.org/wp-content/uploads/2014/03/CKN_Raudenbush_Long-Term-Impacts_v2.pdf

Raudenbush, S.W., & Jean, M. (2012, October 15). How should educators interpret value-added scores? Carnegie Knowledge Network. Retrieved from www.carnegieknowledgenetwork.org/briefs/value-added/interpreting-value-added/

Ravitch, D. (2010). *The death and life of the great American school system: How testing and choice are undermining education.* New York: Basic Books.

Rhode Island Department of Education. (2013). *Rhode Island educator evaluations: Improving teaching and learning (year one report).* Retrieved from www.ride.ri.gov/Portals/0/Uploads/Documents/Teachers-and-Administrators-Excellent-Educators/Educator-Evaluation/Education-Eval-Main-Page/2013_Evaluation_Data_External_Report.pdf

Rich, M. (2012, December 11). U.S. students still lag globally in Math and Science, tests show. *New York Times.* Retrieved from www.nytimes.com/2012/12/11/education/us-students-still-lag-globally-in-math-and-science-tests-show.html?_r=0

Rivkin, S., Hanushek, E., & Kain, J. (2005). Teachers, schools, and academic achievement. *Econometrica, 73*(2), 417–458.

Roethlisberger, F.J., & Dickson, W.J. (1939). *Management and the worker.* Cambridge, MA: Harvard University Press.

Rosenholtz, S. (1989). *Teachers' workplace: the social organization of schools.* New York: Longman.

Rothstein, J. (2014, June 12). California ruling on teacher tenure is not the whole picture. *New York Times.* Retrieved from www.nytimes.com/2014/06/13/opinion/california-ruling-on-teacher-tenure-is-not-whole-picture.html?emc=eta1&_r=0

Rothstein, J., & Mathis, W.J. (2013). *Review of the two culminating reports from the MET project.* National Education Policy Center. Retrieved from http://nepc.colorado.edu/files/ttr-final-met-rothstein.pdf

Sawchuk, S. (2014a, January 7). AFT's Weingarten backtracks on using value-added measures for evaluations. *Education Week.* Retrieved from http://blogs.edweek.org/edweek/teacherbeat/2014/01/weingartens_retrenchment_on_va.html

Sawchuk, S. (2014b, March 28). Tenn. Teachers' union takes evaluation fight into the courtroom. *Education Week.* Retrieved from www.edweek.org/ew/articles/2014/03/28/27tennessee.h33.html?cmp=ENL-EU-NEWS2

Scott, D. (2014, January). *Delving into the data: The mathematics of teacher effectiveness.* Paper presented at Using Observational and Student Achievement Data to Improve Teaching. Tucson, AZ.

Strong, M. (2011). *The highly qualified teacher: What is teacher quality and how do we measure it?* New York: Teachers College Press.

Taylor, E.S., & Tyler, J.H. (2012). The effect of evaluation on teacher performance. *American Economic Review, 102*(7), 3628–3651.

Tennessee Department of Education (n.d.). *Tennessee Educator Evaluation Model: Overview.* Retrieved from http://team-tn.org/evaluation/overview/

Tennessee Department of Education First to the Top. (2012). *Teacher evaluation in Tennessee: A report on Year 1 implementation.* Retrieved from http://team-tn.org/wp-content/uploads/2013/08/Year-1-Evaluation-Report-TNDOE.pdf

Tennessee State Board of Education. (2011). *Teacher and principal evaluation policy.* Retrieved from www.tn.gov/firsttothetop/docs/IV_C_Teacher_and_Principal_Evaluation_Policy.pdf

Tennessee State Board of Education. (2012a). *Acceptable range of results policy for 2012–2013.* Retrieved from http://team-tn.org/assets/misc/E%20-%20Acceptable%20Range_Final.pdf

Tennessee State Board of Education. (2012b). *Number of observations.* Retrieved from http://team-tn.org/assets/misc/A%20-%20Number%20of%20Observations_12_13_Updated.pdf

Tyack, D., & Cuban, L. (1997). *Tinkering toward utopia: A century of public school reform.* Cambridge, MA: Harvard University Press.

Tyler, R.W. (1969). *Basic principles of curriculum and instruction.* Chicago: University of Chicago Press.

U.S. Department of Education. (n.d.). *Great teachers and great leaders.* Retrieved from www2.ed.gov/policy/elsec/leg/blueprint/great-teachers-great-leaders.pdf

U.S. Department of Education. (2010a, March 29). Delaware and Tennessee win first Race to the Top grants. Retrieved from www.ed.gov/news/press-releases/delaware-and-tennessee-win-first-race-top-grants

U.S. Department of Education. (2010b, August 24). Nine states and the District of Columbia win second round Race to the Top grants. Retrieved from www.ed.gov/news/press-releases/nine-states-and-district-columbia-win-second-round-race-top-grants

U.S. Department of Education. (2010c). *Race to the Top guidance and frequently asked questions.* Retrieved from www2.ed.gov/programs/racetothetop/faq.pdf

U.S. Department of Education. (2011, December 23). Department of Education awards $200 million to seven states to advance K-12 reform. Retrieved from www.ed.gov/news/press-releases/department-education-awards-200-million-seven-states-advance-k-12-reform

U.S. Department of Education. (2013a). Race to the Top fund. Retrieved from www2.ed.gov/programs/racetothetop/index.html

U.S. Department of Education. (2013b). *Summary of discretionary funds.* Retrieved from www2.ed.gov/about/overview/budget/budget14/summary/appendix2.pdf

U.S. Department of Education. (2013c, December 17). U.S. Department of Education names five winners of $120 million from Race to the Top-District grant competition. Retrieved from www.ed.gov/news/press-releases/us-department-education-names-five-winners-120-million-race-top-district-grant-c

U.S. Government Accountability Office. (2013). Race to the Top: States implementing teacher and principal evaluation systems despite challenges. Retrieved from www.gao.gov/assets/660/657936.pdf

Weingarten, R. (2010, January 12). A new path forward: Four approaches to quality teaching and better schools. American Federation of Teachers. Retrieved from www.aft.org/newspubs/news/2010/011210a.cfm

Weisberg, D., Sexton, S., Mulhern, J., & Keeling, D. (2009). *The widget effect: Our national failure to acknowledge and act on difference in teacher effectiveness.* Brooklyn, NY: New Teachers Project. Retrieved from http://widgeteffect.org/downloads/TheWidgetEffect.pdf

Whitehurst, G., Chingos, M., & Lindquist, K. (2014). *Evaluating teachers with classroom observations: Lessons learned in four districts.* Brown Center on Education Policy at the Brookings Institution. Retrieved from www.brookings.edu/research/reports/2014/05/13-teacher-evaluation-whitehurst-chingos

3
WHAT DO WE KNOW ABOUT GOOD TEACHING?

Chapter 1 discussed the hectic roles that principals play. In Chapter 2, we noted the additional burdens imposed on principals by Race to the Top (RttT)—especially the call for principals to observe teachers more frequently. Now we address the demand for principals and others to learn the content of research on effective teaching, something that some have suggested principals know little about (Le Fevre & Robinson, 2014; Stein & Nelson, 2003). Hence one might conclude that many principals need to improve their understanding of this literature, especially since this literature goes beyond what most observation systems measure. We provide this needed knowledge, and believe that it can improve teaching. But, we note, learning and applying this information require time and skill.

The history of research on effective teaching has been reviewed frequently (Brophy & Good, 1986; Hattie, 2008). Here we largely ignore the technical details. Instead we present the highlights that capture the specific instructional processes that are consistently associated with student achievement. This research has considerable *value* for those who observe and evaluate teachers and merits consideration when designing teacher evaluation plans. Understanding this literature is essential to improve teaching. It is not sufficient to know that a classroom instrument shows a teacher to have weak management skills. Needed also is information about *how* to improve classroom management. Classroom observation instruments can provide good information, but this information holds little value if evaluators do not understand the research that undergirds the dimensions of teaching that observation systems assess. We provide an understanding of this research base—how it developed and how to use it.

Many research traditions have made major contributions to the field that Dunkin and Biddle (1974) called the study of teaching. Among those paradigms most central to modern evaluations of teaching that use student achievement scores is the process-product paradigm (research that relates classroom process with student achievement). For a review/critique of this research area see Brophy and Good (1986), Good and Brophy (2008), and Konstantopoulos (2014). We pull from this complex literature and others (including teacher expectation effects, teacher caring, student belongingness, and valued-added) in order to present knowledge that links teaching to increased achievement.

Teacher Effects on Student Learning Are Powerful

In today's era of high-stakes teacher evaluation, it is common to discuss how much of a student's achievement growth can be attributed to individual teachers as distinct from previous teachers, home conditions, and degree of wealth/poverty. Non-school factors account for a substantial percentage of students' achievement, but of the factors that educators can influence (e.g., smaller class sizes, new computers, SMART boards, flipped classes), teachers' instructional behaviors exert the single biggest impact on achievement. Researchers often express teachers' impact on achievement as an effect size. Readers not familiar with this term can see Appendix B.

When considering teacher effects we must remember that teachers alone can accomplish only so much. Under the best circumstances teacher effects can account for only 21% of the variance in student achievement (and typically less—see Konstantopoulos, 2014). Better instructional practices can improve learning, but large determinants of students' success reside in issues of poverty/wealth and parental and community socialization.

Children who live in poverty and the schools they attend have fewer resources than those schools that enroll children from more affluent homes (Biddle, 2014). Furthermore, countries whose students' achievement is high in comparison to that of students in the U.S. invest more in schooling than we do. Darling-Hammond (2007) wrote, "Most high-achieving countries not only provide high-quality universal preschool and health care for children, but also fund their schools centrally and equally, with additional funds to the neediest schools" (p. 329). Improving student performance requires improving both educational resources and teaching.

Our comments are not to dampen improvement efforts but to place these efforts in perspective. Yes, even small effects can aggregate over time in important ways. But to achieve the fruits of enhanced learning requires time and sustained effort. We stress this because in their well-intentioned zeal to improve students' learning, educational reformers often overpromised when presenting new reforms. Major reforms were launched and immediate gains promised. The rapid implementation of even potentially good ideas renders them dead on arrival. When sizeable gains are not realized quickly, the reforms are rejected and the field moves to a new fad. Ironically new fads sometimes advance without recognition that these same ideas have failed in the past (e.g., the progressive era is repackaged as open classrooms) or have had some success but were ultimately forgotten and then rediscovered (e.g., direct instruction becomes explicit teaching). Thus, in presenting knowledge about good teaching, we also discuss where ideas for improving practice originate.

General Instructional Variables Related to Student Achievement

The variables we discuss ahead are robust instructional actions that *consistently* relate to student achievement across grades and subjects. Principals and supervisors would do well to ensure that teachers (regardless of experience) possess or quickly acquire these fundamental teacher beliefs and actions. Here we provide a summary of research-based considerations for good teaching. Importantly, some of these instructional actions are not included (or measured well) in current observation systems used to evaluate teaching. For example, appropriate teacher expectations are poorly measured with popular instruments used today and teacher interactions with individual students are not coded at all, masking much data that could be used to improve instruction. The general teaching variables consistently associated with increases in student achievement are presented in Table 3.1.

TABLE 3.1 Instructional Behaviors Frequently Associated with Student Achievement

- **Appropriate Expectations.** Do all students receive an appropriately demanding curriculum? Are teacher expectations positive and forward-looking for students who vary in achievement level, ethnicity, gender, and socioeconomic status?
- **Supportive Classrooms; Seeing Students as Social Beings as Well as Students.** Do teachers encourage students and support them at all times, especially when they struggle? Do teachers and students work in a climate of "we-ness" that supports individual differences?
- **Effective Use of Time.** Do teachers start classes promptly, plan transitions well, and help students focus on key ideas?
- **Opportunity to Learn.** Do teachers present content at the appropriate cognitive level to assure suitable pace and challenge?
- **Coherent Curriculum in Sequence.** Given that content and expectations have been established for student performance, is the curriculum logically sequenced?
- **Active Teaching.** Do teachers actively present concepts and supervise students' initial work, and then encourage them to build and to extend meaningfully on teachers' initial presentations?
- **Balance Procedural and Conceptual Knowledge.** Do teachers encourage students to understand knowledge *and* apply it?
- **Proactive Management.** Do students know what to do, how to do it, and when confused, how to access help?
- **Teacher Clarity, Enthusiasm, and Warmth.** Do teachers focus students on the lesson objectives? Do teachers express that they care about the content being studied as well as the students who study it?
- **Instructional Curriculum Pace.** Do teachers go through the curriculum reasonably briskly? Are teachers attentive to students' concerns and reteach content if necessary?
- **Teaching to Mastery.** Do teachers focus on students learning all material and minimize tangential material?
- **Review and Feedback.** Are students presented with frequent review? Do teachers give frequent feedback to students so that they know if they are making adequate progress and how to correct difficulties when they occur? Do teachers offer students opportunities to apply feedback to improve their work in future lessons or activities?
- **Adequate Subject Matter Knowledge.** Do teachers have adequate subject matter knowledge?

Source: Adapted from Lavigne and Good (2013) and Good and Brophy (2008).

We first discuss in detail two teaching dimensions from Table 3.1 that afford good learning opportunities for students: the need for teachers to develop and create appropriate expectations for student learning, and to create supportive classrooms that recognize that students are social beings as well as learners. These two aspects were selected because they are important and difficult to describe, "see," and measure (both of these aspects of teaching are not measured well in existing observation systems).

Appropriate Teacher Expectations

Good teaching is hard. If teachers do not *believe* that students can learn, why would they spend time designing good lessons, devote time to determine what students have learned (or not), and consider how to build on students' successes and failures? But high expectations are not sufficient for improving learning. Most of us have held high expectations for our New Year's resolutions that were not fulfilled. Plans for sustained weight loss were not carried out. Most who marry expect to have a long relationship with their spouse, but divorce rates suggest that these high expectations often are not realized.

Still, expectations are an aspect of everyday life—we invariably develop expectations when first meeting someone or encountering a new situation, and we use these small bits of information to form a story or a fuller picture (Asch, 1946). Teachers form expectations for students through students themselves (how they dress, speak, and so forth), school records (comments from former teachers, test scores), and family characteristics (zip code address, older siblings).

However, teachers' expectations for students have no effect upon students unless teachers communicate them (e.g., by asking more or less challenging questions). Teacher effects can be direct. For example, when students believed to be less capable are called upon less by their teacher and when their teacher quickly moves on when these students do not respond, the teacher is essentially offering these students fewer opportunities to process or integrate information. Teachers' effects can be indirect. For example, if students internalize the belief that they are less capable than their peers, then their commitment to master difficult classroom tasks is sharply reduced, and reciprocally this makes the task for future teachers to increase student performance much more difficult.

All teachers do not communicate low expectations to students, but research shows that a sizeable number of teachers do on the basis of students' ability, gender, race, ethnicity, socioeconomic status, and physical attractiveness. But the fact that teachers communicate expectations does not mean that students *perceive* them or *believe* them. And some students are more sensitive/vulnerable to teacher expectations than are others.

Research relating teacher expectations and instructional behavior. Based upon research, Good and Brophy (2008) summarized how some teachers differ when interacting with students believed to be more or less capable. These differences appear in Table 3.2.

Clearly, the use of one or two of the behaviors included in Table 3.2 would not suggest that teachers hold low expectations. However, if several of these interactions presented in Table 3.2 are consistent aspects of classroom interactions for some students, it seems important that mentor teachers, coaches, or principals explore the possibility of the communication of low expectations with the teacher.

Likewise, it is important to remember that teachers offer better learning opportunities to those believed to be more capable. Good and Weinstein (1986) organized teachers' expectations in terms of grouping practices and other aspects (e.g., locus of responsibility for learning, feedback and evaluation) and found that students believed to be more capable were afforded more of the following:

- Opportunity to perform publicly on meaningful tasks.
- Opportunity to think.
- Assignments including comprehension and understanding.

TABLE 3.2 Research-Based Examples Showing How Teachers Have Been Found to Behave Differently toward Students They Believe Have Less Potential

- Waiting less time for lows to answer a question (before giving the answer or calling on another student).
- Providing answer to lows or calling on someone else rather than trying to improve their responses (e.g., providing clues).
- Rewarding inappropriate behavior or incorrect answers.
- Criticizing lows more often for failure.
- Praising lows less often for success.
- Paying less attention to lows or interacting with them less frequently.
- Calling on lows less often to respond to questions or asking them only easier questions.
- Seating lows farther away from the teacher.
- Demanding less from lows (e.g., teach less, excessive offers of help).
- Interacting with lows more privately than publicly.
- Monitoring and structuring lows' activities more closely.
- Differential grading of tests or assignments in which lows are not given the benefit of the doubt in borderline cases.
- Less friendly interaction with lows, including less smiling and fewer other non-verbal indicators of support.
- Briefer and less informative feedback to questions of lows.
- Less eye contact and non-verbal communication of attention (e.g., positive head nodding) in interactions with lows.
- Less use of effective but time-consuming instructional methods with lows when time is limited.
- Less acceptance and use of lows' ideas.
- Exposing lows to an impoverished curriculum (limited and repetitive content) and emphasis upon factual recitation rather than application and higher-level thinking tasks.

Source: Good and Brophy (2008).

- Opportunity for self-evaluation.
- Honest-contingent feedback.
- Respect as a learner and individual with unique interests and needs.

Expectations are often communicated to groups of students or to the whole class. Teachers sometimes treat student groups differently (when students are assigned to ability groups or are placed into academic tracks). Students placed in low-ability-based reading groups are often treated in ways that do not fully facilitate their achievement (Eder, 1981; Oakes, 2005; Weinstein, 1976, 2002). Clearly grouping students does not always lead to poor instruction (Alpert, 1974). Still, a voluminous literature describes how students placed in lower groups have less opportunity to learn more advanced material. Much has been written on avoiding or reducing the negative effects of ability grouping (Burris, 2014; Oakes, 2005). However, the differences reported earlier by Good and Weinstein provide a framework for principals to observe for the possibility of differential expectation effects when students are grouped.

Teachers may express low or high expectations for the entire class (Brophy, 1983; Brophy & Good, 1974; Evertson, 1982). Christine Rubie-Davies has conducted a powerful and *productive* program of research, demonstrating that some teachers hold differential expectations for the entire class, and that their high or low expectations for the class have been expressed in ways that influence students' achievement, with a large Cohen's *d* effect size of .86 (Rubie-Davies, 2007, 2014). More information on effect size is presented in Appendix B. How teachers express high and low expectations to the class is similar to how teachers have communicated differential expectations to individual students or groups of students within a classroom believed to be more or less capable—when teachers believe the class as a whole can learn, more content and more challenging material are provided.

Appropriate expectations. The term "high expectations" is misleading. Teachers need to express appropriate expectations that are *positive, supportive*, realistic, and forward-looking. Rubie-Davies, Peterson, Sibley, and Rosenthal (forthcoming) studied a teacher who reported when classes started that her students were far below average for their grade level but they would improve, and they did. Rubie-Davies (2014) wrote, "This example illustrates the notion that the class-level expectation is relative to achievement. For this particular class, an expectation that the students would be achieving at slightly below average levels by the end of the year was a very high expectation" (p. 73). This teacher taught in a school where students generally achieved at very low levels. Thus, high expectations are better seen as relative, as believing that students can do better than they have been doing.

Although there are arguments and evidence that teachers communicate inappropriate expectations in low-income schools (Payne, 2010; Timperley & Robinson, 2001), it is important to note that inappropriately low expectations appear in all types of classrooms and schools, not just those that primarily serve children from low-income homes (although the most egregious communication of poor expectations often occurs in these settings). This is because teacher expectations generally are relative and not absolute comparisons. For example, in some academically advanced high schools, most students are academically talented. However, even in such settings, some students may be perceived by teachers as less talented than their peers, and receive less opportunity than other students.

Teacher efficacy. Teachers hold beliefs about their ability to teach. Teachers may lessen student learning because they believe that students cannot learn or they (the teacher) do not have the ability to teach "difficult to teach" students. Research on teacher efficacy has a long history (Armor et al., 1976). Teacher efficacy (the sum of teachers' responses to two statements) was the strongest measure in a study relating teacher characteristics and student learning.

> *Rand item 1: When it comes right down to it, a teacher really can't do much because most of a student's motivation and performance depends on his or her home environment.* A teacher who agreed with this statement suggests that home factors negate any influence that teachers can exert in school. NOTE this item assesses whether, despite students' difficult backgrounds, they can learn and benefit from teaching/schooling.
>
> *Rand item 2: If I really try hard, I can get through to even the most difficult or unmotivated students.* Teachers who agree with this statement are making a statement that they have the necessary skills and abilities to develop lessons that enhance student learning. NOTE this item assesses whether the teacher believes that he or she can make a difference.
>
> (Tschannen-Moran, Woolfolk Hoy, & Hoy, 1998, pp. 204–205)

If teachers do not believe that students can learn and/or if they do not have the ability to teach certain students, it is likely that either or both of these beliefs will erode teacher motivation and reduce the amount of time that teachers spend in preparing academic lessons and may even shift their priorities to making lessons about fun (e.g., building forts) rather than about learning. Ashton and Webb (1986) found that high-efficacy teachers were more confident and more positive and less negative when interacting with students. Further, high-efficacy teachers were more accepting of student challenges and more effective in stimulating student achievement gains.

Principals should consider that new teachers or those changing schools or grade level may have heightened concerns about their teaching ability, and often lack normative information about what students at their new grade level can do. Principals should consider that teachers with low self-efficacy, even if provided with detailed information about the effects of appropriate teacher expectations on student achievement, may not be motivated to use this information to change instruction unless their efficacy beliefs are altered.

Teacher expectations influence student achievement. Findings from experimental (Darley & Fazio, 1980; Jussim, 1986; Rosenthal & Rubin, 1978) and naturalistic expectations (Brattesani, Weinstein, & Marshall, 1984; Jussim & Eccles, 1992; Madon, Jussim, & Eccles, 1997; West & Anderson, 1976) research show that differential teacher behavior can be related to student achievement. For example, Brattesani, Weinstein, and Marshall (1984) identified teachers (using student reports) who differed significantly in their interaction patterns with high-and low-achieving students and those who did not differentiate much when interacting with these students. The effects of low-differentiation teachers' expectation of student achievement added 9–18% to the predictable variance in student achievement over and beyond what could be predicted on the basis of prior achievement, whereas high-differentiation teachers' expectation added only 1–5%. Simply put, teachers who students believed treated highs and lows very differently obtained less student achievement than teachers who were not believed to treat highs and lows very differently.

Madon, Jussim, and Eccles (1997) in a study involving about 1,500 students in sixth-grade classrooms noted (when students' prior math achievement and motivational scores were controlled) that teachers' over- and underestimates of students' performance were correlated with student achievement. Low teacher expectations predicted achievement more strongly than did high teacher expectations. Furthermore, they found that low achievers were more susceptible to teacher effects than were high achievers. And teachers' overestimates of student ability had a very small influence on student achievement. In short, perhaps in the short run principals' attention to teachers' communication of low expectation should be a *top priority*.

Teachers' expectations and behavior can be changed. Although differential teacher expectations have been related to student achievement, little research has examined whether teachers' expectations can be changed. Situations providing teachers with feedback are highly varied. For example, does the teacher want feedback? Does the teacher judge the feedback provider as being highly knowledgeable about effective teaching? Answers to such questions likely mediate the extent to which feedback actually changes teaching behavior. Abundant research demonstrates that teacher feedback to students can improve performance (Hattie, 2008), but there is less evidence that feedback to teachers improves performance. Furthermore, research collected in various contexts has shown that roughly one-third of the time feedback actually lowers performance (Kluger & DeNisi, 1996). Poor feedback is worse than no feedback, as we will see in Chapter 5.

Changing individual teachers' beliefs or behavior. Good and Brophy (1974) observed in first-grade classes for 40 hours, coding teacher interactions with individual students. They used this information to identify two student groups. One group included students with whom the teachers interacted infrequently, and another group included students teachers did not "stay with" (provide a prompt or new question) when these students did not respond or responded incorrectly. Teachers tended to be aware of students they did not call upon frequently (often because they did not want to embarrass the student) but were largely *unaware* of their qualitative differences in behavior when students did not respond or responded incorrectly. After teachers were informed about these differences, 40 additional hours of observations were collected and these data demonstrated that teachers could change their quantitative behaviors—calling on some students more often—and qualitative behaviors—staying with a student and working to obtain a student response. And importantly, target student behavior changed reciprocally and positively (e.g., students responded more effectively to academic questions).

Changing expectations for a cohort of teachers. Weinstein et al. (1991) conducted a quasi-experimental study that involved collaboration between university researchers and classroom teachers. Research findings were presented at seminars, and teachers had opportunities to discuss why and how needlessly low expectations might be communicated. Furthermore, they considered the motivational problems that low-achieving students face in urban middle schools. The treatment program—to prevent low expectations—focused not only on individual teachers but also on school-wide practices, such as reducing the tracking of students on the basis of achievement. At the end of the year, project students had better grades, fewer disciplinary referrals, and an increased rate of school retention than did control students. However, these gains were not sustained in the following year with a new set of teachers, suggesting the importance of teachers and that students had not internalized more positive beliefs about themselves.

Changing students' group placement. Research has shown that structural changes in schooling can enhance student achievement. Mason, then a junior high principal, and his colleagues (Mason, Schroeter, Combs, & Washington, 1992) conducted a study in which 34 average achieving eighth-grade math students were assigned to pre-algebra classes rather than to general math classes. The teacher knew (in discussion with Mason) that the students had not performed above the cutoff score on the pretest, but she agreed they were sufficiently prepared to benefit from the class. Students placed in pre-algebra classes made better math progress than comparison students who took general math. Importantly, the presence of average students in the pre-algebra course did not hinder the learning of higher-achieving students in these classes. The study demonstrated long-term effects, as students who were allowed to take the pre-algebra course subsequently enrolled in more advanced math classes in high school and obtained better grades than students who took the general math class.

Improving teacher expectations for the entire class. Rubie-Davies, Peterson, Sibley, and Rosenthal (forthcoming) have studied how teachers communicate high or low expectations to the whole class. They recently conducted an experiment showing that teachers changed their expectations and instruction in ways that increased the achievement for the whole class. This work was conducted in New Zealand, where teachers are required annually to participate in extensive professional development. Teachers in the treatment (expectation) group attended four workshops that provided information about how high-expectation teachers taught, and teachers planned instructional strategies based on what high-expectation teachers do. Teachers (including the control group) were observed on three occasions to see if they expressed high and appropriate expectations. At year's end students' mathematical performance in high-expectation treatment classrooms was 28% higher than control group students. This study illustrates that in New Zealand teacher expectations and practice can be changed in ways that directly improve student achievement substantially.

Improving teaching: some considerations for administrators. Some teachers hold and communicate low expectations to individual students, student groups (based on ability), or entire classrooms. When helping teachers who communicate low expectations, you should consider that most teachers cannot reflect upon their teaching while teaching. Teachers may be unaware that they communicate low expectations because classrooms are complex and busy. Teachers ask questions while thinking about the previous student's response, while wondering whether to correct two students who are misbehaving. Teachers must make quick decisions in order to maintain lesson flow while providing appropriate feedback to individual students and engaging the entire class in the lesson. That some teachers behave differently toward students who differ in perceived academic potential, ethnicity, or gender is not necessarily a comment upon teachers' commitment to providing equitable learning environments for all. Most teachers who express low expectations care about students and want them to succeed, but may be using inappropriate strategies (e.g., asking them only easy questions). Principals should realize that inappropriate teaching behavior does not necessarily reflect teacher intent. Thus, what teachers need is conceptual and practical information about problems and opportunities for addressing them. And, like their students, they need emotional support and encouragement as they learn to do new things.

Some principals may express differential expectations for teachers just as teachers do for students. Principals may treat some teachers more favorably (those they like or believe to be more capable), leading to higher teacher evaluation scores. Whitehurst, Chingos, and Lindquist (2014) found that principals gave higher ratings to teachers whose classes were populated with mainly high-achieving students than to teachers whose classes included pupils of less ability. Principals assigned teachers to classes in the first place. Their perception of teachers' ability might have led principals to assign more high-ability students to teachers they believed to be more effective.

Principal observations of teaching are time-consuming, and research has not illustrated that principals can use observational data to improve teaching. However, there is reason for optimism. Many principals lack appropriate training in how to do classroom observations well. Many principals have not been armed with evidence that teacher expectations can be changed in ways that enhance instruction and achievement. Knowledge of good teaching is important, but it must be applied to individual contexts (Johnson, Kraft, & Papay, 2012; Rosenholtz, 1989). Having said this, we provide concrete strategies to consider when working with teachers.

Increasing teacher expectations: some considerations. One way to enhance teachers' expectations is to increase their knowledge of teacher expectation effects. Teachers need to know how teachers communicate inappropriate expectations. Teachers can also benefit from opportunities to talk (with other teachers or principals) about how expectations shape classroom practice. Peer discussions might help teachers to more fully understand that students' past learning trajectories can be improved. However, for some teachers, abstract information may not be sufficient to change their behavior because they do not realize that they treat students differently (I wonder why *other* teachers do that?). Furthermore, teachers' own beliefs about their ability to teach low achievers may be a problem. Providing teachers the opportunity to see other teachers (live or on videotape) teach low-achieving students successfully may help them to realize that these students can learn and that *they* can teach them.

Furthermore, teachers can profitably reflect on their teaching: Do I believe that all students can learn? How do I demonstrate this belief through instruction and assessment? How might I interact differently with students who are performing less well? Can I improve their performance before the year ends? Teachers might reflect upon how their teacher education experiences might have lowered their expectations for some students. Delpit (1995) noted, "We say we believe that all children can learn, but few of us really believe it. Teacher education usually focuses on research that links failure and socio-economic status, failure and cultural differences, and failure and single parent households. It is hard to believe that these children can possibly be successful after their teachers have been so thoroughly exposed to so much negative indoctrination" (p. 172). Principals might do well to think about whether they believe all students can learn, ask teachers to do the same, and then discuss their responses together. Developing a shared focus on stimulating student progress is important.

Another strategy for helping teachers change is to provide them with information about how they teach. Teachers need information about their interactions with the whole class and with individual students. Although some teachers are aware of the frequencies of interactions with individual students, most are not aware of the quality of interactions (e.g., when a student answers incorrectly, what do I do?). Principals or mentors can provide teachers with feedback about the quality of their dyadic interactions with students or encourage teachers to audio- or videotape their own lessons for self-study or to seek feedback from others. And these videotapes could be compared with ones collected later in the year, thus providing a record of growth.

Those evaluating teachers typically use an observational instrument that describes teacher interaction at the *class* level (general classroom climate, types of questions that teachers ask, and the general level of student engagement). Observational systems commonly used would not capture that Julie is disengaged 90% of the time—only that 5% of the class was disengaged during the entire lesson. Much classroom interaction is between individual students and the teacher—in one study nearly 92% of teacher interactions were found to occur with *individual* students (Power, 1971). But we have long known that teachers vary in instructional styles. Lightfoot (1972) found that one second-grade urban classroom teacher asked individual students 75% of her questions, while another second-grade teacher addressed individual students but 35% of the time. Subsequently, research has consistently shown that many teachers treat students differently on the basis of social class, perceived ability and/or language proficiency, gender, ethnicity, and many other attributes (Good & Brophy, 2008). Thus, principals should determine if the pattern of interaction is similar across gender, ethnicity, and socioeconomic status. Attention to these questions also serves a policy need since schools have to report achievement outcomes by groups of students. Questions that principals should consider when conducting classroom observations include the following:

- Do some students receive more challenging questions than other students?
- When students make a mistake, how does the teacher react? Are there signs of disappointment or are there actions that indicate that mistakes are okay, but it is something we must address? Do teachers encourage students (e.g., provide a clue, ask a new question) or do they tend to give up (e.g., provide the answer, call on another student)?
- How does the teacher start and end the lesson? Is there more of an attempt to build student motivation in some classrooms than others? Are some students more likely to be included in summarizing the lesson (What have we learned today? How can we use this material?) than other students?
- Does the lesson account for students' previous knowledge and interests?
- Is there consistently more focus on facts and memory in some classes and more emphasis upon using information in other classes?
- Do teachers provide useful comments on students' written work?

Addressing these questions is very time-consuming. Thus, principals might collect this information in only a few classrooms. Opportunities for more targeted observation include classrooms that are making comparatively little achievement progress, classrooms where observational scores are low, and classrooms that have expressed a keen interest in improving.

Teachers' attitudes toward low-achieving students. Teacher attitudes about students are critical. Teachers must see students as more than their *deficits* and refuse to succumb to instruction based on what students *do not* know. Instead, teachers need to create cultures and instruct in ways that are informed by and promote students' *potential* and *progress*. Clearly, learning gaps need to be addressed. First-grade students with limited vocabulary need to develop a richer vocabulary.

But too often these students are placed together in a low reading group and their work becomes an educational diet of drill, simple stories, and vocabulary development. Students who have limited vocabularies need extended work, but like students with more developed vocabularies they also need challenges to think (How would you have ended the story—what other endings are possible?). Remedial work is often necessary, but teachers need to make remedial instruction meaningful through opportunities for students to think about their work.

Teachers should focus on student *progress*. Reciprocally, teachers should help students to recognize their progress and to value this achievement. Teachers can also help students identify what factors resulted in their success. Principals might facilitate this process by asking teachers to describe the three students who have improved the most from August to October and asking them to explain how they know this. Principals who ask about student progress during teacher conferences are essentially modeling for teachers how to create a climate that values growth.

In secondary schools, principals should look for possible differences in how teachers interact in college prep classes, other advanced classes, and "regular" or remedial classes. Students who fall behind in math often unprofitably are assigned to eighth-grade classes in which they primarily review material that they have failed to master from grade 4 on. Again review may be needed, but it must involve new and more meaningful teaching and learning strategies. As noted, some teachers interact differently with different classes because of the expectations they hold about the potential of the class as a class. Some things to look for in addition to questions we raised earlier might include: How do teachers plan for their more advanced classes? Do students in non-college prep classes have the opportunity to write papers and to make oral presentations? Is there evidence that teachers spend time planning for and evaluating all their classes?

Secondary supervisors in middle schools and high schools should note that expectation effects have been found to be especially strong in grades 1 and 2, in the first year of middle school or junior high, and possibly when students begin high school. This advice is based upon a synthesis of 18 experimental students (Raudenbush, 1984). The increased influence of teachers may be because students are new to the school and teachers, and perhaps previous expectancy cues are not as strong in new settings.

There are no silver bullets for improving performance expectations. In closing, following Good and Brophy (2008), we suggest some general considerations to note when assessing teacher communication with individual and whole classes of students.

- Keep expectations for individual students (or the entire class) current by examining their progress; stress improvement and present performance over past performance.
- Think in terms of stretching students' minds by stimulating them and encouraging them to achieve as much as they can, not in terms of protecting them

from failure or embarrassment (Are students in less advanced classes more likely to be protected while those in advanced classes are more likely to be challenged?).
- When students have not understood an explanation or demonstration, try to diagnose their learning difficulty and follow through by reteaching in a different way rather than repeating the same instruction—or worse, by giving up in frustration.
- When students make mistakes (especially low-achieving students) teachers should convey that it is okay to make a mistake but encourage students to keep thinking and processing information (Do teachers in high-track or low-track classrooms react differently to student mistakes?).

Recognizing and Supporting Students as Social Beings

Appropriate teacher expectations are necessary for good student performance. And good teacher-student relationships are important for building trust. A relationship built upon trust makes it possible to develop and maintain orderly and safe environments, which allow, if not encourage, students to express emerging ideas, to take intellectual risks, and to learn from their failures and their successes. Independent of their utility value (e.g., allowing for smoother classroom management), good teacher-student relations are inherently valuable. Other than parents, students spend more time with teachers than any other adults. Hence, civil, supportive, and prosocial interactions between teachers and youth are important.

Connecting to and communicating with others is a useful function of schooling, especially in a society that is experiencing less affiliation at both the macro and micro level. For example, Putnam (2000) in his book *Bowling Alone* noted that Americans' affiliation with various social groups, including bowling teams, churches, and social clubs, has diminished considerably in the last 50 years. Similarly, Nichols and Good (2004) in their book on American teenagers noted that families seldom eat together, have sustained conversations, or watch the same media.

Readers should understand, then, that the literature we are about to review often had considerations other than student achievement in mind. Researchers' goals were often to make schools more friendly or civil, to value students' learning processes (not just the product), and to encourage students to explore to become more curious. Hence some of the research did not collect achievement data. Still, much of this work has implications for improving student achievement.

A brief history. Here we provide a brief history of research on students as social beings. After we describe this history, we discuss why it matters, and what we can do to improve classrooms. The study of teacher-student relationships has a long history (Becker, 1952; Carter, 1952; Kelley, 1950; Kleinfeld, 1972; Leacock, 1969; Lippit & Gold, 1959; St. John, 1971) and these studies continue today (Hamre & Pianta, 2005; López, 2012; McCaslin, 2006; McKown, 2013; Pianta & Hamre, 2009; Rohrkemper, 1984).

Once, parents and policy makers had little concern whether their child was taught by Miss Burden or Miss Hill. Phil Jackson in his seminal book *Life in Classrooms* (1968) described the lack of societal concern about schooling. Jackson wrote, "This massive exodus from home to school is accomplished with a minimum of fuss and bother. Few tears are shed (except perhaps by the very youngest) and few cheers are raised. The school attendance of children is such a common experience in our society that those of us who watch them go hardly pause to consider what happens to them when they get there" (p. 3).

Things have changed! Now students' achievement—especially the lack of it—is headline news. Parents want good teachers for their children, and some policy makers have contended that the poor achievement of American students is a threat to our economy. When researchers moved into classrooms, their findings (including Jackson's pioneering research) in time led to increased awareness that classrooms were complex and posed important constraints and opportunities for students.

Jackson showed the complexity of classrooms (e.g., teachers have as many as 1,000 interpersonal exchanges a day, and it was understandably difficult for teachers to remember many of these interactions), and noted the complexity that children faced and felt in the daily grind of classroom life (e.g., living in a crowd, waiting one's turn, public evaluation). Much research followed to respond to the complexity of classrooms for teachers and students, including Kounin's seminal research on classroom management (1970). Kounin studied how teachers can cope with multiple students while helping students to adjust to classroom crowds, and limited supplies and time. Brophy and Good (1974) added to knowledge about the rich texture of classrooms by reviewing research demonstrating how teachers formed different relationships with different students. Brophy and Good synthesized what was known about how teachers' attitudes toward students influenced teacher-student interactions and created a broader understanding of the different types of students who populated classrooms and how teachers responded to them.

Brophy and Good (1974) reviewed the work of many scholars, including Judith Kleinfeld (1972), whose writings then seem eerily contemporary now in 2015. In describing Kleinfeld's work they noted that effective teachers assumed a personal interest in students, had informal conversations with them, and were highly supportive of students' attempts to learn, but they provided more than sympathy. Brophy and Good quoted Kleinfeld:

> The essence of the instructional style which elicits a high level of intellectual performance from village Indian and Eskimo students is to create an extremely warm, personal relationship and to actively demand a level of academic work which the student does not suspect he can obtain. Village students thus interpret the teacher's demandingness not as bossiness or hostility, but rather as another expression of his personal concern, and meeting the teacher's academic standards becomes their reciprocal obligation in an intensively personal relationship.
>
> (Kleinfeld, 1972, p. 34)

Notably for some time researchers have argued that good teaching is a blend of demand for student performance and affective support for students. The early work on process-product as summarized by Brophy and Good (1986) and the early work on teacher expectation effects as reviewed in this chapter collectively argued that students perceived as less capable needed more opportunities to contribute to class discussions and to receive more challenging work. Although both of these lines of research included some aspects of climate and support (e.g., Rosenshine and Furst's [1971] work on enthusiasm and warmth, and Good and Grouws' [1975] notions of positive classroom climate), each prioritized achievement in the assumed context of relationships. However, the work we review now changed the figure/ground distinction of academic press and academic support.

Recognizing students as social beings as well as learners. Earlier we noted that Jackson's work brought attention to students but did so from an adult's perspective. Rohrkemper (1985) provided a focus on students from the perspective of *students*. She did this by interviewing students, and her findings highlighted the importance of seeing students not only as learners but also as social beings possessing emotions and social affiliation needs. Rohrkemper and Corno (1988) also examined classroom learning demands from the perspective of the student: how students deal with the lump in their throat when they do not know what to do, what you do when the teacher asks you to respond to your friend's incorrect answer, and how you respond to your own failure, whether academic or social. What is remarkable about their arguments, in addition to their attention to the student perspective, was the era in which they wrote. Many then believed that good teaching was to allow students to achieve success at all costs. In contrast, Rohrkemper and Corno theorized that students could not be protected from failure, especially if students were engaged in authentic learning tasks that challenged their thinking. Not only was failure inevitable but also in some contexts it was constructive and thus desirable.

Others too have noted the importance of Rohrkemper and Corno's pioneering work. Perry, Phillips, and Hutchinson (2006) wrote,

> In their 1988 article for the *Elementary School Journal*, Rohrkemper and Corno wrote, ". . . classroom learning inevitably requires adaptive responses on the part of students. Teachers cannot and should not engineer tasks to try to prevent this, for the experience of modifying either task or themselves to cope with the stress of classroom demands allows students to learn to respond flexibly and to assume control over their own learning."
> (pp. 237–238)

Perry et al. (2006) commented on Rohrkemper and Corno's influence on the field: "Since then, volumes have been written about the need for students to develop skills and attitudes that will enable them to engage in intentional, self-regulated learning (SRL) to prepare for life and work in the twenty-first century" (p. 238).

However, this did not mean that students were left alone to navigate failure. Rohrkemper and Corno (1988) noted various ways teachers could support students, depending upon the type of emotion that students faced, such as task difficulty or boredom, including explicit instructions for how to change instruction, change task, change situation, and help students to make an adaptive response. As one example, "Adaptive strategies that *modify the self* include overcoming detrimental inner speech when anxious, taking a break when frustrated and returning with a 'totally different' approach, managing one's study time more efficiently, and maintaining the intention to learn when confronted with difficult learning" (Rohrkemper & Corno, 2006, p. 308). This perspective helps administrators understand that all students face classroom challenges and that students need teacher support as they deal with classroom tasks and their emotions. McCaslin (pka Rohrkemper) wrote more extensively about the important role that teachers had in coregulating with students as they coped and learned. McCaslin's work has moved on to consider other emotions, including pride, shame, and guilt, and how students cope with them (see McCaslin, Vriesema, & Burggraf, in press). She has further argued persuasively that a major reason that reform fails is because policy makers frame the "problem" in ways that ignore learners as social beings (McCaslin, 1996, 2006, 2009; McCaslin & Lavigne, 2010).

Students' need for belonging. Considerable literature asserts that students need to feel a sense of belongingness in the school community. Osterman (2000) reviewed this literature by addressing three questions: Is a perception of belonging important in a school setting? Do students generally perceive themselves to be a member of the school community? How do schools influence a sense of community? In brief, she reports that research on students' belongingness in schools establishes that the benefits are evident and strong. She notes, "These concepts of commitment and engagement are closely linked to student performance, and more importantly, to the quality of student learning" (p. 359). Student perception of belongingness varies among students. Some students receive positive and supportive environments, while other students experience indifference and even alienation (Anderman & Maehr, 1994; Newmann, 1981; Wehlage et al., 1989). And despite the pleas for schools to do more (e.g., Anderman & Maehr, 1994; Goodlad, 1984; Noddings, 1992), schools generally have done little to support students' social and emotional needs.

Teacher caring. One reason students come to feel that they belong in schools is because teachers care. Noddings (1992) argued that teachers create caring classrooms by modeling (displaying how to care), dialogue (connecting to students and understanding students as individuals), practice (caring), and confirmation (affirming our best selves). Most importantly care is bidirectional—teacher care is only as valuable as students' perceptions that they are cared for. Oberg De La Garza, Roberts, and Lavigne (2013) reported that research on students' reports of caring indicates that teachers express care in various ways, including: maintaining an orderly classroom, treating students as individuals (Ferreria & Bosworth,

2001), knowing their students well, holding high expectations for achievement (Alder, 2002) and behavior (Wentzel, 1997), and liking to help students (Howard, 2001). Although correlational, there is abundant evidence to show that caring is consistently associated with positive student outcomes. Oberg De La Garza et al. (2013) reported that perceptions of teacher caring have been associated with many student outcomes, including: lower levels of delinquent behavior and drug use (Battistich & Hom, 1997); fewer negative behaviors, such as cheating (Murdoch, Miller, & Kohlhardt, 2004); and academic effort and greater student responsibility (Wentzel, 1997). Undoubtedly and importantly the research on teacher caring and teacher expectations overlaps (e.g., high expectations for achievement). Similarly, the literatures on student belongingness and teacher caring converge in supportive ways (e.g., treating students as individuals).

Increased attention to the needs of students of color. The literature we reviewed described the need for students generally to have supportive expectations from teachers and to enjoy warm relations with them. Although the educational needs for Black and other students of color have always been a part of the literature to some degree, the frequency and intensity of research and concern have increased over time. The expectation literature spoke directly to the fact that teachers often reported lower expectations for minority or students of color and the negative effects of their low expectations were stronger for these students than other students (Jussim, Eccles, & Madon, 1996; McKown & Weinstein, 2003). Some scholars have contended that problems for minority students stem not from teachers' conceptions of their academic abilities but rather from teachers' conceptions of their color and culture (Banks, 1997). These concerns argue that teachers need to demonstrate to students that they care for the cultural assets they bring to the classroom.

Concerns for the needs of Black students have not gone unnoticed, and much attention has been paid to research showing that achievement levels and graduation rates of Black students are lower than for White students (Jencks & Phillips, 1998). Earlier efforts to narrow the achievement gap showed progress in the 1970s and 1980s, but now the gap is widening. Barton and Coley (2009) note that the explanations for this are complex and varied (e.g., decline of the nuclear family, concentrations of poverty, and fewer employment opportunities). Some argue that the low performance is partially due to teachers' low expectations for Black students' achievement. And these beliefs, such as the belief that students of color are unmotivated or have behavioral issues (Villegas & Lucas, 2002), have been shown to be related to the disproportionate representation of Black and Latino males in special education classrooms (Klingner et al., 2005). However, some issues may be in how students respond to the stereotypes placed on them by the broader society. Claude Steele's (1997, 2010) work has provided one explanation for the achievement gap. He observed at the University of Michigan that Black students, including those with high SAT scores, received lower grades and dropped out of school much more frequently than did White peers. In his discussions with Black students he sensed that they wondered if they belonged (and if they ever would) at Michigan.

Subsequently, he found that stereotype threat existed in other groups (e.g., women who underperformed in advanced math classes). In short, Steele demonstrated that stereotype threat undermines students' performance when they perform in domains in which they are not expected to do well. Steele (2010) explained how:

> It's this: stereotype and identity threats—these contingencies of identity—increase vigilance toward possible threat and bad consequences in the social environment, which diverts attention and mental capacity away from the task at hand, which worsens performance and general functioning, all of which further exacerbates anxiety, which further intensifies the vigilance for threat and the diversion of attention.
>
> (pp. 125–126)

Steele argued that his research offers practical implications for practice, such as changing the way feedback is delivered to improve minority students' motivation and performance. For example, Cohen, Steele, and Ross (1999) found that Black students benefitted when feedback suggested that they were being held to high standards while also assuring students they had the capacity to be successful. Further, Steele recommends fostering intergroup conversation among students from different backgrounds to improve students' sense of belonging and performance.

Others have documented that reducing stereotype threat can improve achievement. Cohen, Garcia, Apfel, and Master (2006) showed in two experiments that the psychological threat that some Black students perceive could be lessened by self-affirmations that students expressed in classroom writing assignments. The interventions improved the grades of Black students and reduced the racial gap in grades by 40%.

Hanselman, Bruch, Gamoran, and Borman (2014) followed the procedures of Cohen et al. (2006) with seventh-grade students. In this study they also demonstrated the importance of racial context in school settings. Students completed a 15–20-minute writing assignment four times in a year. Self-affirmation students chose their most important values from a list of 11 items (e.g., why I like being with family and friends or sports) and wrote about why these values were *personally* important. Control students received this same list but were asked to write about why these values might be important to others. In high-potential threat schools (low minority enrollment), intervention effects were large—a full grade improvement for treatment students. However, in low-potential threat schools (high minority enrollment) the intervention had a slight negative effect. Furthermore, the findings differed by subject matter as the gains were more pronounced in English than mathematics classes.

Over time many suggestions have been made for helping culturally and racially diverse students by altering the curriculum or changing teacher actions. Banks (1997) made the case for multicultural education and suggested five characteristics of multicultural education: content integration (students from all races are discussed in the curriculum); knowledge construction (recognizing the value assumptions included in terms like "the western movement"); prejudice reduction (helping teachers and students to recognize sources of bias); equity pedagogy (teachers' openness to diverse instructional needs of their students); and empowering school and societal cultures (recognizing that Blacks or Hispanics could never get enough votes to be elected student body president or a cheerleader in schools where they were but a small percentage of the student body). Ladson-Billings (1994) theorized that teachers' behavior may help students to develop a more culturally relevant perspective rather than socializing students into an "American identity." Teachers do this by helping students to make connections between their community, national, and global identities.

Culturally relevant teaching (CRT). Over time increasing attention has been given to the educational needs of other minority groups, including indigenous youth, Hispanic youth, and immigrant youth (Castagno, McKinley, & Brayboy, 2008; López, Heilig, & Schram, 2013). The enhanced focus upon the needs of Latino/a students has emerged in part because they are the largest minority group in Grades K–12 (22.3%; NCES, 2010), and are the fastest growing (Fry & López, 2012). And, just as the Black-White achievement gap has received significant consideration, now the Latino-White achievement gap is taking the stage (McKown, 2013). The growing demographic divide between aging White and younger minority Americans has educational and political consequences. Meckler (2014) quoted William Frey (a demographer at the Brookings Institution): "It suggests that even greater priority should be given to providing these younger minorities education opportunities and other resources to be successful as members of the labor force" (p. 5).

However, concerns for attention to the needs of Latino/a students go beyond the fact that they are increasing in number. These students often bring not only cultural differences to the classroom but also language skills that differ from their peers. Historically these potential *assets* are seen only as *liabilities* and students are often asked to ignore their language and culture.

One way to prioritize minorities' education is through CRT. According to López (2014), defining CRT and analyzing the degree of its presence in classrooms are difficult because it is derived from a rich and diverse literature (Au & Jordan, 1981; Delpit, 1995; Roberts, 2010). Many believe that CRT was influenced by researchers, including Au and Jordan (1981) and Cazden and Leggett (1981), who argued that the educational needs of traditionally marginalized students needed to be addressed. These arguments stressed that these students had been exposed to "deficiency ideologies" and that more attention needed to be paid to "cultural mismatches" and "cultural differences." The CRT literature has shifted the instructional focus from deficits or differences to assets (e.g., viewing students' non-English language as an advantage rather than a limitation). However, some CRT theorists, such as Ladson-Billings (1995), go beyond concerns about students' academic success and cultural competence and suggest that students need to develop a critical consciousness (e.g., a willingness to challenge the status quo). However, some CRT supporters (e.g., Sleeter, 2011) have raised questions about the research base to support this assertion. Others, such as López, have expressed concerns for developmental issues related to CRT and one particular component—the emancipator dimension (e.g., Do 4-year-old students benefit from knowing that they are a member of an oppressed group?).

López (2014) reviewed CRT research and advanced six considerations relevant to creating environments where students of color can succeed academically. First is the communication of high academic expectations; much research shows that students of color are often exposed to a less demanding curriculum. Second is the need to acknowledge the worth of the cultural heritage of every student. When teachers model tolerance and respect for individual differences, they also positively influence the development of students' ethnic identity. Third is the need to consider students' culture and preferences for instructional strategies but in ways that do not trivialize students by approaching instruction in reductionist ways (the fact that many Latinos value a teaching practice does not mean that all Latinos do). Fourth is to assure that cultural information, resources, and materials be reflected in all school subjects (e.g., including some literature that includes protagonists who share their culture). Fifth is a belief that home experiences can be incorporated into the curriculum, allowing teachers to learn from their students, their families, and their culture. Sixth is recognizing that the use of students' native language supports their achievement. López notes that when applicable, students' native language should be viewed as a strength and incorporated as students develop academic English proficiency. We write this acknowledging that some state laws may prohibit this recommendation.

CRT perspectives present rich considerations but ones that are difficult to measure and validate. For example, López argued that it is important to recognize the differences within groups of students because the failure to do so leads to harmful reductionist teaching (e.g., providing all Latino students frequent cooperative work because some benefit from it). Others have urged against the use of simplistic ideas and stereotypes. Oberg De La Garza et al. (2013) have demonstrated that some Latino students interpret the *same* teacher behavior differently (e.g., as a sign of support *or* as a sign of not caring). Clearly, students not only perceive teacher actions but also interpret teacher actions (Rohrkemper, 1985). Research has shown that high and low achievers and female and male students sometimes interpret teacher intentions and behavior differently (Copper & Good, 1983; Weinstein & Middlestadt, 1979).

Essentially our point is this: some aspects of good teaching apply to most students and in many subject areas. But it is also important to realize that some students have needs in addition to these general considerations that may be important. Clearly all students benefit from some degree of social and instructional support. Yet CRT perspectives suggest that students of color may need more social support, especially support that values their culture. Despite the fact that American schools are established on historically white, middle-class norms of schooling, teachers who follow CRT ideas seek to help culturally and linguistically diverse students feel that their identity, beliefs, and assets *do* belong in schools and classrooms.

Teachers as providing both instructional and emotional support. Robert Pianta and colleagues have further unified thinking about classroom learning by noting that students need both instructional support and emotional support. Like others (Kleinfeld, 1972; McCaslin, 1996; Noddings, 2007) before them, they note that students have need for emotional support because they are social beings. Pianta, La Paro, and Hamre (2008) developed the Classroom Assessment Scoring System (CLASS) to measure the degree of emotional and instructional support that students receive in classrooms, using concepts from both the effective teaching literature (e.g., Brophy & Good, 1986) and various intervention efforts to improve schools (as explicated in Hamre & Pianta, 2005).

Their work has generally illustrated that when students are provided with high levels of both emotional and instructional support they often achieve more than students not receiving this support (Hamre & Pianta, 2005; NICHD ECCRN, 2005; Pianta, Belsky, Houts, & Morrison, 2007; Pianta & Hamre, 2009; Ruzek, Hafen, Hamre, & Pianta, 2014). The value of providing both instructional and emotional support has been extended to examine effective teaching in English Language Learners classrooms (Reyes, Brackett, Rivers, White, & Salovey, 2012). However, the extent to which the CLASS uniquely captures minority students' conception of support has been questioned (López, 2012). We return to this issue.

In sum, teachers can support students' need for belongingness (Osterman, 2000) by providing emotional support (Kleinfeld, 1972; Rohrkemper & Corno 1988) and care (Noddings, 1984, 1992), and addressing CRT concerns (López, 2014). The CLASS enables researchers to measure both teachers' caring and their ability to provide good instruction (Pianta, La Paro, & Hamre, 2008). Despite the important theoretical arguments that identify the need to see students as social beings and to recognize students' emotional needs and good advances in measurement, it is difficult to define specifically those teacher actions that embody these actions/beliefs and how they are best expressed in ways that students perceive as positive support.

The search for the independent variable: How do teachers provide emotional support? We examine some recent research using the CLASS to explore how teacher support (instructional, management, and emotional) impacts students. Do students benefit in the same way from teacher support as measured on the CLASS? Furthermore, we wonder what threshold level teachers must reach (as measured on the CLASS) to show support in a way that improves achievement.

Reyes et al. (2012) used the CLASS to explore student engagement and academic achievement as measured by report card grades that included seven scores (e.g., effort and conduct). The study found that one dimension of the CLASS—emotional support—was associated with student engagement and teacher-assigned grades, but that the other two CLASS dimensions (management and instruction) were not. In another study, Reese, Jensen, and Ramirez (2014) studied the effects of CLASS on K–2 Latino students in three rural elementary schools. The students in the school were largely Latino (94%) and from low-income homes (98%). Many teachers self-reported as Spanish speakers (60%). The findings indicated that students benefitted from teacher emotional support but not from management or instructional support. They reported, "Teachers rendering more emotional support, for example, were more likely to use Spanish, a majority of students' native language, to communicate affection, enthusiasm and assistance to support students' emotional and academic needs" (Reese et al., 2014, p. 519).

Lewis, Ream, Bocian, Cardullo, and Hammond (2012) tested the hypothesis that students' beliefs that their teachers cared for them would increase their self-efficacy in math and in their math achievement. This study included 84 fifth- and sixth-grade classrooms; 799 of the students were fluent English speakers, and 667 were English learners. Teacher caring was defined by students' responses to three statements: "Our math teacher takes a personal interest in students; our math teacher cares about how we feel; our math teacher listens to what I have to say." Although teacher caring was positively associated with increases in students' motivation for all students, teacher caring impacted the math performance of only those Hispanic students who were still learning English.

In another study involving low- to middle-income students including 49 Latino and 44 White students, Garza (2009) found that students described teacher care as the provision of instructional scaffolding, a kind disposition, availability, personal interest in students, and affective academic support. The themes were important to *all* students. However, within these patterns Latino high school students most highly valued the provision of teacher scaffolding, whereas White students most valued teacher actions that reflected a kind disposition. Roughly speaking, this indirectly suggests that Latino students were more responsive to instructional support and that White students were more responsive to emotional support. Appendix C provides an interesting report of students' statements, indicating how "they knew" that teachers cared for them.

However, a different pattern was found in research elsewhere. Recall in Chapter 2 we reported that Strong (2011) in a follow-up to his third experiment found that one scale from the CLASS—instructional support—correlated with teaching effectiveness, but the classroom management and emotional support scales did not. So how do we make sense of these varied findings?

- Strong (2011) found that instructional support scale predicted student achievement.
- Reyes et al. (2012) found that the emotional support scale was associated with higher teacher grades; Reese et al. (2014) found that teachers rated high

on the emotional support scale were found (on the bases of field notes) to express more affection to students.
- Lewis et al. (2012) found that the emotional support scale was associated with high student self-efficacy beliefs in math, but the impact of emotional support was associated with increased math performance only for students who were less proficient in English.
- Garza (2009) found that White students reported their perception of teacher caring was most influenced by teachers' emotional support, whereas Hispanic students reported instructional support.

Hence, across these studies it is hard to generalize about the unique needs that students have for emotional versus instructional support. Our inability to generalize is not only on the basis of inconsistencies in findings, but also because of differences in sample sizes, level of schooling, the geography of setting (rural/urban), the percentage of minority students present in schools, and teacher characteristics. Furthermore, we believe an important finding emerging from this small review is that the CLASS scores for instructional support were exceedingly *low* both in terms of the standards by the developers and in comparison to scores on the other two scales in two studies (Reese et al., 2014; Reyes et al., 2012). So one might ask: was instructional support unimportant in improving learning, or was the lack of its impact due to the quality of support being insufficient? To reiterate, we believe more work needs to be done establishing what the *quality* of the independent variables is.

Given the extant state of research, we acknowledge that there might be some uniquely important instructional considerations for some learners, but in general, the data reviewed here and across a diverse set of literatures provides support for concluding that emotional, instructional, and management support is beneficial to most students. Also, as we mentioned earlier in reviewing the teacher expectation literature, part of the issue may be who receives the instructional or emotional support from teachers. Although some teacher expressions of warmth or personalization may be expressed to the whole class, much teacher affect is expressed to individual students and some students may receive considerable affect and others little or none. Students' beliefs about belongingness or teachers' emotional support may well be impacted by how teachers support them directly, uniquely, or indirectly. For example, does the teacher make personal comments to some students and not others? Does a teacher address some students consistently first and others last? Does the teacher comment to some students about dress and appearance while noting other students' work ethic and academic success? Those who attempt to help teachers to improve might examine individual differences in how teachers express their affect to students. We have known for a long time that teacher-student relationships are varied and complex (Brophy & Good, 1974).

A Brief Summary of the Research

When we presented our considerations following our review of teacher expectations literature, we noted that there were no magic bullets for how teachers can best express appropriate expectations. Here, too, we note that there is no formula for how teachers can best recognize students as social being and communicate that they care about students (in ways that students perceive and believe). But this does not mean that this information cannot be applied—it suggests that this rich knowledge must be applied in context. Two important considerations flow from our review. This broad research area has yielded a rich perspective that including concepts and instructional actions can enhance student achievement when applied appropriately in a particular context.

From the teacher expectation literature (TE) we have seen the importance of rejecting the deficit view of students that defines them in terms of their weaknesses, and rather that teachers need to focus on students' potential. Some students may need appropriate remedial work, but all students need the chance to learn and benefit from teachers' explicit beliefs and intentions that all students can learn and make progress and that all students need choice and challenge. Teachers must expect and demand good work from students.

Obviously, the TE and seeing students as social beings (SSB) perspectives overlap on some issues. For example, one of the strongest ways students perceive teacher care is that teachers not only make instructional demands but also provide instructional scaffolding with affective support. More generally the SSB view suggests the need for teachers to be available to students, to be flexible in negotiating student needs/requests, and to show that they personalize instruction to show they know and care for students. In short, these two research traditions suggest that as teachers push students academically, they also need to provide support and recognize their students as people and as learners.

How Can Principals Use This Information?

As with the teacher expectation literature, the first step is for principals to help teachers become *aware* of the diverse literature that shows that students must be seen and treated both as learners and as social beings. Beyond this, teachers need *feedback* and opportunities to explore how they address students' instructional and emotional needs in their classroom. Teachers might benefit from study groups or the opportunity to be observed and to observe other teachers with an eye toward enhancing their communication of appropriate support to students. Principals and mentor teacher observations might focus attention on dimensions of teacher support that appear to be related to positive outcomes for students, including the following:

- Do teachers demonstrate affective support for their students?
- Do teachers display kind dispositions and warmth to students?
- Are teachers available and approachable for student needs?
- Do teachers demonstrate their knowledge of individual students and their personal interest?
- Do teachers explain to students the importance of the content they study and demonstrate that they value the content being presented?
- Do teachers display a willingness to work with students when they make mistakes, and do they do so in a way that encourages students to think (that is not simply giving students the right answer or calling on someone else to do so)?
- Do teachers demonstrate their awareness of students' diversity and aspects of the community that have relevance to content that is being studied in schools?

However, these guidelines need to be applied with balance. For example, too much support for students might be suffocating to some students.

Other Aspects of Effective Teaching

Now we briefly describe other teaching practices that commonly relate to student achievement gains. These aspects of good teaching are comparatively easier to describe. Most of these important practices were identified in the process-product research (Brophy & Good, 1986) and *consistently* confirmed in subsequent, recent research.

Using Time Well

Time is a precious commodity, and its effective use in classrooms cannot be overstated as teachers' good use of time impacts student achievement. Teachers vary in using time well, and these variations are often huge (Berliner, Fisher, Filby, & Marliave, 1978; Fisher et al., 1978). These researchers established that on average only 58% of available time was actually used studying academic topics and that 18% of time was spent on non-academic topics. The extreme class-to-class variation merits attention as in some second-grade classrooms students received on average roughly 18 minutes on math instruction, whereas other classrooms averaged 48 minutes on math instruction. Furthermore, there was considerable variation in students' engagement—students were engaged 50–90% of the time. Poor use of time continues to be documented. Smith (2000) studied time allocations in 70 social studies, math, and language arts classes. Three hundred observations were collected in grades 2, 5, and 8. Similar to earlier work, 23% of allocated time was used for non-instructional purposes. Importantly, more effective teachers used time better than less effective teachers—non-instructional time in less effective teachers' classrooms was 30% but only 14% in more effective teachers' classes. Smith concluded that students in less effective teachers' classrooms received only two-thirds of the time actually allocated for instruction.

Of course, any variable, including time usage, has no meaning in and of itself. For example, if students are using the entire period completing review work that they already know how to do, time is wasted. Furthermore, there are many reasons that all available time should not be used on instruction activities. Asking students about their personal interests, school events, and national media issues is a social exchange that helps to personalize classrooms and to make them comfortable and enjoyable. Still, the marked variations that we described earlier seem to indicate that excessive amounts of time away from academic topics suggest that teachers are not attentive to students' instructional needs. Further, we believe that some students see this and perceive that these teachers do not care enough to prepare well for class. Principals evaluating teachers should be sensitive to how teachers use time and how they involve students in lessons.

Maintaining a Good Instructional and Curriculum Pace

More effective teachers tend to go through the curriculum more quickly than do other teachers. Good, Grouws, and Beckerman (1978) found that more effective fourth-grade math teachers (teaching students of similar ability) averaged 1.13 pages per day, whereas less effective teachers averaged .71 pages per day. Over time, some students receive more material than others. This does not mean that faster is better! Good teachers tend to increase pace (especially in elementary schools) with small steps that reduce student frustration and allow for students to make continuous progress. The relationship between curriculum pace and achievement is more apparent in some subjects than in others. Subjects that allow for a quicker pace are those that are more linear and hierarchical (e.g., math). One reason that a faster pace is associated with amount learned in math is because there is much redundancy in the math curriculum (Polikoff, 2012). Understandably, good teachers move through review content more quickly than new material.

Opportunity to Learn

If students are not exposed to concepts, they will not learn them. As simple as that sounds, students are often tested upon material that they have not studied! As noted, there is extraordinary variation in curriculum content in the United States. Sometimes students in the same school but in different classrooms receive content that varies strikingly (Porter & Polikoff, 2009). Teachers decide how long to spend on a particular unit of instruction and choose the cognitive level at which the material is addressed. Accordingly, some students' work is focused on skill and drill, whereas in other classrooms students have opportunities to think about content and to apply it to practical issues (this research relates back to our discussion of teacher expectation effects, where some students receive more opportunity to learn advanced content).

Much has been made of the findings that international students do considerably better on tests than do American students. This is directly related to our discussion on time and opportunity to learn. Clearly, students elsewhere spend considerably more time on core academic subjects than we do. Furthermore, sometimes international students have the opportunity to learn content that our students do not. The classic case is algebra; students in other countries (e.g., Japan) have the opportunity to learn algebra at an earlier age than do our students. Hence, on international tests taken in the eighth grade, it is not surprising that our students do poorly in algebra, given that they have not studied it.

Balance Procedural and Conceptual Knowledge

American education often moves from fad to fad; one clear example of faddism is swings in advocacy from procedural knowledge to conceptual knowledge. Contentious debates have abounded in reading—moving through eras dominated by phonics and periods dominated by whole language and the importance of understanding. In mathematics, we have gone from cycles where understanding of mathematics was critical to eras when drill and practice dominated. These extreme either-or debates are self-defeating.

Good et al. (2013) noted that it is unreasonable to want students to understand mathematical concepts if they cannot use ideas in practical ways or to want students to do math if they do not understand the math that they do. Hiebert and Grouws (2007) reviewed the literature and convincingly argued that successful mathematics teaching requires an emphasis on both understanding and skill efficiency (procedural knowledge). Too much emphasis on drill and skill to the neglect of conceptual learning is unproductive (Rakes, Valentine, McGatha, & Ronau, 2010), and emphasis upon conceptual knowledge without procedural knowledge is also unproductive (Hiebert & Grouws, 2007; National Mathematics Advisory Board, 2008).

It seems self-evident to assert that teachers need to provide a balanced curriculum. Yet many teachers overemphasize drill and practice (especially when they believe they are teaching less talented students). And as we have frequently noted, all students need work that makes them think, and understand and apply academic content. Some teachers err in the other direction—extensive time doing group work and discovery-oriented activities. In proportion, these activities are reasonable, and often important, but students also need to learn basic concepts and skills.

This also relates to research on teaching to mastery and active teaching literatures. After deciding what students will have the opportunity to learn, teachers need to teach content to the point where students have fully mastered it. This typically means students have attained both skill and conceptual knowledge so that they understand and can apply the content they have mastered. To help students fully integrate content, teachers must actively model procedural skills for students and engage students in ways that make their understanding visible to the teacher. Teaching to mastery and active teaching are instructional strategies that have been consistently related to student achievement.

Proactive Management

For 45 years we have known that teachers who are effective managers (those whose students are primarily engaged and seldom if ever engaged in major misbehavior) are so because of their ability to prevent misbehavior. After misbehavior occurs, most teachers lose time because after correcting the misbehavior they must regain other students' attention and reestablish the lesson flow. Kounin (1970) observed that more and less effective managers varied in several simple but powerful ways. The system of good management he identified had these characteristics: alerting (allowing students to anticipate what will happen), accountability (following through on announced actions), "withitness" (showing students that the teacher is aware of their behavior), smoothness of transition (explicit communication about how to transition from one task to another), and variety in seat work. Kounin found that effective managers are *proactive* teachers—establishing clear classroom structures that allow students to pursue tasks productively.

Work by Emmer, Evertson, and colleagues (Anderson, Evertson, & Brophy, 1979; Emmer, Evertson, & Anderson, 1980; Evertson & Weinstein, 2006) has shown that effective classroom management practices can be taught to other teachers in ways that improve student behavior, and there exists a direct relationship between Kounin's variables and student involvement. Emmer and Evertson have extended Kounin's basic principles by illustrating the importance of teachers' use of proactive management at the start of the year. They noted that some teachers teach (and reteach) the management system every day, whereas other teachers take some time at the beginning of the year to be sure that management principles are understood and followed. Essentially, proactive management is critically important and must be taught in *secondary* schools as well as elementary schools.

Management principles have been related to student achievement. Freiberg, Huzinec, and Templeton (2009) conducted an experiment in 14 elementary schools in an urban school district. The performance of 350 upper elementary students was compared with that of 350 matched control group students. Treatment teachers exposed their students to a prosocial classroom and instructional management treatment program (that included Kounin management variables and certain other prosocial variables). On average treatment students were ranked at the 67th percentile in mathematics and the 64th percentile in reading, whereas the control students scored at the 50th percentile in both subjects. These data clearly show the importance of good management. Notably, the treatment did not contain any academic content so it was clear that good management *alone* was related to better achievement in reading and mathematics.

Chapter 5 provides more advice about how principals can help teachers to become better managers.

Adequate Subject-Matter Knowledge

A commonly held belief is that good teaching is as simple as finding teachers who have solid subject-matter knowledge and allow them to teach. However, despite this belief (both among educators and policy makers), there is considerable literature to show that even advanced teacher knowledge does not correlate highly with student learning. This seems counterintuitive, as it would seem likely that a teacher who understands algebra thoroughly would be able to teach rational numbers, early algebra concepts, division with remainders, and other concepts. But to use mathematical knowledge teachers have to understand students as social beings and they need to know about student learning and development. If teachers are to effectively use mathematical (or chemistry) knowledge they must know how students think and the type of examples that students need to understand at different grade levels. If teachers do not present content with enthusiasm and warmth, student learning can be less than if teachers had these skills. However, having said this, it is essential that teachers have at least adequate subject matter knowledge if they are to teach well (recall the study by Hill, Umland, Litke, and Kapitula [2012] that we described in Chapter 2—teachers with low knowledge of mathematics also had students with low achievement) and to help students conceptually understand the content they study.

Teacher Clarity/Teacher Enthusiasm

Since the early 1970s, researchers have consistently found a positive relationship between teacher clarity and student learning (Rosenshine & Furst, 1973). Teacher clarity enables students to understand what is most important about the content they study and prepares students for how they will complete assignments. Teacher clarity saves time and provides more instructional time. Teachers who repeat assignments (especially if they do so inconsistently) will eventually have to deal with many student questions, and thus considerable momentum and opportunity for learning are lost. Confused students not only disengage but also often attract other students to off-task activities.

Clarity has frequently been studied, and many specific examples of how to avoid vagueness can be found in Good and Brophy (2008). Hines, Cruickshank, and Kennedy (1985), on the basis of extensive research using videos of classroom instruction, suggested that clarity falls into three major categories: teacher stresses the important aspects of content (repeats key terms, summarizes important points); teacher explains content through use of examples (written, visual, practical); and teacher assesses understanding (defines new words, asks students questions, examines their work).

Teachers who are enthusiastic about the content they teach involve students in the lesson, and this increases student learning and retention of concepts. It is highly unlikely that students would be interested in content if their teachers were not. Teachers can demonstrate enthusiasm by displaying: a sincere interest in the content, vigor, and surprise and other emotions that are occurring. Teachers can model interest in student responses and their express interest in aspects of the content. Earlier we noted the importance of seeing students as social beings, and students are much more likely to be engaged when teachers show interest in them. Brophy (2010) noted that many teachers do not convey why it is important to learn content and fail to provide logical reasons for studying content. He suggested that students are more likely to value content when teachers obviously enjoy the material they present. Research has consistently shown that models (like teachers) influence others not only by what they say but also through their actions. Indeed, students pay much more attention to what teachers *do* than to what they *say*.

Review Frequently

We have stressed the advantages of using time well and moving through the curriculum at a good pace. But it is also important for teachers to take time to review frequently. Although review takes time away from learning new content, it helps to consolidate learning gains in ways that assist students to remember what they have learned. Rosenshine (2012) summarized research on review and noted that its value is supported by various traditions, including research on how effective teachers teach and cognitive science research. Research shows that we have limited space in our working memory that we can use to focus on the task at hand. Thus, students, in completing academic work, need to be able to retrieve information from long-term memory into short-term or working memory. The better organized our long-term memory is, the easier it is to find needed information. Information becomes more organized when it is reviewed frequently. Some may equate review with drill, but review can take many forms, including student-led review and weekly or monthly review, and review can be in the form of discussion and application activities.

Value-Added Research: A New Research Paradigm

As we finished writing our book in July 2014, findings from the Measures of Effective Teaching (MET) Project were published (Kane, Kerr, & Pianta, 2014). The MET Project, a major research study funded by the Bill & Melinda Gates Foundation, involved observations of teaching, student achievement, and student surveys that were collected in six urban school districts and involved roughly 3,000 teachers and 100,000 students. This study provided useful information about the technical and practical issues involved in using observational systems and policy information, such as the match between observational systems and state achievement tests (Polikoff, 2014). Accordingly we include some of these findings in our book chapters.

Here we briefly consider: Have the MET findings linking classroom instruction to student achievement helped expand our knowledge base for explaining how instruction increases student achievement? The answer is *no*. The findings simply replicate what has been known for some time (Brophy & Good, 1986; Good & Brophy, 2008; Lavigne & Good, 2013) and is summarized in this chapter. Even though the study yielded no new knowledge, it is useful because it *replicates* extant knowledge about good teaching. This replication is important because the effective teaching literature described earlier was collected some time ago and classroom demographics of teachers and students have changed. Hence, the MET replication enhances our understanding that many of the basic and desirable teacher student relationships and instructional processes that support achievement have remained stable over time.

Since we have already discussed aspects of good teaching, our attention to MET findings is limited to illustrating examples of how themes we have already described are reconfirmed by the MET Project. For example, Ferguson and Danielson (2014) used data from about 1,900 classrooms, involving grades 4 through 8 instruction in math and English. They examined the relationship between classroom observational (Danielson's Framework for Teaching), student survey (7 C's) and student achievement data. These measures are described in Appendix D. The researchers reported that the combination of student survey data and observed teaching demonstrates that *classroom management* is the strongest predictor of student achievement. They further reported, "In addition, for each framework, the teaching component associated with clarity is the strongest predictor of effective classroom management" (Ferguson & Danielson, 2014, p. 131). In related research Raudenbush and Jean (2014) analyzed the 7 C's survey instrument to see if some aspects of the 7 C's are more predictive of student achievement than others. They report, "We found that teachers whose classrooms are well controlled and intellectually challenging produce comparatively large learning gains" (Raudenbush & Jean, 2014, p. 191). However, Raudenbush and Jean noted that some issues of application of 7 C's are problematic. They reported that control (.202), challenge (.219), and clarify (.090) were positively correlated with student achievement but that other dimensions, captivate (-.266) and consolidate (-.098), were negatively correlated. Hence, using the class mean for the 7 C's can be highly misleading as some dimensions are negatively related to achievement.

Summary

We have described what is known about good teaching that applies to many situations and that impacts students' performance on standardized tests. We have made it clear here and elsewhere (Lavigne & Good, 2013) that good teaching also requires attention to student outcomes beyond good scores on standardized tests, and noted that that the extant research base is limited. Still the information we provided is a needed foundation for other, more ambitious instructional and learning goals.

There are a plethora of claims about what works. Some of these claims may be accurate and important, but most are not and lack research support. Here we presented information describing teaching practices that have been consistently related to student achievement. Principals and others concerned with enhancing teaching should be sure that teachers have the skills and dispositions we described in this chapter.

Much research illustrates that the opportunities students have for learning largely determine what they learn. And opportunities teachers provide for learning are often a function of teacher expectations for individual students or the class as a whole. We have seen that students seen as less capable often receive less content, less challenging content, and less choice in what they learn, but they do receive considerable drill and repetition. As noted, the affective climate that students receive also varies. The degree of emotional support that teachers provide to students depends on the extent to which teachers see students as both social beings and learners. In short, teacher beliefs about students influence how teachers use time and manage classrooms, and determine the extent to which teachers provide students with a mastery-oriented curriculum that blends both conceptual and procedural knowledge. We have provided some considerations for principals to help tap into these beliefs and related practices when working with teachers to improve teaching and learning.

Given our purpose here—to describe what supports achievement for most students in a range of grade levels and subject matter areas—we do not explore in depth differences such as issues of good instruction in math versus social studies, gender, grade level, and other important learner characteristics (e.g., dispositions, past achievement). But we do acknowledge these limitations, and note that research has long shown that students sometimes vary in important ways in reacting to a particular set of instructional actions (see Good, Grouws, & Ebmeier 1981). Principals might attend to these issues more fully after attending to general instructional needs of all students and the variables described in this chapter. Although there are important distinctions in the social and learning needs that students have, we assert that there is a core of teacher instructional actions, dispositions, and beliefs that most if not all students benefit from. We do provide a broad canvass of variables that in combination have important effects on students' opportunity to learn.

References

Alder, N. (2002). Interpretations of the meaning of care: Creating caring relationships in urban middle school classrooms. *Urban Education, 37*, 241–266. doi:10.1177/0042085902372005

Alpert, J. (1974). Teacher behavior across ability groups: A consideration of the mediation of Pygmalion effects. *Journal of Educational Psychology, 66,* 348–353.

Anderman, E. M., & Maehr, M. L. (1994). Motivation and schooling in the middle grades. *Review of Educational Research, 64*(2), 287–309.

Anderson, L., Evertson, C., & Brophy, J. (1979). An experimental study of effective teaching in first-grade reading groups. *Elementary School Journal, 79,* 193–223.

Armor, D., Conry-Oseguera, P., Cox, M., King, N., McDonnell, L., Pascal, A., ... & Zellman, G. (1976). *Analysis of the school preferred reading program in selected Los Angeles minority schools* (Rep. No. R-2007-LAUSD). Santa Monica, CA: Rand. (ERIC No. Ed 140 432).

Asch, S. (1946). Forming impressions of personality. *Journal of Abnormal and Social Psychology, 41,* 258–290.

Ashton, P., & Webb, R. (1986). *Making a difference: Teachers' sense of efficacy and student achievement.* New York: Longman.

Au, K., & Jordan, C. (1981). Teaching reading to Hawaiian children: Finding a culturally appropriate solution. In H. Trueba, G. Guthrie, & K. Au (Eds.), *Culture and the bilingual classrooms: Studies in classroom ethnography* (pp. 69–86). Rowley, MA: Newbury House.

Banks, J. (1997). *Educating citizens in a multicultural society.* New York: Teachers College Press.

Barton, P. E., & Coley, R. J. (2009). *Parsing the achievement gap II.* Retrieved from www.ets.org/Media/Research/pdf/PICPARSINGII.pdf

Battistich, V., & Hom, A. (1997). The relationship between students' sense of their school as a community and their involvement in problem behaviors. *American Journal of Public Health, 87*(12), 1997–2001.

Becker, H. (1952). Social-class variations in the teacher-pupil relationship. *Journal of Educational Sociology, 25,* 451–465.

Berliner, D., Fisher, C., Filby, N., & Marliave, R. (1978). *Executive summary of Beginning Teacher Evaluation Study.* San Francisco: Far West Laboratory.

Biddle, B. (2014). *The unacknowledged disaster: Youth, poverty, and education failure in America.* Rotterdam, The Netherlands: Sense.

Brattesani, K., Weinstein, R., & Marshall, H. (1984). Student perceptions of differential teacher treatment as moderators of teacher expectation effects. *Journal of Educational Psychology, 76,* 236–247.

Brophy, J. (1983). Research on the self-fulfilling prophecy. *Journal of Educational Psychology, 75,* 631–661.

Brophy, J. (2010). Cultivating student appreciation of the value of learning. In R. Marzano (Ed.), *On excellence in teaching* (pp. 301–318). Bloomington, IN: Solution Tree Press.

Brophy, J., & Good, T. (1974). *Teacher-student relationships: Causes and consequences.* New York: Holt, Rinehart, Winston.

Brophy, J., & Good, T. (1986). Teacher behavior and student achievement. In M. Wittrock (Ed.), *Handbook on research in teaching* (3rd ed., pp. 328–375). New York: Macmillan.

Burris, C. (2014). *On the same track: How schools can join the twenty-first century struggle against resegregation.* Boston, MA: Beacon Press.

Carter, R. (1952). How invalid are marks assigned by teachers? *Journal of Educational Psychology, 43,* 218–228.

Castagno, A., McKinley, B., & Brayboy, J. (2008). Culturally responsive schooling for indigenous youth: A review of the literature. *Review of Educational Research, 78*(4), 941–993.

Cazden, C., & Leggett, E. (1981). Culturally responsive education: Recommendations for achieving LAU remedies. In H. Trueba, G. Guthrie, & K. Au (Eds.), *Cultural and the bilingual classrooms: Studies in classroom ethnography* (pp. 69–86). Rowley, MA: Newbury House.

Cohen, G., Garcia, J., Apfel, N., & Master, A. (2006). Reducing the racial achievement gap: A social-psychological intervention. *Science, 313*, 1307–1310.

Cohen, G., Steele, C., & Ross, L. (1999). The mentor's dilemma: Providing critical feedback across the racial divide. *Personality and Social Psychology Bulletin, 25*, 1302–1318.

Cooper, H., & Good, T. (1983). *Pygmalion grows up: Studies in the expectation communication process.* New York: Longman

Darley, J. M., & Fazio, R. H. (1980). Expectancy confirmation processes arising in the social interaction sequence. *American Psychologist, 35*, 867–881.

Darling-Hammond, L. (2007). The flat earth in education: How America's commitment to equity will determine our future. *Educational Researcher, 36*(6), 318–334.

Delpit, L. (1995). *Other people's children: Cultural conflict in the classroom.* New York: New Press.

Dunkin, M., & Biddle, B. (1974). *The study of teaching.* New York: Holt, Rinehart and Winston.

Eder, D. (1981). Ability grouping as a self-fulfilling prophecy: A micro-analysis of teacher-student interaction. *Sociology of Education, 54*, 151–162.

Emmer, E., Evertson, C., & Anderson, L. (1980). Effective classroom management at the beginning of the school year. *Elementary School Journal, 80*, 219–231.

Evertson, C. (1982). Differences in instructional activities and higher- and lower-achieving junior high English and math classes. *Elementary School Journal, 82*, 329–350.

Evertson, C., & Weinstein, C. (Eds.) (2006). *Handbook of classroom management: Research, practice and contemporary issues.* Mahwah, NJ: Erlbaum.

Ferguson, R., & Danielson, C. (2014). How Framework for Teaching and Tripod 7Cs evidence distinguish key components of effective teaching. In T. Kane, K. Kerr, & R. Pianta (Eds.), *Designing teacher evaluation systems: New guidance from the Measures of Effective Teaching Project* (pp. 98–144). San Francisco, CA: Jossey-Bass.

Ferreria, M. M., & Bosworth, K. (2001). Defining caring teachers: Adolescents' perspectives. *Journal of Classroom Interaction, 36*(1), 24–30.

Fisher, C., Filby, N., Marliave, R., Cahen, L., Dishaw, M., Moore, J., & Berliner, D. (1978). *Beginning teacher evaluation study.* San Francisco, CA: Far West Regional Educational Laboratory.

Freiberg, H., Huzinec, C., & Templeton, S. (2009). Classroom management—a pathway to student achievement: A study of 14 inner-city elementary schools. *Elementary Journal, 110*, 63–80.

Fry, R., & Lopez, M. (2012). *Hispanic student enrollments reach new highs in 2011.* Washington, DC: Pew Hispanic Center.

Garza, R. (2009). Latino and white high school students' perceptions of caring behaviors: Are we culturally responsive to our students? *Urban Education, 44*, 297–321.

Good, T. (2014). What do we know about how teachers influence student performance on standardized tests: And why do we know so little about other student outcomes? In A. L. Lavigne, T. L. Good, & R. M. Marx (Eds.), High-stakes teacher evaluation: High cost—big losses [Special Issue]. *Teachers College Record, 116*(1).

Good, T., & Brophy, J. (1974). Changing teacher and student behavior: An empirical investigation. *Journal of Educational Psychology, 66*(3), 390–405.

Good, T., & Brophy, J. (2008). *Looking in classrooms* (10th ed.). New York: Pearson.

Good, T., & Grouws, D. (1975). Teacher rapport: Some stability data. *Journal of Educational Psychology, 67*(2), 179–182.

Good, T., Grouws, D., & Beckerman, T. (1978). Curriculum pacing: Some empirical data. *Journal of Curriculum Studies, 10*, 75–81.

Good, T., Grouws, D., & Ebmeier, H. (1981). Active mathematics teaching. New York: Longman.

Good, T. L., & Weinstein, R. S. (1986). Schools make a difference: Evidence, criticisms, and new directions. *American Psychologist, 41*, 1090–1097.

Good, T. L., Wood, M. B., Sabers, D., Olson, A. M., Lavigne, A. L., Sun, H., & Kalinec-Craig, C. (2013). Strengthening grade 3–5 students' foundational knowledge of rational numbers. *Teachers College Record, 115*(7), 1–45.

Goodlad, J. I. (1984). *Place called school.* New York: McGraw-Hill.

Hamre, B., & Pianta. R. (2005). Can instructional and emotional warmth in the first-grade classroom make a difference for children at risk of school failure? *Child Development, 76*, 949–967.

Hanselman, P., Burch, S., Gamoran, A., & Borman, G. (2014). Threat in context: School moderation of the impact of social identity on racial/ethnic achievement gaps. *Sociology of Education, 87*, 106–124.

Hattie, J. (2008). *Visible learning: A synthesis of over 800 meta-analyses relating to achievement.* New York: Routledge.

Hiebert, J., & Grouws, D. (2007). The effects of classroom mathematics teaching on students' learning. In F. Lester (Ed.), *Second handbook of research on mathematics teaching and learning* (pp. 371–404). Greenwich, CT: Information Age.

Hill, H. C., Umland, K., Litke, E., & Kapitula, L. R. (2012). Teacher quality and quality teaching: Examining the relationship of a teacher assessment to practice. *American Journal of Education, 118*, 489–519.

Hines, C., Cruickshank, D., & Kennedy, J. (1985). Teacher clarity and its relationship to student achievement. *American Educational Research Journal, 22*, 87–99.

Howard, T. C. (2001). Telling their side of the story: African-American students' perceptions of culturally relevant teaching. *Urban Review, 33*(2), 131–149.

Jackson, P. (1968). *Life in classrooms.* New York: Holt.

Jencks, C., & Phillips, M. (1998). *The black-white test score gap.* Washington, DC: Brookings Institution Press.

Johnson Moore, S., Kraft, M., & Papay, J. (2012). How context matters in high-need schools: The effects of teachers' working conditions on their professional satisfaction and their students' achievement. *Teachers College Record, 114*(10), 1–39.

Jussim, L. (1986). Self-fulfilling prophecies: A theoretical and integrative review. *Psychological Review, 93*, 429–445.

Jussim, L., & Eccles, J. (1992). Teacher explanations: Construction and reflection of student achievement. *Journal of Personality and Social Psychology, 63*, 947–961.

Jussim, L., Eccles, J., & Madon, S. (1996). Social perception, social stereotypes, and teacher expectations: Accuracy and the quest for the powerful self-fulfilling prophecy. In M. P. Zanna (Ed.), *Advances in experimental social psychology* (pp. 281–388). New York: Academic Press.

Kane, T., Kerr, K., & Pianta, R. (Eds.) (2014). *Designing teacher evaluation systems: New guidance from the Measures of Effective Teaching Project.* San Francisco, CA: Jossey-Bass.

Kelley, H. (1950). The warm-cold variable in first impressions of people. *Journal of Personality, 18*, 431–439.

Kleinfeld, J. (1972). *Instructional style and the intellectual performance of Indian and Eskimo students.* Final Report, Project No. 1-J-027, Office of Education, US Department of Health, Education and Welfare.

Klingner, J. K., Artiles, A. J., Kozleski, E., Harry, B., Zion, S., Tate, W., … Riley, D. (2005). Addressing the disproportionate representation of culturally and linguistically diverse students in special education through culturally responsive educational systems. *Education Policy Analysis Archives, 13*(38), 1–43. Retrieved from http://epaa.asu.edu/epaa/v13n38

Kluger, A., & DeNisi, A. (1996). The effects of feedback interventions on performance: A historical review, a meta-analysis, and a preliminary feedback intervention theory. *Psychology Bulletin, 119*, 254–284.

Konstantopoulos, S. (2014). Teacher effects, value-added models, and accountability. In A. L. Lavigne, T. L. Good, & R. M. Marx (Eds.), High-stakes teacher evaluation: High cost—big losses [Special Issue]. *Teachers College Record, 116*(1).

Kounin, J. S. (1970). *Discipline and group management in classrooms.* New York: Holt, Rinehart, & Winston.

Ladson-Billings, G. (1994). *The dreamkeepers: Successful teachers of African American children.* San Francisco, CA: Jossey-Bass.

Ladson-Billings, G. (1995). But that's just good teaching! The case for culturally relevant pedagogy. *Teaching into Practice, 60*, 159–165.

Lavigne, A., & Good, T. (2013). *Teacher and student evaluation: Moving beyond the failure of school reform.* New York: Routledge.

Leacok, E. (1969). *Teaching and learning in city schools.* New York: Basic Books.

Le Fevre, M., & Robinson, V. (2014). The interpersonal challenges of instructional leadership: Principals' effectiveness in conversations about performance issues. *Educational Administration Quarterly.*

Lewis, J., Ream, R., Bocian, K. Cardullo, R., & Hammond, K. (2012). Con Cariño: Teacher caring, math self-efficacy, and math achievement among Hispanic English learners. *Teachers College Record, 114*, 42.

Lightfoot, S. (1972). *An ethnographic study of the status structure of the classroom.* Unpublished doctoral dissertation, Harvard University.

Lippit, R., & Gold, M. (1959). Classroom social structure as a mental health problem. *Journal of Social Issues, 15*, 40–49.

López, F. (2012). Moderators of language acquisition models and reading achievement for English Language Learners: The role of emotional warmth and instructional support. *Teachers College Record, 114*(8), 1–30.

López, F. (April, 2014). *Addressing the need for explicit evidence on the role of culturally responsive teaching and achievement among Latino youth: Preliminary findings for the Spencer/National Academy of Education Postdoctoral Fellowship.* Poster presented at the 2014 annual meetings of the American Educational Research Association, Philadelphia, PA.

López, F. A., Heilig, J. V., & Schram, J. (2013). A story within a story: Culturally responsive schooling and American Indian and Alaska Native achievement in the National Indian Education Study. *American Journal of Education, 119*, 513–538.

Madon, S., Jussim, L., & Eccles, J. (1997). In search of the powerful self-fulfilling prophecy. *Journal of Personality and Social Psychology, 72*, 791–809.

Mason, D., Schroeter, D., Combs, R., & Washington, K. (1992). Assigning average-achieving eighth graders to advanced mathematics classes in an urban junior high. *Elementary School Journal, 92*, 587–599.

McCaslin, M. (1996). The problem of problem representation: The Summit's conception of students. *Educational Researcher, 25*, 13–15.

McCaslin, M. (2006). Student motivation dynamics in the era of school reform. *Elementary School Journal, 106*, 479–490.

McCaslin, M. (2009). Co-regulation of student motivation and emergent identity. *Educational Psychologist, 44*, 137–146.

McCaslin, M., & Lavigne, A. (2010). Co-regulation approach to research on student motivation. In T. Urdan & A. Karabenick (Eds.), *The decade ahead: Applications and context of motivation and achievement* (pp. 211–149). Bingley, UK: EmeraldBooks.

McCaslin, M., Vriesema, C., & Burggraf, S. (in press). Making mistakes: Emotional adaptation and classroom learning. *Teachers College Record*.

McKown, C. (2013). Social equity theory and racial-achievement gaps. *Child Development, 84*(4), 1120–1136.

McKown, C., & Weinstein, R. (2003). The development and consequences of stereotype consciousness in middle childhood. *Child Development, 74*, 498–515.

Meckler, L. (2014, June 26). Generational race gap grows. *Wall Street Journal*. p. A5.

Murdock, T. B., Miller, A., & Kohlhardt, J. (2004). Effects of classroom context variables on high school students' judgments of the acceptability and likelihood of cheating. *Journal of Educational Psychology, 96*(4), 765–777.

National Mathematics Advisory Panel. (2008). *Foundations for success: The final report of the National Mathematics Advisory Panel*. Washington, DC: U.S. Department of Education.

Newmann, F. M. (1981). Reducing student alienation in high schools: Implications of theory. *Harvard Educational Review, 51*(4), 546–565.

NICHD ECCRN. (2005). A day in third grade: A large-scale study of classroom quality and teacher and student behavior. *Elementary School Journal, 105*, 305–323.

Nichols, S., & Good, T. (2004). *America's teenagers—myths and realities: Media images, schooling, and the social cost of careless indifference*. Mahwah, NJ: Erlbaum.

Noddings, N. (1984). *Caring: A feminine approach to ethics and moral education*. Berkeley: University of California Press.

Noddings, N. (1992). *The challenge to care in schools: An alternative approach to education*. New York: Teachers College Press.

Noddings, N. (2007). Caring as relation and virtue in teaching. In R. Walker & P. Ivanhoe (Eds.), *Working virtue: Virtue ethics and contemporary moral problems* (pp. 41–60). Oxford: Oxford University Press.

Oakes, J. (2005). *Keeping track: How schools structure inequality* (2nd ed.). New Haven, CT: Yale University Press.

Oberg De La Garza, T., Roberts, A., & Lavigne, A. L. (2013, November). *Cross-cultural relationships: Fostering belonging and achievement of Latino students in U.S. schools*. Paper presented at the annual meeting of the World Education Research Association, Guanajuato, Mexico.

Osterman, K. (2000). Students' need for belonging in the school community. *Review of Educational Research, 70*, 323–367.

Payne, C. (2010). *So much reform, so little change*. Cambridge, MA: Harvard Education Press.

Perry, N. E., Phillips, L., & Hutchinson, L. (2006). Mentoring student teachers to support self-regulated learning. *Elementary School Journal, 106*(3), 237–254.

Pianta, R., Belsky, J., Houts, R., Morrison, F., & NICHD ECCRN. (2007). Opportunities to learn in America's elementary classrooms. *Science, 315*, 1795–1796.

Pianta, R., & Hamre, B. (2009). Conceptualization, measurement, and improvement of classroom processes: Standardized observation can leverage capacity. *Educational Researcher, 38*, 109–119.

Pianta, R., La Paro, K., & Hamre, B. (2008). *Classroom Assessment Scoring System* (CLASS). Baltimore, MD: Paul H. Brooks.

Polikoff, M. (2012). The redundancy of mathematics instruction in US elementary and middle schools. *Elementary School Journal, 113*, 230–251.

Polikoff, M. (2014). Does the test matter? Evaluating teachers when tests differ in their sensitivity to instruction. In T. Kane, K. Kerr, & R. Pianta (Eds.), *Designing teacher evaluation systems: New guidance from the Measures of Effective Teaching Project* (pp. 278–303). San Francisco, CA: Jossey-Bass.

Porter, A., & Polikoff, M. (2009). National curriculum. In T. Good (Ed.), *21st century education: A reference handbook* (Vol. 2., pp. 434–442). Thousand Oaks, CA: SAGE.

Power, C. (1971). *The effects of communication patterns on student socio-economic status, attitudes and achievement in science.* Unpublished doctoral dissertation, University of Queensland.

Putnam, R. D. (2000). *Bowling alone: The collapse and revival of American community.* New York: Simon & Schuster.

Rakes, C., Valentine, J., McGatha, M., & Ronau, R. (2010). Methods of instructional improvement in algebra: A systematic review and meta-analysis. *Review of Educational Research, 80*, 372–400.

Raudenbush, S. (1984). Magnitude of teacher expectancy effects on pupil IQ as a function of the credibility of expectancy induction: A synthesis of findings from 18 experiments. *Journal of Educational Psychology, 76*, 85–97.

Raudenbush, S., & Jean, M. (2014). To what extent do student perceptions of classroom quality predict teacher value added? In T. Kane, K. Kerr, & R. Pianta (Eds.), *Designing teacher evaluation systems: New guidance from the Measures of Effective Teaching Project* (pp. 170–202). San Francisco: Jossey-Bass.

Reese, L., Jensen, B., & Ramirez, D. (2014). Emotionally supportive context for young Latino children in rural California. *Elementary School Journal, 114*, 501–526.

Reyes, M., Brackett, M., Rivers, S., White, M., & Salovey, P. (2012). Classroom emotional climate, student engagement, and academic achievement. *Journal of Educational Psychology, 104*(3), 700–712.

Roberts, M. A. (2010). Toward a theory of culturally relevant critical teacher care: African American teachers' definitions and perceptions of care for African American students. *Journal of Moral Education, 39*(4), 449–467.

Rohrkemper, M. (1984). The influence of teacher socialization style on students' social cognition and reported interpersonal classroom behavior. *Elementary School Journal, 85*, 245–275.

Rohrkemper, M. (1985). Individual differences in students' perceptions of routine classroom events. *Journal of Educational Psychology, 77*, 29–44.

Rohrkemper, M., & Corno, L. (1988). Success and failure on classroom tasks: Adaptive learning and classroom teaching. *Elementary School Journal, 88*, 296–312.

Rosenholtz, S. J. (1989). *Teacher's workplace: The social organization of schools.* New York: Longman.

Rosenshine, B. (2012). *Principles of instruction: Effective teaching practices that all teachers should know.* Retrieved from www.aft.org//sites/default/files/periodicals/Rosenshine.pdf

Rosenshine, B., & Furst, N. (1971). Research on teacher performance criteria. In B. O. Smith (Ed.), *Research in teacher education* (pp. 37–72). Englewood Cliffs, NJ: Prentice Hall.

Rosenshine, B., & Furst, N. (1973). The use of direct observations to study teaching. In R. Travers (Ed.), *Second handbook of research on teaching* (pp. 122–183). Chicago, IL: Rand McNally.

Rosenthal, R., & Rubin, D. B. (1978). Interpersonal expectancy effects: The first 345 studies. *Behavioral and Brain Sciences, 3*, 377–386.

Rubie-Davies, C. M. (2007). Classroom interactions: Exploring the practices of high- and low-expectation teachers. *British Journal of Educational Psychology, 77*, 289–306.

Rubie-Davies, C. M. (2014). *Becoming a high expectation teacher: Raising the bar*. London: Routledge.

Rubie-Davies, C. M., Peterson, E., Sibley, C., & Rosenthal, R. (forthcoming). A teacher expectation intervention: Modelling the practices of high expectation teachers. *Journal of Psychological Sciences*.

Ruzek, E., Hafen, C., Hamre, B., & Pianta, R. (2014). Combining classroom observations and value-added for the evaluation and professional development of teachers. In T. Kane, K. Kerr, & R. Pianta (Eds.), *Designing teacher evaluation systems: New guidance from the measures of effective teaching project* (pp. 205–233). San Francisco, CA: John Wiley & Sons.

Sleeter, C. (2011). An agenda to strengthen culturally responsive pedagogy. *English Teaching Practice and Critique, 10,* 7–23.

Smith, B. (2000). Quantity matters: Annual instructional time in an urban school system. *Educational Administration Quarterly, 365*(5), 652–682.

Steele, C. (1997). A threat in the air: How stereotypes shape intellectually identity and performance. *American Psychologist, 52,* 613–629.

Steele, C. (2010). *Whistling Vivaldi: How stereotypes affect us and what we can do*. Issues of our time. New York: W.W. Norton.

Stein, M., & Nelson, B. (2003). Leadership content knowledge. *Educational Evaluation and Policy Analysis, 25,* 423–448.

St. John, N. (1971). Thirty-six teachers: Their characteristics, and outcomes for black and white pupils. *American Educational Research Journal, 8,* 635–648.

Strong, M. (2011). *The highly qualified teacher: What is teacher quality and how do we measure it?* New York: Teachers College Press.

Timperley, H., & Robinson, V. (2001). Achieving school improvement through challenging and changing teachers' schema. *Journal of Educational Change, 2,* 281–300.

Tschannen-Moran, M., Woolfolk Hoy, A., & Hoy, W. K. (1998). Teacher efficacy: Its meaning and measure. *Review of Educational Research, 68*(2), 202–248.

Villegas, A. M., & Lucas, T. (2002). Preparing culturally responsive teachers: Rethinking the curriculum. *Journal of Teacher Education, 53*(1), 20–32.

Wehlage, G. G., Rutter, R. A., Smith, G. A., Lesko, N., & Fernandez, R. R. (1989). *Reducing the risk: Schools as communities of support*. New York: Falmer Press.

Weinstein, R. (1976). Reading group membership in first grade: Teacher behaviours and pupil experience over time. *Journal of Educational Psychology, 68,* 103–116.

Weinstein, R. (2002). *Reaching higher: The power of expectations in schooling*. Cambridge, MA: Harvard University Press.

Weinstein, R., & Middlestatd, S. (1979). Student perceptions of teacher interactions with male high and low achievers. *Journal of Educational Psychology, 71,* 421–431.

Weinstein, R., Soule, C., Collins, F., Cone, J., Mehorn, M., & Simontacchi, K. (1991). Expectations and high school change: Teacher-researcher collaboration to prevent school failure. *American Journal of Community Psychology, 19,* 333–364.

Wentzel, K. R. (1997). Student motivation in middle school: The role of perceived pedagogical caring. *Journal of Educational Psychology, 89*(3), 411–419.

West, C., & Anderson, T. (1976). The question of preponderant causation in teacher expectancy research. *Review of Educational Research, 46,* 613–630.

Whitehurst, G., Chingos, M., & Lindquist, K. (2014). *Evaluating teachers with classroom observations: Lessons learned in four districts*. Brown Center on Education Policy at the Brookings Institute. Retrieved from www.brookings.edu/research/reports/2014/05/13-teacher-evaluation-whitehurst-chingos

4
RESEARCH ON IMPROVING TEACHING AND STUDENT ACHIEVEMENT
The Role of the Principal

In Chapter 3, we learned that knowledge about teacher expectations and students as social beings and teaching actions like good management and time use can help principals provide teachers with useful feedback for improving teaching. Now, we discuss *how* knowledge of effective teaching practices and observation and feedback work jointly to improve student achievement. Consequently, this chapter addresses these questions: Does feedback matter? How and when does it matter? The questions are basic, yet the answers are essential. Recall that RttT assumes by rewarding highly effective teachers and eliminating ineffective teachers, and providing feedback on instruction, student achievement will improve. Will providing teachers with feedback about their teaching improve instruction in meaningful ways? What is known about principals' effects on student achievement? We describe effective principal practice as measured by student achievement outcomes because one way principals achieve effects on student achievement is through instruction. Accordingly, then, we discuss what is known about how teachers modify their instruction in response to feedback. Finally, our focus narrows to the task assigned to many of our readers—observing and providing feedback to teachers. The evidence provided here is valuable but weaker than that presented in Chapter 3. One major difference is that much of the teacher effectiveness literature is based upon direct observation of teaching, whereas the literature on principals' feedback to teachers is based on self-report or teachers' responses to questionnaires. Research on feedback is vast, but much of it has been established in the context of teachers providing feedback to students, in experimental lab conditions utilizing college students, or in corporate settings. With that said, we make a modest attempt to summarize existing research, assessing if and how principals (and others) can use it to inform practice.

Principal Effects

In an era of accountability, the focus is to hold teachers and principals more accountable for student learning. We know much about the effects of teachers on students, but what is known about principal effects? Do principals matter? If not, can they be helped to matter?

Conceptual Frameworks and Related Findings

Administrators' effects on student achievement can happen directly or indirectly (Pitner, 1988). In a *basic direct effects model*, principal leadership is related to student achievement outcomes—a simple bivariate relationship. As principals are rated as more effective, as measured by principal self-report or teachers' perceptions (e.g., "The principal has confidence in the expertise of teachers," "The principal takes personal interest in the professional development of teachers" [Sebastian & Allensworth, 2012]), student achievement increases (principal leadership → student achievement). But defining the characteristics of effective leadership is not easy. In a *simple indirect model*, principal leadership influences student achievement outcomes, but is mediated (or explained) by school-level variables (e.g., school climate, teachers, staff). For example, perhaps principals can increase student achievement through targeted professional development (PD) or through the implementation of a new policy that changes school climate. An indirect model might look something like this: principal leadership → school climate → student achievement. Other models suggest that antecedent variables—preceding variables, or in the case of education, contextual variables (e.g., student demographics of school, school funding, parent support)—explain how and when principals matter (Hallinger, Bickman, & Davis, 1996). In a *basic antecedent effect*, antecedent variables influence principal leadership, which in turn influences student achievement (e.g., parent support → principal leadership → student achievement). In an *antecedent plus mediated variables effects model*, antecedent variables influence principal leadership, which then influences student achievement, while being mediated through other variables (parent support → principal leadership → school climate → student achievement). We will discuss these types of effects ahead. But given that principals rarely provide direct instruction to students, the commonly accepted belief is that principals' effect on student achievement occurs in indirect and complex ways.

Direct effects. Principals' direct effects on student achievement are small, when present. Ogawa and Hart (1985) studied 124 elementary and 151 high school principals, and found that principals account for 2–8% of the variance in student achievement scores. In a meta-analysis of 37 studies, Witziers et al. (2003) found that principal leadership effects on student achievement varied from -.18 to .26 (the overall average effect: principals explain less than 2% of the variance in student achievement). Some have documented larger effects. In a meta-analysis of 70 studies, in some studies principals had significant and large effects (.50), with leadership ability resulting in a difference of nearly 19 percentile points in student achievement (Waters, Marzano, & McNulty, 2004). But recent research mirrors earlier findings suggesting that principal characteristics explain a small (3.9%) amount of variance in student achievement outcomes (Knoeppel & Rinehart, 2008).

Does context matter? Do principal effects differ by school characteristics or content area? In a meta-analysis of 37 international studies, principal effects were found in elementary but not in secondary settings (Witizers et al., 2003). Similarly, Ogawa and Hart (1985) found principals to have a greater effect on sixth-grade student mathematics (7.92% of the variance) than twelfth-grade (2.66%). In higher grades, principals have been found to have greater effects on reading (sixth grade: 5.66%, twelfth grade: 6.01%), and in elementary schools others have found no direct effects of principals on student reading achievement (Hallinger et al., 1996).

Taken together, and with few exceptions (see studies reviewed by Waters et al. 2004), principals' direct effects on student achievement are small and vary by context. And, as expected, these effects are smaller than teacher effects (see Chapter 3). This limited knowledge about principals' direct effects makes the job of a principal incredibly difficult. Despite this, principals may benefit by capitalizing on the indirect ways in which they can influence student achievement, particularly through instruction. Perhaps direct effects on teaching and learning will improve as principals better understand teacher effects literature and how to use it.

Indirect effects. Do principals indirectly affect student learning? Through factors like school climate and staff development (Supovitz, Sirinides, & May, 2010), principals have small indirect effects on student achievement. In a study of 99 Chicago schools, Sebastian and Allensworth (2012) found that via school climate, principal leadership is associated with the overall quality of instruction. Schools with more effective leaders were more likely to be safe and have a "college-going culture," as rated by teachers. Understandably, students in these schools had better behavior and grades. But this happened through an important mechanism—teachers. Teachers who felt they received high-quality PD and that the instructional programming in the school was clear and well aligned demonstrated higher levels of academic demand and classroom order. Furthermore, teachers who perceived the school climate as good were more likely to demonstrate higher levels of instruction. In a study of 22 primary schools in Greece, Kythreotis, Pashiardis, and Kyriakides (2010) found that although principals influenced classroom culture, they did not influence school culture. The authors suggested that principals might have better luck changing individual teachers' personal orientation rather than the culture of teachers. This point underscores principals' task of providing feedback to individual teachers. Perhaps the change of a few individual teachers in time may change the culture.

Antecedent effects models. Lee and Hallinger (2012) examined antecedent effects in a study of 5,927 principals across 34 societies. They found that principals in societies with a higher GDP per capita spent longer hours on the job. They also spent more hours on instructional leadership (5.99 hours) in an average week compared to their peers in lower GDP societies. Hallinger et al. (1996) studied 87 elementary schools and found that principal effects occur through school climate variables, but are simultaneously driven by school context. Principals in higher socioeconomic SES schools were rated by teachers as more active instructional leaders than in lower SES schools ($r = +.39$). Principals perceived as more active leaders were more likely to work in schools with parents who were rated as more involved in their child's education ($r = +.31$). And female elementary principals were rated as more active instructional leaders than their male counterparts ($r = -.20$). In short, the model revealed that these three antecedent variables influenced principals' instructional leadership, which then related to a clear school mission ($r = +.35$). A clear school mission, in turn, was significantly related to student opportunity to learn ($r = +.67$) and teacher expectations for students ($r = +.36$), resulting in positive effects on student achievement in reading. This example illustrates the complexity of indirect and antecedent effects, but also underscores the value of opportunities to learn and teacher expectations (recall Chapter 3).

This literature yields four messages: (1) albeit small, principals do matter; (2) antecedent variables can determine how principals matter; (3) principals matter the most through their influence on school climate and mission, and teachers, who in turn influence student learning; and (4) principals may benefit from achieving school-wide change through teachers rather than achieving teacher change through school-wide initiatives. Having established that principals *can* matter, what do they *do* that matters?

Leadership

Current conceptualizations of principals have focused on leadership style—transformational and instructional. Transformational leaders facilitate change. They motivate others, support intellectual stimulation, and provide support to empower individual faculty (Leithwood, 1994; Robinson, Lloyd, & Rowe, 2008). Instructional leaders define a school's mission, manage the instructional program, and promote a positive school-learning climate (Hallinger, 2003). Some research advocates for instructional leadership over transformational leadership. Robinson, Lloyd, and Rowe (2008) studied the effect of leadership style on student achievement outcomes in 27 studies. Findings revealed a moderate mean effect size (.42) for instructional leadership, while transformational leadership had a much smaller effect size (.11). The authors also created an "other" category (with a mean effect size of .30). But at least one recent study contradicts Robinson et al.'s (2008) meta-analysis, finding that principals' self-reported skills related to organizational management are stronger predictors of student-level value-added than instructional leadership skills (Grissom & Loeb, 2011). Interestingly, instructional activities (e.g., coaching, formal teacher evaluations) *did not* predict student achievement growth, and they were significantly and negatively related to teacher satisfaction. These findings contradict common beliefs and RttT, in practice. But poor feedback may be more harmful than no feedback, and, as we show later, some teachers perceive quick evaluations (e.g., walk-throughs) negatively. These findings raise concerns about how administrators spend their time on supervision and evaluation. In short, it's not that simple to establish which leadership style is most effective, and even more difficult to determine what effective principals *do*.

Practices. Research examining the relationship between principal practice and school achievement is sparse. Robinson et al. (2008) noted, "The fact that there are fewer than 30 published studies in English that have examined the links between leadership and student outcomes indicates how radically disconnected leadership research is from the core business of teaching and learning" (p. 667). Unfortunately, policy makers either are not aware of this void or do not care. Despite this lack of knowledge, principals are held accountable for student learning. In Appendix E, in no particular order, we provide a list of "effective" principal practices (as measured by student achievement) that reflect a total of 109 studies across multiple countries drawn from two meta-analyses (Waters et al., 2004; Witziers et al., 2003) and 4 additional studies that have been conducted since then (Grissom et al., 2013; Grissom & Loeb, 2011; Kythreotis et al., 2010; Shatzer, Caldarella, Hallam, & Brown, 2014). Before principals can use this list wisely, it would be helpful to establish the importance of these practices relative to one another. Indeed, Waters, Marzano, and McNulty (2004) have done just that. They identified a total of 66 leadership practices that fall within 21 leadership responsibilities that are significantly related to student achievement (these are included in Appendix F). We see that some practices, such as situational awareness (e.g., awareness of school problems) ($r = .33$), intellectual stimulation (e.g., up-to-date on effective practices) ($r = .32$), and monitoring effectiveness ($r = .28$), have a strong relationship with student achievement, whereas others, such as visibility (e.g., visiting classrooms), less so ($r = .16$). This list does not endorse spending more time in classrooms. Given this, should principals apply Appendices E and F to practice? Not necessarily, but they do provide some considerations.

Let's consider a study that examined time use and challenged the value of instructional leadership. Horng, Klasik, and Loeb (2010) examined the relationship between principals' time use and student achievement in 65 principals in the Miami-Dade County Public Schools. One category of time use was day-to-day instruction (e.g., informal coaching, teacher evaluation, and classroom observation). Principals spent little (5.58%) time on day-to-day instruction, and time spent on these activities decreased from elementary school to high school settings, from low-performing to high-performing settings, and from high-poverty to low-poverty settings. But does time spent on coaching and evaluating teachers matter for student achievement?

Study findings revealed that day-to-day activities were weakly or not at all related to increased student achievement. These findings are somewhat surprising, given the current emphasis on improving teaching through high-quality supervision. However, three factors lessen the value of these data. First, data were collected in a state attuned to student achievement accountability, but before the increased demands of RttT. So, the finding that principals spent little time on supervision and evaluation may be understandable. Accountability advocates might argue that principals did not attend to instruction because they were not held accountable for doing so. Second, data were collected before principals were trained in evaluation as required by RttT. Perhaps findings would have been different had principals received specific and additional training. Finally, the study describes how time was used but not its quality—did principals visit classrooms but provide no feedback? Poor feedback? These data do not provide compelling evidence that principals' time on supervision has limited value. Furthermore, we cannot ignore that in at least one study examining principal and teacher logs in 51 schools (May & Supovitz, 2011), the frequency of a principal's instructional leadership activities with a teacher was directly related to that teacher's self-report of instructional improvement.

Despite these challenges, there is value in what we *do* know. Research on teacher effects that underscores the value of work with individual teachers (Kythreotis et al., 2010) has value. We established that good teaching is the greatest school factor that contributes to student learning. As such, and in reflecting on the role of school leaders, the greatest gains may be achieved by investing further in helping principals to facilitate teachers. First, though, we must prepare principals to do so.

Preparation. Some argue that graduates of principal preparation programs are ill-equipped to manage the supervisory tasks required of them today (Hess, 2006). We have illustrated that principals historically have not spent significant time observing teachers and still do not. Perhaps this is because principal preparation programs spend little time on this component. We wonder: Are principals prepared well in this aspect of their job?

The traditional preparation programs that produce nearly 84% of all principals (U.S. Department of Education [USDOE], 2013) are feeling the heat. Critiques include that principal preparation programs lack vision, purpose, and cohesion (USDOE, 2013), and do little to prepare school leaders to improve curriculum, instruction, and student achievement (Hess & Kelley, 2005). Further, in a study of 31 principal preparation programs and 210 syllabi, Hess and Kelley (2007) found that preparation programs did little to address recent educational reforms or to require principals to be well versed in improving student achievement, suggesting that principals are not prepared for their jobs. School leaders agree. Farkas, Johnson, and Duffet (2003) surveyed 1,006 superintendents and 925 principals and found that 72% of superintendents and 67% of principals reported their graduate preparation programs failed to prepare them to be successful in today's schools. Levine (2005) found that 47% of principals reported that their coursework was dated and irrelevant.

More recently, Styron and LeMire (2009) studied the perceptions of 374 high school principals in four states and found more support for preparation programs. Principals reported (in some form of agreement) that they felt well prepared in understanding and interpreting school data (74%), assessing test data for individual student achievement (69%), and managing the school accountability plan (69%). Similarly, Hernandez, Roberts, and Menchaca (2012) studied 768 graduates from Texas principal preparation programs and found that graduates reported (in some form of agreement) that they were well prepared in: data-driven decision making (84%), research and best practices (95%), staff development (98%), curriculum and instructional leadership (89%), and personnel management (84%).

Taken together, the unpromising findings about instructional leadership practices and their relationship to student achievement outcomes reflect a glass that is half full. These data suggest that principal effects are modest under the most favorable conditions. However, it is useful to note that most studies were conducted before RttT. Principals are now required to complete training in order to evaluate teachers. And there is some evidence that preparation programs are beginning to address the demands of educational reform. Equally promising is that principals feel they have lots of control over teacher evaluation (96% agreement)—more than other factors (e.g., establishing curriculum, setting discipline policy, deciding how budget will be spent) (USDOE, 2013). Yet it remains to be seen what principals could do when armed with new knowledge and skills in an area where they feel they have significant agency.

Improving Instruction: Teacher Change

Research has confirmed that teachers and principals matter. We know much about *effective* teaching practices, but comparatively little about meaningfully *improving* instruction. But do principals know and use this knowledge? In response to this question—about how to use the knowledge base—we address theory and research on teacher change. We consider questions about teacher change: Does it happen? How? And what is the principal's role?

Models of Teacher Change

Teacher change models assume that teachers *can* change. Some have adopted the belief that *most* teachers are resistant to change. This belief was the prevalent perspective until the early 1990s (see, e.g., Duffy and Roehler, 1986; Lortie, 1975). Others argue that resistance is teachers' response to situational and contextual factors. In some urban schools, teachers' resistance to change can be high (Payne, 2010) as teachers are skeptical after years of failed reform (Kennedy, 2005). Others argue that resistance is developmental. Teachers later in their career become more set in their ways. Mid-career teachers may experience self-doubt and feel disenchanted by their attempts to improve practices. Veteran teachers may become dogmatic and resist change as they begin to exit the profession (Huberman, 1989). Similarly, teachers stabilize in their ability to demonstrate student achievement gains, plateauing in their effectiveness between the third and sixth year of teaching (Henry, Bastian, & Fortner, 2011; Rivkin, Hanushek, & Kain, 2005). These findings suggest that some teachers (teachers earlier in their careers) may be more likely to change than veteran teachers. But previous experimental work has demonstrated that through instructional (Good & Grouws, 1979) and management treatments (Freiberg, Stein, & Huang, 1995) veteran teachers modify their practices to improve student achievement. Furthermore, expert teachers perceive and process classroom experiences differently than their novice peers. Experts are more likely to comment and reflect upon complex classroom interactions related to learners, whereas novices tend to focus on surface-level features related to the teacher (e.g., amount of content covered)(Chi, Glaser, & Farr, 1988; Glaser & Chi, 1988). Although not all teachers become experts, some teachers change and improve with experience. Nevertheless, current conceptualizations of teachers are built upon the premise that teachers *should* and *can* change. The current climate of accountability endorses this belief and further promotes it. Under this perspective, notions of change are primarily rooted in terms of improving student achievement or else.

How does change occur? Stein and Wang (1988) propose "The Process of Teacher Change" (see Figure 4.1). According to Stein and Wang, teachers can establish their self-efficacy, in part, through feedback from student outcomes and instructional leaders. The perceived value teachers place on the program is established through teachers' perceptions of program efficacy and its relation to their professional goals. Although this model was created with the implementation of innovative programs in mind, the components apply to changes in general instructional practice. Principal feedback should underscore the value of the recommended feedback and support teachers in implementing such practices.

Guskey (1986, 2002) has conducted significant work on teacher change for over 30 years. Guskey's "Model of Teacher Change" has four steps (professional

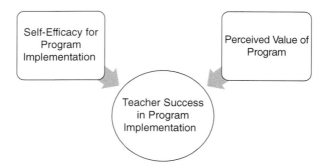

FIGURE 4.1 The Process of Teacher Change
Source: Adapted from Stein and Wang (1998).

development → teachers' practices → student learning → teachers' beliefs and attitudes). His model recommends retaining only practices that teachers find useful in helping students to attain learning outcomes. We reported earlier that teachers bring to the classroom beliefs about learners, and that these beliefs and practices can change. According to Guskey's model, this might happen if some practice demonstrates results contrary to a teacher's preconceived notions and expectations (e.g., seeing that a practice helps disadvantaged students excel).

Models can help administrators when thinking about how to help teachers improve practice and to understand why a teacher has or has not adopted a particular practice. Yet the fact that teachers who have been adequately trained can apply new programs (Wang & Gennari, 1983) does not mean that classroom-level implementation quality and quantity are similar across teachers. Actually, findings indicate the opposite (Han & Weiss, 2005). Finally, implementation does not equate to change or sustained change (Duffy & Rochler, 1986); in part this may be true because teachers do not believe the change will work.

Do Teachers Change Their Practices in Meaningful Ways?

Teacher change occurs voluntarily or involuntary through various mechanisms like: professional learning communities, program implementation, interventions or treatments, self-analysis, feedback, observation and analysis of teacher models, and study of an observation system. We closely examine the research areas of PD and feedback because these are the most common change mechanisms that principals can use.

Professional development (PD). Research reviews have shown PD to be generally ineffective in changing teachers' practices (Cohen & Hill, 2000). But we believe this is less related to teachers' capacity for change and more related to quality of PD. Professional development has been criticized for not tapping into teacher motivation, applying the processes that result in teacher change (Guskey, 1986), providing teachers with adequate time or resources, or engaging teachers in a way that promotes change (Loucks-Horsley, Hewson, Love, & Stiles, 1998). The traditional form of PD that most teachers (79%) participate in is of short duration (usually 2–4 days) and few contact hours (Garet et al., 2001). Implementation success rates are only 15% (Meyer, 1988). Garet et al. (2001) illustrate that effective PD (as measured by student achievement gains) extends over time and is conducted for long periods of time per session. These longer activities allow for more active learning (e.g., classroom implementation, observation, review of students' work) and coherence (e.g., alignment with standards, communication with other teachers). They also improve teachers' content knowledge and skills. Other characteristics of effective PD include the following:

- School-wide and context-specific
- Encouragement and support in change from school leaders
- Follow-up

- Research-based and up-to-date knowledge
- Adequate funding for materials, substitutes to allow for peer observation, etc. (Richardson, 1998)
- Focused on specific content and how students learn (Kennedy, 1998)

But even PD programs that meet these criteria can fail. Duffy and Roebler (1986) in a 4-year study of grades 2, 3, and 4 reading teachers' participation in a staff development on reading strategies (including 12 hours of instruction, and individual on-site coaching) found that all participating teachers endorsed the training, but primarily used the new strategies only when they were observed. This is an issue that administrators need to be aware of and may be one of many reasons why sometimes observation data and achievement data do not align. Duffy and Roebler argued that we often assume if we provide teachers with a sensible suggestion, they will use it. Instead, the authors found something very different.

> Teachers, like all learners, are "boundedly rational" (Shulman & Carey, 1985). That is, they combine information received from teacher educators and researchers with what they already know, re-structure it, and make it fit their perception of reality . . . Second, there are at least four sets of "filters" that constrain teacher decision-making. Teachers restructure new information in terms of their conceptual understandings of curricular content, their concept of instruction, their perceptions of the demands of the working environment, and their desire to achieve a smoothly flowing school day.
> (Duffy and Rochler, 1986, p. 57)

These findings illustrate that the early change models do not address components necessary for change. For example, teachers may report they are using a principal's feedback in instruction, but principals may not see it as teachers often implement a "restructured understanding." This is not to say that teachers are wrong—teachers often want to use feedback, but in the context of knowledge about their learners. Feedback providers should take into consideration teachers' perceptions of classroom contexts when they follow up with teachers to observe feedback implementation.

Feedback. Administrators need to understand the characteristics of effective feedback, and how/why such feedback is valued, interpreted, and used (or not) by teachers to improve practice. Here are some considerations:

- **Provider**. Who provides the feedback? Peer? Researcher? Principal? Students? Parents?
- **Method of delivery**. Is the feedback provided written? Verbal? Using visuals such as tables or reviewing video?
- **Type**. Is the feedback quantitative (e.g., number of higher-order questions asked, percentage of time spent in discussion)? Or is it qualitative (e.g., descriptions of classroom climate)? Or both?

- **Frequency**. Is feedback provided systematically—on a daily, weekly, or monthly basis? Or randomly?
- **Context**. Is feedback provided publicly or privately?
- **Content**. Is feedback directed toward process variables (e.g., teaching practices) or product (e.g., student learning outcomes)? Or both?
- **Quality**. Is feedback specific? Actionable? Addresses factors that are within a teacher's control?

We use extant research to discuss these considerations. First, we describe what is known about feedback from studies that include feedback providers *other* than the principals for both preservice teachers and practicing teachers. We do this because the literature on principal feedback to improve teaching is sparse. Then, we examine one context in which principals offer feedback—postobservation conferences.

Research on preservice feedback. Besides a few experimental studies, most studies on feedback during teacher preparation are small, qualitative cases. Research on student teachers indicates that feedback can improve their instruction. Freiberg, Waxman, and Houston (1987) examined the effects of feedback on student teachers' instruction by randomly assigning 20 student teachers to one of three conditions: (1) control (the usual feedback from their supervisor and cooperating teacher); (2) feedback (control plus an analysis of their teaching profiles from three observations and one workshop on profile interpretation); or (3) experimental (feedback plus three workshops on application of profiles to practice). Student teachers were observed using the Stallings Observation System (SOS; Stallings, 1986). Although there were no significant differences across the three groups, trends illustrated that students in the experimental group implemented change in the desired direction, showing improvements in interactive instruction and declines in organizing statements and off-task behavior.

In another study, Harris (1989) randomly assigned 51 students to one of three conditions: (1) control; (2) full (feedback from the SOS plus five workshops on interpreting findings and application); or (3) feedback only. The full treatment group improved on 8 of 11 variables—with significant improvements for student monitoring, students in interactive instruction, and student off-task behavior. The feedback-only group showed improvement on nine variables (with significant change for teachers' interactive instruction, teachers' managing, and students in interactive instruction). When significant, changes were small, yet these two studies establish that feedback can improve student teachers' instruction.

These studies provided no information on quality of the feedback—what suggestions were student teachers given for improvement? Ahn Le and Vásquez (2011) examined the qualities of feedback from the recipients' perspective in a study on preparing English language teachers. Six postobservation conversations between five mentor teachers, one internship instructor, and five MA student interns were analyzed using discourse analysis. Interns reported several strategies to be helpful, including several effective methods previously established through research: using questions, providing compliments before criticisms or specific suggestions, using mild advice and suggestions, providing feedback in a comfortable atmosphere, and establishing a balance of both negative and positive feedback. This study identifies feedback characteristics that student teachers perceived as helpful, but does not tell us if such feedback altered instruction / student learning significantly. Research on in-service feedback fills some of these gaps.

Research on in-service feedback. What happens after teachers enter the classroom? Do they receive feedback? Does feedback make a difference? Yeany and Padilla (1986) provided a synthesis of practices and research and documented that teaching practice could be improved. Practice and analysis with a peer or feedback from a supervisor had the greatest effect (mean effect size 2.30) on teachers' behaviors compared to other methods of improving instruction, such as study of an analysis system (.79), observing poor and effective models of instruction (1.10), analyzing models of instruction (1.15), and practice and self-analysis (.72). These findings show that teachers can change and indicate that feedback can be a powerful mechanism for change. But do changes in teaching enhance learning?

Leach and Conto (1999) examined the effectiveness of an in-service training with or without feedback on teachers' and students' behaviors in a four-phase study:

- **Phase 1** (pre-intervention): Observers established their presence in classrooms and established coder reliability.
- **Phase 2** (baseline): Data were collected during language arts and mathematics lessons across a 5-day period on teacher and student behaviors (related to the workshop). Student engagement rates were collected for six students per teacher—three target students (generally off-task students) and three non-target students.
- **Phase 3** (workshop): Teachers participated in a half-day in-service workshop on classroom instruction and management practices related to student academic engagement. Teachers received written copies of workshop materials, and postworkshop data were collected on teachers' practices and students' behavior.
- **Phase 4** (feedback): Teachers received feedback. Three conditions were rotated across teachers: (1) outcome (students' academic engagement rates); (2) process (measured by teachers' practices); and (3) outcome and process. Observations followed each feedback rotation, separated by periods of no feedback. Lessons were observed during 4 consecutive days weekly throughout the 13-week study.

Postworkshop data indicated temporary improvements. Prior to the workshop, target and non-target students were academically engaged in 50–70% of the coded intervals. On Day 1 following the workshop, students' academic engagement rates improved from baseline in classrooms in both target and non-target students for all teachers (mean increases ranged from 3.0% to 10.4%). Although improvements were statistically significant, there was a downward trend in students' academic engagement rates following Day 1. In terms of teachers' behavior, there was brief documented improvement *only* in some variables. Minimizing transition time was stressed during the workshop, but Day 1 data indicated an *increase* in time spent on transitions, as measured in minutes! Another surprising trend was the decrease in positive teacher interactions with students. Negative teacher interactions with students, curriculum-relevant academic interactions, and non-academic teacher interactions were stable. The changes in curriculum-relevant academic and non-academic interactions were primarily a function of changes in one teacher. Visual scanning was the only observed increase, demonstrating an upward trend following additional observation days postworkshop.

After the introduction of feedback, teachers and students demonstrated immediate and cumulative changes. Improvements were seen in students' academic engagement rates for target and non-target students for all feedback conditions. Most teachers' practices changed as intended. The time of delay transition decreased and visual scanning increased. Positive interactions with students increased while negative interactions remained stable and low. Academic interactions demonstrated gains postworkshop, but illustrated differences across feedback conditions with the greatest gain seen in the outcome-plus-process feedback condition. Non-academic interactions decreased, and teachers demonstrated a downward trend in this practice with cumulative reductions. The largest gains were mostly seen after the first feedback, and some variables appeared to be easier to change (such as visual scanning) than others. There were no differences of the effects of conditions on teachers' practices. And most practices did not change between conditions.

These findings suggest that feedback *does* matter. They also bring to light that feedback on process, outcome, and a combination of both has the same probability of promoting change in teachers' practices. However, it is clear that follow-up *and* feedback are needed. Furthermore, since teachers generally maintained any improvements across no-feedback periods in Phase 4, it is possible that administrators could provide feedback weekly or even less frequently while still maintaining important gains in teacher and student behavior—the latter, of course, would need to be tested. And, given that some practices are easier to change than others, it is important that observers and evaluators remember that teachers may improve in some practices and not others, and that some teachers may respond to feedback differently than others; this may interact with the specific practice they are asked to improve and its perceived difficulty.

Research on principal feedback. After reviewing the first ten volumes of the *Journal of Curriculum and Supervision*, Short (1995) found 82 articles that addressed instructional leadership, but only a few articles on conferences with teachers. One reason for the limited research is that principals spend limited time supervising and evaluating teachers. Likewise, teacher evaluations are viewed as cursory—with many teachers receiving high scores compounded by processes for remediation and removing teachers that are ineffective, slow, or impossible to implement (Weisberg, Sexton, Mulhern, & Keeling, 2009).

Given that research is limited, can it tell us anything? Do principals supervise and evaluate well? An audit conducted in six school districts (1987–1991) found that the few times that principals did visit teachers, teachers reported rarely receiving helpful suggestions and noted that principals primarily engaged in chitchat and discussion unrelated to teaching (Frase & Streshly, 1994). Perhaps principals need to be merely present (more frequently) and provide instructional feedback. Yet Tuckman and Oliver (1986) found that not to be the case. In their study, 286 vocational high school teachers were separated by years of experience and subjected to one of four conditions: student feedback, supervisor (principal, assistant principal) feedback, student-plus-supervisor feedback, or no feedback. Feedback was established through a survey that both students and principals completed, including items rating the teacher on aspects like content knowledge, ability to explain, fairness, and ability to get students to think for themselves. Four-opened questions were included, seeking out what was like and disliked about the course/class and suggestions for improvement. Written feedback was provided—graphs, tables, and responses from the open-ended questions. Teachers assigned to the student feedback condition showed positive instructional changes as measured by students' ratings. In the student-plus-supervisor condition, principal feedback (although no different than the student feedback) added no effect to the effects of student feedback, and when provided alone, teachers demonstrated shifts opposite of the desired outcomes! Less experienced teachers tended to be more responsive to student feedback, showing greater gains than more experienced teachers. And less experienced teachers were most negatively impacted by supervisor feedback. Clearly, more research is needed to better understand why principal feedback had such a negative impact on teaching. We illustrated in Chapter 3 that a teacher's self-efficacy, which is often lower in the beginning years, may be one variable that mediates instructional improvement following feedback. And exploring the quality of feedback is vital. We wonder: Would study outcomes have been different if feedback were based on the variables described in Chapter 3 (which may have been perceived as more relevant by teachers)? What if feedback were provided in a face-to-face conference? Further, we do not believe that these findings necessarily undermine the value of a principal's role in instructional improvement. We believe that feedback (and its potency) is both poorly understood and underutilized by principals. Yet our optimistic beliefs beg for empirical support.

Blase and Blase (1999) examined teachers' perceptions of principals' instructional leadership behaviors that changed their instructional practices. Elementary, middle, and high school teachers ($N = 809$) responded to two open-ended questions: What characteristics (e.g., strategies, goals) of school principals positively influence classrooms teaching? What characteristics adversely influence classroom teaching? Two major themes emerged—talking with teachers to promote reflection and supporting professional growth. Five strategies promoted reflection:

(1) making suggestions; (2) providing feedback; (3) modeling; (4) using inquiry and soliciting advice and opinions; and (5) giving praise. Teachers provided specific practices and descriptions for both making suggestions and providing feedback. See Table 4.1 for a summary of these related practices.

Six strategies promoted professional growth: (1) emphasizing the study of teaching and learning; (2) supporting collaboration among teachers; (3) developing coaching relationships with teachers; (4) encouraging and supporting program redesign; (5) applying principles of adult learning, growth, and development; and (6) implementing action research to inform decisions. Teachers indicated that these behaviors and practices impacted their motivation, satisfaction, and sense of security. Teachers also reported positive effects on their innovation and creativity, instructional focus, risk taking, and planning.

Principals can indirectly affect student achievement through many processes—one being the growth and development of teachers—by structuring and providing relevant PD, including feedback to teachers and coaching. To reiterate, some practices (e.g., coaching and evaluation) are linked to positive student achievement gains, but if they occur, the effects are small. We have limited knowledge about what characteristics of feedback from principals alter teachers' practices, and in

TABLE 4.1 Teachers' Perspectives on Instructional Practices That Promote Instructional Improvement

Theme	Strategies	Specific practices
Talking with teachers to promote reflection	Making suggestions	Listening
		Sharing their experiences
		Using examples and demonstrations
		Providing teacher choice
		Challenging outdated or destructive policies
		Encouraging risk taking
		Providing professional literature
		Acknowledging teachers' strengths
		Maintaining focus on instructional improvement
	Providing feedback	Focusing on observational data
		Providing detailed and specific feedback
		Expressing care, interest, and support
		Providing praise
		Establishing a problem-solving orientation
		Responding to concerns about student behavior
		Addressing teacher-student interaction
		Expressing availability for follow-up

Source: Adapted from Blase and Blase (1999).

some cases, no feedback might be the most effective! Other challenges include that research suggests that informal classroom observations (e.g., walk-throughs)—although highly popular—are negatively related to student achievement growth, and this is particularly true in high schools (Grissom et al., 2013). Perhaps principals are not providing teachers with feedback, but instead are instead using walk-throughs to "check in." In a study of 17 elementary schools, intrusive forms of supervision were negatively associated with teachers' perceptions of the principal as a helpful advisor. The frequency of meetings principals had with teachers was of less concern to teachers. What mattered most to teachers was principals' accessibility, attentiveness to teacher concerns, and collaborative problem solving on instructional issues within the context of mutual respect. These process/style variables principals displayed related to teachers perceiving administrators as a valuable source of feedback (and someone teachers sought out for advice) (Friedkin & Slater, 1994). Thus, principals' decisions of when and how they observe teachers and provide feedback are important factors in teachers' growth and development. There appears to be ample opportunity for principals to improve in how they establish and maintain collaborative relationships with teachers.

Unfortunately, there is limited knowledge about the extent to which teachers change their practice following feedback after observations. This is due, in part, to the limited amount of follow-up that occurs in typical evaluations. Also, given new requirements, principals face the challenge of large amounts of time spent with initial evaluation that might make follow-up nearly impossible. Furthermore, most pilot studies and initial reports from RttT states look at improvement from the lens of appropriately removing ineffective teachers. Any research examining improvement in instruction is based within surveys on principals' and teachers' satisfaction with teacher evaluation and their perceptions of instructional change without any real evidence that this occurs. Yet there may be value in examining research on the processes that occur during evaluation structures, such as pre- and postconferences and coaching,

A Closer Look at Improving Instruction: The Instructional Conference

Blase and Blase (1996) examined the micropolitical strategies used by 100 administrators during teacher conferences. The authors studied how administrators leveraged their formal and informal power in instructional conferences to achieve organizational goals. Four strategies emerged: personal orientation, conversational congruence, formal authority, and situational variables. "Success" was measured by supervisors' and teachers' ratings, and successful conferences were characterized by shared meanings and similar agendas. The use of personal orientation captured cognitive and affective frameworks (e.g., values), conference participants' interpersonal histories (e.g., shared events), and individual agendas (e.g., objectives).

In successful conferences, teachers and supervisors generally agreed on the instructional methods, and discussed the value of methods and reasons for implementing particular methods. In successful conferences, there was goal consistency. In terms of conversational congruence, in effective conferences supervisors and teachers shared professional jargon and terminology and research references, and there were shared definitions around the practices and concepts discussed. Formal authority was used infrequently, and successful supervisors were less likely to use status or rewards to guide discussion. Instead, they used comments that engaged reflective and critical talk (e.g., "Tell me a little bit about this class"; "You listed a lot of problems; what do you see as their strengths?"). Successful conferences were more about empowerment rather than control, and fostered trust, reflection, and risk taking.

Responding to poor performance. Historically, principals have struggled to deal with teacher incompetence, due in part to restrictions like the difficulty in removing ineffective tenured teachers. In an interview/survey study of 150 superintendents and 30 principals the most common response to teacher ineffectiveness was to avoid confrontation and tolerate. When interventions occurred, issues were often reduced to make the process easier to cope with (Bridges, 1992). LeFevre and Robinson (2014) noted principals may forgo improvement in teaching and learning with poor-performing teachers in order to uphold positive relationships. Unfortunately, if the culture has historically been to provide inflated and globally positive ratings, anything to the contrary may be seen as unusually harsh and teachers may respond negatively. LeFevre and Robinson (2014) assessed how principals interacted with poor teacher performance, following a hypothetical parent complaint. Twenty-seven principals in their first position were asked to respond to a scenario of a complaint by a parent of perceived poor classroom management by meeting with the teacher to discuss the issue. Principals' interactions with teachers were rated on several skills: (1) expressing a grounded point of view; (2) seeking deeper understanding of teachers' perspectives; (3) checking their own understanding with that of the teacher; (4) helping the teacher consider an alternative point of view; (5) examining their own assumptions; and (6) agreeing with the teacher on next steps. On a five-point Likert scale, principals were rated the weakest in checking their own understanding with the teacher ($M = 1.96, SD = .85$), and the strongest in expressing their own point of view ($M = 3.33, SD = 1.18$). But, overall, principals were found to demonstrate low to moderate interpersonal effectiveness. These findings are concerning, but may suggest that new principals have not had the opportunity to deal with these issues and preparation programs did not include these skills. Now that principals are held accountable on effective teacher evaluations and these evaluations may go to court, we may see a significant increase in preparation and PD for school leaders to enhance this aspect of their job.

A Closing Note on Teacher Change and Instructional Improvement

One issue that challenges RttT changes is that teachers are often trying to achieve different goals than reformers. In analyzing teachers' thinking and intentions related to their practices, Kennedy (2005) found that teachers had many intentions for their practices—averaging nearly 20 intentions per lesson! Teachers' intentions were numerous, diverse, and sometimes contradictory. Although reform ideals were present in teachers' thinking, they were practically absent in the context of the complexity of schools and competing intentions and goals that teachers noted were important to their practices (Kennedy, 2005, p. 61). Considering this reality, Guskey (2002) offered three key considerations about teacher change. First, change is a gradual and difficult process, ridden with anxiety and risk. And it often requires more work. Administrators can't expect that feedback is implemented immediately or even is successful once implemented. Furthermore, even if teachers agree with the feedback, change in practice is likely slow and evolving and substantial changes in students, if possible, will likely mirror this process and may not be significant. Sustained change is hard to achieve. For example, in studies of school-based smoking and substance use prevention programs, it is typical that 70–90% of teachers who receive training initially implement the program, but after a year (with no follow-up), implementation drops to 20–60% (McCormick, Steckler, & McLeroy, 1995; Rohrbach, Graham, & Hansen, 1993). These challenges have also been documented in studies of feedback on classroom instruction—when feedback is withdrawn, observed instructional change returns to baseline (Leach & Ingram, 1989). In order to sustain change, Guskey provides two last recommendations—teachers need regular feedback on student learning and continued follow-up and support.

Conclusion

This chapter addressed the extent to which and how principals can influence classroom instruction and student learning. We considered different forms of principal effects. Direct effects, when found, tend to be small and more evident in some contexts than others. But small effects over time can add up and thus merit consideration. Indirect effects (through school climate and leadership) tend to be larger than principals' direct effect on student achievement. However, these effects were highly varied (sometimes yielding big positive effects and other times modest but negative effects). These varied findings make recommendations problematic not only because of the inconsistencies across studies but also because the data are largely self-reported and lack grounding in direct observation. Some have argued that principals do not have detailed knowledge about the effective teaching literature or how to apply this knowledge and hence have little skill to impact instruction and learning (thus the weak impact of principals we found is what you would expect). Accordingly, we reviewed research on school leaders' preparation and found that many programs were not preparing administrations well for evaluating and improving teaching, but we found some recent evidence to suggest that some preparation programs are better received by their graduates. Perhaps in time better training of administrators will improve their ability to enhance teaching and learning. We addressed other issues, such as whether teachers can change and whether they are willing to do so. Here we explored models explaining teacher change and considered related variables, such as the teacher's self-efficacy and value placed on such change. There is reasonable evidence that teachers are willing and can change if they *believe* the changes to be desirable. We also explored the type of feedback and support that enhanced teacher change for both preservice and in-service teachers. After examining PD and in-service literatures, we considered what was known about how principals provide feedback to teachers in ways that teachers find useful. In Chapter 5 we apply Chapters 1–4 to practical issues that school leaders face in supervising and evaluating teachers.

References

Anh Le, P.T., & Vásquez, C. (2011). Feedback in teacher education: Mentor discourse and intern perceptions. *Teacher Development, 15*(4), 453–470.

Blase, J., & Blase, J. (1996). Micropolitical strategies used by administrators and teachers in instructional conferences. *Alberta Journal of Educational Research, 42*(4), 345–360.

Blase, J., & Blase, J. (1999). Principals' instructional leadership and teacher development: Teachers' perspectives. *Educational Administration Quarterly, 35*(3), 349–378.

Bridges, E.M. (1992). *The incompetent teacher* (revised and extended version). Oxford: Routledge.

Chi, M.T.H., Glaser, R., & Farr, M. (Eds.) (1988). *The nature of expertise.* Hillsdale, NJ: Erlbaum.

Cohen, D.K., & Hill, H.C. (2000). Instructional policy and classroom performance: The mathematics reform in California. *Teachers College Record, 102*(2), 294–343.

Duffy, G., & Rochler, L. (1986). Constraints on teacher change. *Journal of Teacher Education, 37*(1), 55–58.

Farkas, S., Johnson, J., & Duffet, A. (2003). *Rolling up their sleeves: Superintendents and principals talk about what's needed to fix public schools.* New York: Public Agenda.

Frase, L.E., & Streshley, W. (1994). Lack of accuracy, feedback, and commitment in teacher evaluation. *Journal of Personnel Evaluation in Education, 1,* 47–57.

Freiberg, H.J., Waxman, H.C., & Houston, W.R. (1987). Enriching feedback to student-teachers through small group discussion. *Teacher Education Quarterly, 14*(3), 71–82.

Freiberg, H.J., Stein, T., & Huang, S. (1995). The effects of classroom management intervention on student achievement in inner-city elementary schools. *Educational Research and Evaluation, 1*(1), 33–66.

Friedkin, N.E., & Slater, M.R. (1994). School leadership and performance: A social network approach. *Sociology of Education, 67,* 139–157.

Garet, M.S., Porter, A.C., Desimone, L., Birman, B.F., & Yoon, K.W. (2001). What makes professional development effective? Results from a national sample of teachers. *American Educational Research Journal, 38*(4), 915–945.

Glaser, R., & Chi, M.T.H. (1988). Introduction: What is it to be an expert? In M.T.H. Chi, R. Glaser, & M.J. Farr (Eds.), *The nature of expertise* (pp. xv–xxiix). Hillsdale, NJ: Erlbaum.

Good, T.L., & Grouws, D.A. (1979). The Missouri mathematics effectiveness project: An experimental study in fourth-grade classrooms. *Journal of Educational Psychology, 71*(3), 355–362.

Grissom, J.A., & Loeb, S. (2011). Triangulating principal effectiveness: How perspectives of parents, teachers, and assistant principals identify the central importance of managerial skills. *American Educational Research Journal, 48*(5), 1091–1123.

Grissom, J.A., Loeb, S., & Master, B. (2013). Effective instructional time use for school leaders: Longitudinal evidence from observations of principals. *Educational Researchers, 42*(8), 433–444.

Guskey, T.R. (1986). Staff development and the process of teacher change. *Educational Researcher, 15*(5), 5–12.

Guskey, T.R. (2002). Professional development and teacher change. *Teachers and Teaching: Theory and Practice, 8*(3/4), 381–391.

Hallinger, P. (2003). Leading educational change: Reflections on the practice of instructional and transformational leadership. *Cambridge Journal of Education, 33*(3), 329–351.

Hallinger, P., Blickman, L., & Davis, K. (1996). School context, principal leadership, and student reading achievement. *Elementary School Journal, 96*(5), 527–549.

Han, S. S., & Weiss, B. (2005). Sustainability of teacher implementation of school-based mental health programs. *Journal of Abnormal Child Psychology, 33*(6), 665–679.

Harris, A.H. (1989). *A search for sources of treatment effects in a teacher effectiveness training program*. Paper presented at the Annual Meeting of the American Educational Research Association. San Francisco, CA.

Henry, G.T., Bastian, K.C., & Fortner, C.K. (2011). Stayers and leavers: Early-career teacher effectiveness and attrition. *Educational Researcher, 40*(6), 271–280.

Hernandez, R., Roberts, M., & Menchaca, V. (2012). Redesigning a principal preparation program: A continuous improvement model. *International Journal of Educational Leadership Preparation, 7*(3), 1–12.

Hess, F. (2006). Looking beyond the schoolhouse door. *Phi Delta Kappan, 87*(7), 513–515.

Hess, F.M., & Kelly, A.P. (2005). The politics of principal preparation reforms. *Education Policy, 19*(1), 155–180.

Hess, F.M., & Kelly, A.P. (2007). Learning to lead: What gets taught in principal-preparation programs. *Teachers College Record, 109*(1), 221–243.

Horng, E.L., Klasik, D., & Loeb, S. (2010). Principal's time use and school effectiveness. *American Journal of Education, 116*, 491–523.

Huberman, M. (1989). On teachers' careers: Once over lightly, with a broad brush. *International Journal of Educational Research, 13*(4), 347–362.

Kennedy, M.M. (1998). *Form and substance in in-service teacher education* (Research Monograph No. 13). Arlington, VA: National Science Foundation.

Kennedy, M.M. (2005). *Inside teaching: How classroom life undermines reform*. Cambridge, MA: Harvard University Press.

Knoeppel, R.C., & Rinehart, J.S., (2008). Student achievement and principal quality: Examining the relationship. *Journal of School Leadership, 18*(5), 501–527.

Kythreotis, A., Pashiardis, P., & Kyriakides, L. (2010). The influence of school leadership style and culture on students' achievement in Cyprus primary schools. *Journal of Educational Administration, 48*(2), 218–240.

Leach, D.J., & Conto, H. (1999). The additional effects of process and outcome feedback following brief in-service teacher training. *Educational Psychology, 19*(4), 441–462.

Leach, D.J., & Ingram, K.I. (1989). The effects of information and feedback on teachers' classroom behavior and students' academic engaged time. *Educational Psychology, 9*, 167–184.

Lee, M., & Hallinger, P. (2012). National contexts influencing principals' time use and allocation: Economic development, societal culture, and educational system. *School Effectiveness and School Improvement, 23*(4), 461–482.

Le Fevre, M., & Robinson, V. (2014). The interpersonal challenges of instructional leadership: Principals' effectiveness in conversations about performance issues. *Educational Administration Quarterly*, 1–38.

Leithwood, K. (1994). Leadership for school restructuring. *Educational Administration Quarterly, 30*(4), 498–518.

Levine, A. (2005). *Educating school leaders*. New York: Education Schools Project.

Lortie, D. (1975). *Schoolteacher*. Chicago, IL: University of Chicago Press.

Loucks-Horsley, S., Hewson, P.W., Love, N., & Stiles, K.E. (1998). *Designing professional development for teachers of science and mathematics*. Thousand Oaks, CA: SAGE.

May, H., & Supovitz, J. A. (2011). The scope of principal efforts to improve instruction. *Educational Administration Quarterly, 47*(2), 332–352.

McCormick, L.K., Steckler, A.B., & McLeroy, K.R. (1995). Diffusion of innovations in schools: A study of adoption and implementation of school-based tobacco prevention curricula. *American Journal of Health Promotion, 9*, 210–219.

Meyer, L. (1988). Research on implementation: What seems to work. In S.J. Samuels & P.D. Pearson (Eds.), *Changing school reading programs* (pp. 41–57). Newark, DE: International Reading Association.

Ogawa, R.T., & Hart, A.W. (1985). The effect of principals on the instructional performance of schools. *Journal of Educational Administration, 23*(1), 59–72.

Payne, C. (2010). *So much reform so little change*. Cambridge, MA: Harvard Education Press.

Pitner, N.J. (1988). Leadership substitutes: Their factorial validity in educational organizations. *Educational and Psychological Measurement, 48*, 307–315.

Richardson, V. (1998). How teachers change: What will lead to change that most benefits student learning? *Focus on the Basics: Connecting Research to Practice, 2*(C). Retrieved from www.ncsall.net/index.html@id=395.html

Rivkin, S.G., Hanushek, E.A., & Kain, J.F. (2005). Teachers, schools, and academic achievement. *Econometrica, 73*, 417–458. doi:10.1111/j.1468-0262.2005.00584.x

Robinson, V.M.J., Lloyd, C.A., & Rowe, K.J. (2008). The impact of leadership on student outcomes: An analysis of the differential effects of leadership types. *Educational Administration Quarterly, 44*, 635–674.

Rohrbach, L.A., Graham, J.W., & Hansen, W.B. (1993). Diffusion of a school-based substance abuse prevention program: Predictors of program implementation. *Preventive Medicine, 22*, 237–260.

Sebastian, J., & Allensworth, E. (2012). The influence of principal leadership on classroom instruction and student learning: A study of mediated pathways to learning. *Educational Administration Quarterly, 48*(4), 626–663.

Shatzer, R.H., Caldarella, P., Hallam, P.R., & Brown, B.L. (2014). Comparing the effects of instructional and transformational leadership on student achievement: Implications for practice. *Educational Management Administration & Leadership, 42*(4), 445–459.

Short, E.C. (1995). A review of studies in the first 10 volumes of the *Journal of Curriculum and Supervision*. *Journal of Curriculum and Supervision, 11*(1), 87–105.

Shulman, L., & Carey, N. (1984). Psychology and the limitations of individual rationality: Implications for the study of reasoning and civility. *Review of Educational Research, 54*(4), 501–524.

Stallings, J.A. (1986). Using time effectively: A self-analytic approach. In K. Zumwalt (Ed.), *Improving teaching* (pp. 15–27). Alexandria, VA: Association for Supervision and Curriculum Development.

Stein, M.K., & Wang, M.C. (1988). Teacher development and school improvement: The process of teacher change. *Teaching and Teacher Education, 4*(2), 171–187.

Styron, R.A., & LeMire, S.D. (2009). Principal preparation programs: Perceptions of high school principals. *Journal of College Teacher and Learning, 6*(6), 51–61.

Supovitz, J., Sirinides, P., & May, H. (2010). How principals and peers influence teaching and learning. *Educational Administration Quarterly, 46*(1), 31–56.

Tuckman, B.W., & Oliver, W.T. (1986). Effectiveness of feedback to teachers as a function of source. *Journal of Educational Psychology, 59*(4), 297–301.

U.S. Department of Education. (2013). Characteristics of public and private elementary and secondary principals in the United States: Results from the 2011–2012 Schools and Staffing Survey. Retrieved from http://nces.ed.gov/pubs2013/2013313.pdf

Wang, M.C., & Gennari, P. (1983). Analysis of the design, implementation, and effects of a data-based staff development program. *Teacher Education and Special Education, 6,* 211–226.

Waters, T., Marzano, R.J., & McNulty, B. (2004). Developing the science of educational leadership. *ERS Spectrum, 22*(1), 4–13.

Weisberg, D., Sexton, S., Mulhern, J., & Keeling, D. (2009). *The widget effect: Our national failure to acknowledge and act on difference in teacher effectiveness.* Brooklyn, NY: New Teachers Project. Retrieved from http://widgeteffect.org/downloads/TheWidgetEffect.pdf

Witziers, B., Bosker, R.J., & Krüger, M.L. (2003). Educational leadership and student achievement: The elusive search for an association. *Educational Administration Quarterly, 39,* 398–425.

Yeany, R.H., & Padilla, M.J. (1986). Training science teachers to utilize better teaching strategies: A research synthesis. *Journal of Research in Science Teaching, 23*(2), 85–95.

5

CONSIDERATIONS FOR PRINCIPALS WHEN WORKING WITH TEACHERS TO IMPROVE PRACTICE

Principals are busy, and we have shown that historically they have spent little time supervising teachers. Yet policy makers are urging principals to spend more time in classrooms because they now know that teachers matter for student learning and because we have "better" tools for assessing individual teachers' effects on student learning. Are principals prepared to do this? We noted that principal preparation programs have not devoted much time to helping principals develop observational and feedback skills. So it is not surprising that little data supports the belief that principals can improve teaching and learning. Furthermore, some argue that principals do not understand the literature on effective teaching. Such problems do not deter policy makers who at least implicitly suggest that principals' lack of knowledge can be bypassed by giving them an observation instrument that can do the thinking for them. Unfortunately, their beliefs in the utility of classroom observation instruments are flawed. Simply put, these instruments weakly predict teacher effects on student achievement (even when used by well-trained raters), provide inconsistent results, tell us virtually nothing about teacher interactions with individual students, and provide limited information to improve instruction.

Considering these challenges, we wondered how to best help principals with this high-priority activity. From research conducted in Illinois (Lavigne & Chamberlain, 2014), we discovered that those assigned observational and supervision tasks were given few tools and strategies. State training required evaluators to be reliable on the chosen observation instrument (Danielson's Framework for Teaching) and to know appropriate rules and regulations, but surveyed principals and assistant principals reported wanting more—scripts for feedback, and how to supplement existing instruments and conduct meaningful postobservation conferences. Chapter 5 was driven by these needs and our belief that supportive supervision can improve student achievement. We also observed that principals were making important decisions. Principals used additional observers for teacher observations, but there was no consistent strategy across principals about how best to utilize additional observers. We thought it helpful to provide practitioners with considerations for making such decisions. We believe that policy makers' and the media's negative perceptions of American education make principals' important work more difficult by mandating the use of observational instruments that fail to provide principals with useful information for improving teaching and learning, particularly for those students who are achieving at the lowest level. Accordingly, we provide advice about other ways principals can collect data and communicate more effectively with teachers.

We begin with general considerations—how principals can manage their time and the decisions that need to be made prior to the start of the school year. Then we examine observation and feedback through the lens of a formal observation cycle. We discuss preparing to observe and providing effective feedback, and carefully consider the needs of beginning teachers since significant time will be devoted to these teachers.

Principals' Management of Time

Principals have more tasks to do than time allows. Indeed, some have argued that it is exceedingly difficult for principals to control their schedules as "fires" suddenly appear and demand attention. Recall in Chapter 1 we reported that 50% of principal's observed activities were interrupted and that 81.4% of activities that principals engaged in ranged from 1 to 4 minutes. However, "emergencies" must be managed if uninterrupted time is to be protected for doing improvement work with teachers.

Proactively Protect Time

Our first consideration: "be as proactive as possible." *If* you decide to allocate more time to provide meaningful feedback to teachers, you must determine what activities you will delay, ignore, or delegate. Principals are bombarded with information about how to improve schooling. New programs like expanded parent involvement activities or using student data to make instructional decisions "promise" great returns on your time. Advocacy for using student data to make instructional decisions abounds, but has no supporting evidence. Consider this sentence contained in a 70-page report by the U.S. Department of Education, entitled *Using Student Achievement Data to Support Instructional Decision-Making* (2009). "Overall, the panel believes that the existing research on using data to make instructional decisions does not yet provide conclusive evidence of what works to improve student achievement." Recall that the report was entitled *Using Student Achievement Data* … ! Most readers would infer that the recommendations in the report are supported by data—otherwise why disseminate the information? This is not to say that attention to student data is not valuable, but that the value of using student data for decision making is often exaggerated (for an explanation, see Appendix G). In short, we believe you need to protect your time and be wary of empty promises. Now we turn to suggestions for using your time effectively.

Consider Your Context and Resources for Teacher Supervision

There is no answer to the question "how *best* can I allocate time," but some opportunities seem more promising than others. General formulas for allocating time have limited value because the appropriate way to make time allocation decisions is to analyze your *context*. For example, in a school with a history of high achievement compared with a newly reconstituted school replete with beginning teachers and those transferring from other schools, there are different problems and potential that call for different time distributions.

Table 5.1 illustrates that the task of supervising teachers varies for the principals at School A and B. Table 5.1 summarizes the principal's working beliefs about the quality of the teaching staff at the end of August *after* initial observations and feedback conferences have occurred (more on this later). School A has 20 teachers—4 at each grade K–5 level. School B has 30 teachers, 6 at each K–5 level. School A's 20 teachers are composed of 10 beginning teachers, 2 teachers new to the school, and 8 returning teachers. School B's 30 teachers include 10 beginning teachers, 4 new teachers, and 16 returning teachers. Clearly B has more teachers to supervise but the level of teaching proficiency in School B is higher than at School A, where a higher percentage of teachers are new and more teachers are struggling.

The average length of a day in an elementary school is 6.7 hours. Of course, teachers and principals stay longer, but students are being instructed about 6.5 hours a day, so classes in theory can be observed 32.5 hours a week (but you may prefer not to observe Friday late afternoon or early Monday morning). You need to determine how much time to spend on observation and feedback, and how that time can be protected at all costs (who assumes the responsibilities you delegate). These decisions have to be made considering the number of teachers, their quality, and the number of others who can supervise teachers.

TABLE 5.1 A Comparison of Levels of Teaching Experience and Proficiency at Two Elementary Schools

Teacher	School A	School B	School A	School B	School A	School B
	Performing		Coping		Struggling	
Beginning	3	4	3	4	4	2
New to school	0	2	0	2	2	0
Returning	4	11	2	4	2	1

So, after *deciding* how much time you will allocate to and how to protect time for supervision, you must decide how to allocate time across teachers. We believe that dividing time equally among teachers is not a good strategy—some teachers need more help than others. So you will want to consider which teachers get the most attention and the least. Starting with beginning teachers is a good first step because investing time helping them reduce management issues can allow them to get off to a better start. Further, a good start saves future time because if management problems are not nipped in the bud they become bigger issues—requiring more time to address.

Preparing to Observe and Provide Feedback to Teachers

Prior to the start of the school year, principals need to make many decisions about teacher supervision. Beyond the decisions already discussed, principals need to decide who else will be involved in the observation process and who to observe first. Additionally, we provide some general suggestions for establishing appropriate and supportive expectations for teachers before principals observe their instruction.

Additional Observers

If the opportunity to have additional observers presents itself, take it! School leaders are overworked and find it difficult to manage the demands of new teacher evaluation models alongside other administrative tasks. This may result in cutting corners—something that is not a good strategy if it means presenting teachers with electronic or written feedback instead of face-to-face conferences. Involving other observers can provide some relief, among other benefits. Additional observers (e.g., peer observer, department chair, assistant principal, other qualified individuals inside or outside the building) can serve as a reliability check to the primary observer (oftentimes the principal). This offers important protection since in-school administrators tend to provide more biased (Whitehurst, Chingos, & Lindquist, 2014) and higher ratings than those outside of the building (Bill & Melinda Gates Foundation, 2013). And, if reliability is the goal, MET findings have illustrated that the reliability of lessons rated by in-school administrators is best enhanced by *an additional* observer, rather than by more observations (Bill & Melinda Gates Foundation, 2013).

But we caution readers that high reliability can be misleading. And multiple observers may do more harm than good. Consider the power of first impressions (also known as halo effects). Immediately after meeting a teacher, the principal forms an impression about a teacher's effectiveness on factors related (or not) to a teacher's instruction—dress, personality, or demeanor. These impressions taint the first observation. The evaluator unknowingly seeks information that validates his or her perceptions about that teacher's effectiveness. The primacy effect soon follows. Perceptions established (and related ratings) during the first observation endure despite a teacher's demonstration otherwise. What results is that administrators are fairly reliable observers—and, indeed, principals have been shown to have higher reliability (.61) than central administrative staff (.49) when rating teachers' instruction (Whitehurst et al., 2014)—but their ratings might not be accurate. Likewise, two observers could rate a teacher as low on a particular observation item, but for very different reasons, and subsequently offer feedback and improvement plans that vary sharply. In this scenario, reliability is high. And, indeed, the two observers agree that the teacher needs to improve upon a particular practice, but cannot agree why.

This is not to say that reliability is unimportant. Principals must clarify the supervision process and expectations with all involved individuals. And we believe that most of the trainings required by states under RttT are not enough. Those given the great responsibility and opportunity to observe teachers and provide feedback should work with a master coder and with others who will be rating the teacher to establish consistency in scoring, and importantly, clarity in the rationale and evidence used to provide particular scores. Beyond state requirements and prior to the start of the school year, principals might find it helpful to observe, score, and discuss video-recorded lessons with others who will observe teachers in the school building. Other helpful strategies include: take notes in the same ways (establish what evidence is noteworthy for particular observation items), use the language of the observation protocol, attend to interactions between a teacher and individual students (recall Chapter 3), do continued practice on observation items that are difficult to score reliably (Bell et al., 2014), and reach consensus on what additional elements warrant observation and feedback (see ahead for suggestions).

So, how can multiple observers be employed in ways that maximize benefits and reduce harm? As a principal, you must consider: How much time are you willing to spend on supervision? Who else is qualified and willing to observe? How much time can additional observers commit and how will their time be protected? After making these decisions, there are other considerations: Will observers be allocated across teachers or across observations (formal, informal)? Will you observe half of the teachers and your assistant principal the other half? Or will you both observe all teachers at least once? Who will be responsible for formal observations? Informal? Of course, when there are multiple observers (e.g., department chair, principal, assistant principal) you need to decide who takes primary responsibility for observing struggling or beginning teachers. General considerations for making decisions about using additional observers include: How confident are you in your own observational skills? What are your own areas of expertise? Principals, like all of us, have strengths and limitations, and surely some principals have more skills and dispositions for doing supervision than others or in particular grades or subject areas. Likewise, you should assess the expertise and background of the additional observers, including strengths in teaching. You will want to decide if additional observers will be responsible for solely conducting a full observation cycle (pre- and postconference + observation), or if they will also mentor and coach the teachers they observe. In some schools there may be mentor teachers who are willing to help and are capable of doing so. But you must consider that the literature makes clear that good teachers are not always good mentors.

We suggest that elementary and middle school principals conduct the initial brief instructional assessment with beginning teachers, new teachers, and returning teachers who have individualized improvement plans. Since in most cases, the principal will do the final evaluation, this seems particularly important in order to set clear expectations and clarify teacher concerns. Secondary school principals should do this as well unless they have delegated this authority to subject area department heads.

Who Do I Observe First?

Principals deal with at least three types of teachers—beginning teachers, experienced teachers who are doing well, and experienced teachers who struggle to some extent. Teachers experiencing the most difficulty should receive the most attention and help. Teachers needing help are those with low value-added achievement scores and those who perform low on teacher observation ratings. However, we assume that struggling returning teachers were identified in the spring and have improvement plans in place. If you are a new principal, helping teachers who were rated lowest in the previous year should receive attention first.

Given these considerations, a good strategy, as noted, is to observe all beginning teachers first and then teachers who have teaching experience but are new to your school. Our rationale for this is that new teachers may be experienced, but it is likely that you do not have access to their past performance data, and nor do you know if their prior effectiveness will transfer to the new school setting. Second, most principals will deal with many new and inexperienced teachers, as American students are increasingly taught by beginning teachers (see Chapter 1). Some new teachers are terrific, but most need experience and professional development. Work by Susan Johnson (2004) and others clearly shows that third-year teachers on average are more effective than first-year teachers.

Many beginning teachers will have not had experience at the grade level they teach. Some completed student teaching in a first-grade high SES setting, but their first-year assignment is in a fifth-grade class in a high-poverty urban school. Regardless of the match between previous school experience and first job, new teachers must prepare lessons for 180 or so instructional days, and this requires considerable time preparing class activities and student assessments.

Beginning teacher audit. Unless the number of beginning teachers is unmanageable, it is desirable for principals to make an initial observation of first-year teachers and to stay for the entire lesson. This allows you a chance to see the whole cycle: How does the teacher introduce the lesson and is the value/purpose of the lesson clear to students? Are students involved and accountable for class activities and are several different students active participants? How does the teacher transition from one part of the lesson to the next? How does the teacher end the lesson? Does the lesson seem to be interesting and accessible to students? If appropriate, does it include a summary? Is there sufficient evidence to allow the teacher to determine if most students understood the lesson? Is there any evidence that students are treated differently as a function of race or gender? Answers to these framing questions also provide a solid foundation for the feedback session. After the initial conference and developing a better understanding of what teachers did and why, you are in a position to advance working hypotheses—which teachers are performing, coping (several strengths but some weaknesses), and struggling (high support needs).

It is critical that teachers get feedback about the quality of lesson and what can be done to improve it. But also take the time to engage teachers in thinking about a sequence of lessons or a unit of instruction. What comes next and why? How will you know if students have mastered the material? We will return to this point later.

This activity can be time-consuming if there are many beginning teachers. But this initial assessment enables you to obtain a profile of teacher needs. Importantly, beginning teachers will get needed feedback promptly, and this allows them to move forward more quickly than they would without feedback. And you may identify some common problems that can be addressed in a focused workshop. When working with new teachers, do not forget that they need social support and teachers who struggle need information about what they do well in addition to what they do poorly.

Before observing beginning teachers. Given the many needs of beginning teachers, principals should help them before the year begins (when possible). We summarize some considerations from Huling-Austin (1986) about how principals can help new teachers.

1. Principals should provide beginning teachers with considerable preparation time. Teachers need course schedules, textbooks, and curriculum guides to plan their year. They also need physical access to their classroom in order to organize it before students arrive. And they need to know what resources they have access to—a copier? Page limits?
2. Principals can adjust the demands on first-year teachers by reducing/eliminating extra duties or extra curriculum assignments for teachers. Experienced teachers, especially in high schools, lobby principals for more desirable courses (e.g., honors English), leaving beginning teachers with the most difficult and least interesting choices. Too often the students with the fewest academic skills are taught by beginning teachers.
3. Before school begins all teachers should be introduced to beginning teachers. It is especially important that beginning teachers meet those who teach the same subject matter in secondary schools and those who teach the same

and adjoining grades in elementary schools. To the extent possible, beginning teachers should be assigned a mentor teacher who is well prepared for the role.
4. When there are several beginning teachers the principal or assistant principal might profitably plan special orientation meetings to provide detailed information about administrative procedures (that other teachers in the school know about). Here, new teachers could ask questions about their individual needs/concerns. Subsequently, principals could hold brief weekly meetings with beginning teachers for the first several weeks to discuss topics like classroom management, holding conferences with parents, use of test data, and so forth.
5. Principals should be visible during the first few weeks of school and accessible to teachers, especially beginning teachers.

Responding effectively to these considerations likely varies with the level of the school, the number of beginning teachers, and the number of experienced teachers who are capable and willing to be mentor teachers. Having said this, one general organizing principle is to address what most beginning teachers want or need to know. Veenman (1984) reviewed 83 studies and found that beginning teachers reported that class management/discipline represented the most frequent and serious problem—a problem that has remained stable over time and is a challenge for new teachers in other countries (Britton, Paine, & Raizen, 1999). Hence, one important orientation topic could be classroom management—how to prevent it and deal with it (school policies and classroom strategies). Another likely topic in this era of high-stakes teacher accountability (Lavigne & Good, 2014) would be a careful discussion with beginning teachers of observational and other evaluative tools that will be used in evaluating teachers. Furthermore, beginning teachers frequently report that relationships with parents are of high concern. Hence principals might arrange for sessions that provide guidelines or actual demonstration of parent-teacher conferences or allow a teacher to observe a conference with a teacher who excels in conducting parent-teacher conferences.

Although many school districts have orientation meetings for beginning teachers, too few individual schools do. Principals would do well to provide orientations to the school, fellow teachers, and its resources, expectations, and policies. We know of schools that routinely provide new teachers with a tour of the community that the school serves (this is especially important when many teachers live far away from the school). Being familiar with the neighborhood allows teachers to make their awareness and support for the community evident.

Seeing Teachers as Learners Who Also Need Social Support

Just like students, teachers need to know that they are valued for who they are as well as what they do. New teachers (and those new to the school) will have many personal and professional concerns. Will I fit in? Will you value my teaching? Principals can help teachers work through these issues by creating supportive observation and feedback environments.

The uncertainties inherent in any new job often make performance feedback desirable, as we want to know: How am I doing? Can I get better? How? Most teachers experience a predictable developmental cycle as they enter and move through teaching. In her seminal work, Fuller (1969) demonstrated that beginning teachers were initially swamped by self-concerns—will students listen and obey me? Will I be liked? Only after these concerns were worked through were teachers able to address students' needs more centrally. How can I help them to understand and value the content? Fuller's findings continue to be validated by more recent research. And despite efforts to help alter teacher concerns before they enter the field, such efforts have had little impact. Thus, most teachers have to work through their developmental concerns on the job. Your validation of their concerns (as opposed to dismissing them as relatively immature) may help them to shift their priorities to students more quickly than would be the case without validation.

Often too much is expected of beginning teachers, who from day one are expected to do the same things that teachers with much experience do. Help beginners to know that they are not expected to be experts in all aspects of the job and realize that this belief is maladaptive and unrealistic. And let teachers know that you want to see them doing productive basic lessons when you observe and not complicated project work. Principals should let beginning teachers know that it is good to ask questions and to seek advice and resources. The sooner beginners know that they are not alone the better, because then they can seek feedback about those issues that delay their development. Furthermore, principals should make their interest in beginning teachers very clear from the first day of school—I want you to be successful, my visits to your room are intended to be supportive and helpful, I hope you have a good career with us. And, to reiterate, teachers need to know what they do *well* in addition to what needs to improve.

Clarifying role expectations. Some new teachers have few expectations about their professional relationship with their principals, assistant principals, and other administrators, but some have well-formed expectations that might or might not be accurate. Principals would do well not to rely upon teacher education programs (or other teachers) or previous employers to define the principal-teacher relationship. And since more than a third of "beginners" have previous work experience, another reason to spend time with these teachers is because they may have preexisting notions of how to interact with their supervisors and some of these conceptions might be a misconception in the new setting. Misconceptions are difficult to change; thus, the sooner clarification begins the better. Teachers need principals to provide a clear set of expectations for classroom performance outcomes, how to deal with problems, and how to acquire needed resources. In some schools teachers are encouraged to admit problems and to seek help if they experience problems, but in other schools teachers are expected to solve their own problems. Should teachers seek help from you or from other teachers? Teachers should not be left to wonder about whom to approach about instructional issues. They need to know how to seek help and/or obtain resources that they need to teach effectively.

Furthermore, as discussed in Chapter 4, principals' leadership skills can be described in various ways (e.g., transformational). Share your leadership style with teachers. They need to know how you work to: make the school safe, and support a culture that promotes student progress and the belief that all students can learn. Earlier we provided a list of practices that school leaders could consider in deciding how to allocate their time. In preparing and communicating expectations for teachers, it would be useful for principals to review these practices (e.g., recognizes school accomplishments and failures, establishes clear expectations for teachers and students, possesses clear goals for the school, and so forth). Thus, all teachers should understand the principal's beliefs and practices when the school year begins.

You might also review some of the ideas that we shared in Chapter 3 about appropriate teacher attitudes and your beliefs about a focus on progress (e.g., asking teachers about which students are making the most progress and why). Hopefully you encourage teachers to understand that effective teachers communicate to students their belief that all students can learn and place emphasis upon progress and growth rather than past performance. Furthermore, these positive expectations for student progress should be coupled with the expectation that classrooms should be friendly, recognize students as learners and social beings, and respect the diversity of all cultures that are represented within the classroom.

Observing and Providing Feedback to Teachers: The Formal Observation Cycle

Now that we have provided a summary of important things to do prior to the start of the school year, we discuss what happens during the school year, with a close examination of the formal observation cycle.

The Preobservation Conference

We will assume that prior to the start of the formal observation cycle, you have discussed expectations with teachers and teachers are aware of the observation and feedback processes at the school. We also assume that teachers have established personal goals with you prior to this observation. As part of the preobservation conference, collect relevant artifacts: a lesson plan, information about where the lesson plan fits within a larger unit, and any materials that will be used during the lesson (e.g., assessments, PowerPoints, worksheets). Some questions to guide a preobservation conference include: What will I observe? What are the objectives of the lesson—what do you want students to know when the lesson ends? How will your lesson help all students achieve the objectives? How will you engage students in learning? What will you being doing during the lesson? What will your students being doing? How will you assess student learning during the lesson? Finally, principals might return to goals that were set with the teacher prior to the first formal observation and discuss how lesson components help the teacher to achieve these goals. Principals should ask if the teacher has concerns about particular students or areas of content or instruction.

The Formal Observation

General suggestions. Management is a consideration for all teachers, but we assume most returning teachers have the basics of classroom management down; if not, they can benefit from this feedback as well. Given the problems of observation measures (described ahead), you might want to keep a narrative record that documents what teachers did in the classroom and how well. In addition to your running record of classroom events, you may want to include questions or a checklist as part of your data collections. We will not review all of the material in Chapter 3, but here are a few reminders of important considerations.

Appropriate expectations. Do all students receive and appropriately demanding curriculum? Do teachers emphasize progress? Do teachers emphasize improvement and present performance over past performance? When students make mistakes do teachers encourage them to keep thinking and processing information? Do most students have the opportunity to perform publicly on meaningful tasks?

Supportive classrooms. Do teachers behave in ways that demonstrate that they see students as social beings as well as learners? Do teachers demonstrate affective support and display kind dispositions toward all students? Do teachers demonstrate their respect for students' diversity and do they demonstrate their knowledge of individual students and their awareness of their specific interests?

Effective use of time and opportunity to learn. Earlier when discussing beginning teachers we talked about the importance of starting classes promptly, planning transitions well, and helping students to focus on key ideas. We have seen that opportunity to learn is a powerful predictor of student achievement. Accordingly it is important to determine if teachers present content at the appropriate cognitive level to assure suitable pace and challenge. The expectation literature has illustrated that students believed to be less capable often receive less challenging and interesting content.

Balanced curriculum. Effective instruction includes a balanced curriculum that reflects opportunities for students to learn procedural and conceptual information, and the opportunity to apply information in ways that allow students to understand how their knowledge can be used in completing their work and raising new questions. We do not suggest that every day 50% of the lesson should be spent on procedural knowledge and 50% on conceptual development. Some days, all the time might be spent on developing ideas or on practice and review. We believe that over a learning unit, the goal is to provide opportunities to understand and to apply ideas. What this means in practice varies with student age, the complexity of the content, and whether the information has been studied previously. Clearly this distinction cannot be met in a single observation, but data collected in one observation can lead to productive conversations about balance. "I noticed today that all the time was focused on facts and skill development, and from what I could tell, students found this information useful and they were very involved in the lesson." When and how will students get a chance to use this information?

Review. Good teachers help students to integrate information, and one good way of doing this is to periodically review key concepts and ideas so that students have access to relevant concepts as they address problem situations. For example, it is difficult for students to solve novel problems about how best to use space if students cannot remember key concepts, like how to find area or perimeter. Although the lesson you observe may not involve review, you can talk with teachers about when and how they will review key concepts.

More generally your assessment essentially poses a series of questions, like: Did the lesson start on time? Is there some stated reason about the value and the purpose of the lesson? Does it appear that meaningful content is being presented? Is the management sufficient so that productive discussions can take place? Do students know the important content that they are to learn? And do they have an opportunity to share their thinking with peers and the teacher to receive helpful but supportive feedback? Does the lesson have some sense of continuity and direction (do students understand how this lesson fits in with those that preceded it and that will follow)? Does the teacher (and students) know if lesson content has been understood? We believe that collecting data around framing questions provides the story of the lesson, and its flow often yields richer information for improving teaching than do formal observation systems.

Observing beginning teachers. Given that many beginning teachers need help with classroom management, it makes sense that an early observation and feedback session provides extensive information about how they prevent and respond to problems. How is time used? Do classes start on time? Are there clear transitions between one part of the lesson to the next? Do students know what they should attend to and how they can demonstrate their active participation? We know that efforts to help teachers to use time productively have been consistently associated with good student achievement in many studies. It is especially beneficial to help teachers understand what causes poor time use. Do teachers make students wait unnecessarily as they hand back papers or classroom activity forms? Do some students consistently demand attention? Are teachers' directions insufficient for students to understand how to perform seat work or group work? You provide an important role by helping teachers to know if they use time well, and if not, what they can improve. Again, specific strategies for improvement are needed—e.g., "You failed to check student seat work even though you told them work on your own for 10 minutes and then we'll see how we are doing" is much more helpful than "You used only 20 minutes of allocated time productively."

Good use of time is important because most students want to learn and to participate. Good time management helps students to fulfill their intentions. But minds wander if there are voids in lessons. If lessons fail to start on time, some students start conversations or begin to prepare for other classes. Once students disengage, it takes time to refocus their attention. Critical transitions in lessons occur at two other points: When the teacher moves from a whole-class setting to individual or group work and at the end of the lesson, when some individuals and groups finish before others. Teachers need to be sure that students know what they are to do in seat work activities *before* they are released. As groups or individual students finish seat work, there should be something for them to do. Of course, the ideas we shared earlier for working with teachers apply to beginning teachers as well.

Teachers who serve unique groups of students. If your goal is improved achievement, one good place to start is to improve English Language Learners' (ELLs) test scores. In some RttT states, teachers are grouped by assignment or role. And each role/group has a different teacher evaluation model. In other cases, districts and those responsible for observing and evaluating teachers have the challenging task of determining how special education teachers and ELL specialists are evaluated. Holdheide, Goe, Croft, and Reschly (2010) summarize a number of issues related to this challenge:

1. Most districts use observation instruments adopted by the state. And often because of contractual restrictions, districts may not be permitted to use different instruments to observe teachers who teach unique populations. This position limits the value of feedback.
2. Most commonly used observation instruments claim to assess the needs of diverse learners, but may not do this well, limiting principals' ability to provide helpful, specific, and relevant feedback to teachers (Lavigne & Oberg De La Garza, forthcoming).
3. Special education teachers and ELL specialists are often underqualified, and, hence, may benefit the most from observation and feedback specific to their needs.
4. Schools and districts are held accountable, in part, on the progress of particular student groups. So there is an even greater impetus to find a solution to the challenge of providing feedback to those teaching unique student populations.

There is significant room for improvement in evaluating teachers who serve distinct populations. And in a study of 1,100 state and district directors of special education, half felt that special education teachers should be evaluated differently than other teachers (Holdheide et al., 2010). Data support this claim. Even if districts use statistical models that putatively "correct" for special education students, teachers with more special education students still end up having lower value-added scores than teachers with fewer special education students (McCaffrey & Buzick, 2014). So what can principals do? Depending on the level of flexibility, there are options to consider for supervision.

- Select an entirely different observation instrument.
- Supplement existing observation instrument with additional items.
- Include prompts in the observation narrative.
- Use alternative measures and/or additional artifacts.

Improving instruction for ELLs. We discuss these options in this context of ELL specialists or general education teachers who teach a majority of these students. Application of suggestions we note ahead are based on the assumptions that: (1) some knowledge of effective teacher practices exists for these teachers, and (2) observers possess this knowledge to provide useful feedback. Understand that the effective teaching literature for ELL teachers is less developed than that for general practices (see Chapter 3). If administrators are not knowledgeable about ELLs, this provides an ideal opportunity to involve observers with relevant expertise.

Earlier we discussed CRT considerations for thinking about the needs of culturally and linguistically diverse learners and described six considerations for classroom instruction (López, 2014). Applying those six considerations when supervising teachers of ELLs, observers should look for evidence that teachers: (1) hold high academic expectations for students; (2) acknowledge the worth of the cultural heritage of every student; (3) use students' culture and preferences for planning and implementing instruction; (4) include cultural information, resources, and materials across all subjects; (5) incorporate home experiences into the curriculum; and (6) use students' native language.

Pulling from the work of López and others, Lavigne and Oberg De La Garza (forthcoming) have coupled CRT with research-based literacy practices to create questions for principals to use during observations. Given the focus on literacy, these questions can be used across subject areas to provide feedback to teachers. When conducting a preconference, observers might ask: Does the lesson plan reflect the use of texts (for both the teacher and students) in English and students' native language(s)? Does the lesson plan address equity or diversity? Does the lesson plan include the use of multicultural literature when modeling research-based literacy strategies? Does the lesson plan scaffold goals with student knowledge in ways that support student academic success? During the observation, the observer may want to determine: Does the teacher express high expectations for reading, writing, and speaking in English and native language(s)? Does the teacher attend to students' language interaction patterns, in general, and as culturally embedded? (See Lavigne and Oberg De La Garza, forthcoming, for a full list and a supplementary rubric.) Beyond these suggestions, readers can visit the Classroom Qualities for English Language Leaners in Language Arts Instruction website (https://people.stanford.edu/claudeg/cqell/about), which includes an observation instrument that describes both generic and ELL-specific practices in elementary classrooms (Goldenberg, Haertel, Coleman, Reese, & Rodriguez-Mojica, 2013).

Postobservation Conference and Providing Feedback to Teachers

Feedback. Educators consistently tout the salubrious effects of feedback and for good reason. Hattie (1999) synthesized the effect sizes of feedback on *student* achievement in nearly 180,000 studies. The average effect of feedback on achievement was .79, ranking it in the top five of ten highest influences on achievement outcomes—larger than socioeconomic status (.44) and school (.40). In short, *feedback can be powerful*.

But realize that, although the powerful effects of teacher feedback on students have been well documented, the effects of principal feedback on teacher performance have received little research attention. Recall we summarized research on teacher change and found that teachers can change their practices following feedback, but few studies described those feedback characteristics that promoted improvement. Even less is known about feedback effects on teacher effectiveness and student achievement. So we look elsewhere. Cross-disciplinary research on feedback illustrates a complicated process, including significant interactions between subsequent performance and direction of feedback (e.g., positive, negative), content of feedback (e.g., goal, task), and other variables, including the recipient's self-esteem. For example, when the complexity of the activity is low, positive feedback does not improve performance, and negative feedback increases performance only slightly. But when the task is highly complex (like most activities in teaching), positive feedback is related to improvement, yet negative feedback does little to alter performance. And in one-third of studies on feedback, feedback actually *lowered* performance (Kluger & DeNisi, 1998)! And, inaccurate feedback does more damage than no feedback. We stress that the literature on feedback is large, diverse, and often contradictory. We present only a few promising considerations that emerge from this complicated literature.

Hattie and Timperly (2007) provide a good guide for thinking about how to provide feedback. First, does feedback contain *feed-up*? Is the teacher asked: What [are your] goals? What are you hoping to accomplish by the end of the year? When feedback is goal-directed, teachers are often more responsive to positive feedback and change is more sustaining. What is the *feedback* process? What progress is being made? How are data shared with teachers? And third is *feed-forward*: What activities will enable progress? Ahead we consider other characteristics that influence the effectiveness of feedback.

Characteristics of effective feedback. Table 5.2 provides a list of characteristics of effective feedback and related questions that feedback providers can consider as they plan teacher feedback.

TABLE 5.2 Selected Characteristics of Effective Feedback

- **Source.** Is feedback provided by multiple sources? Is one source of feedback teachers' own ratings of self? Feedback provided in consultation (discussing feedback with the teacher versus providing only a written summary) with self-reflection supports cognitive dissonance and a focus on problem solving (Brinko, 1990), and helps establish the feedback provider as supportive (Friedkin & Slater, 1994).
- **Accurate and Persuasive.** Is there clear evidence to support the feedback? Global rubrics that seek to rate effective instruction may be perceived as subjective even if observers have been trained. Observers need to provide justification for a given score and have evidence to explain why the teacher was not rated differently.
- **Specific and Concrete.** Is feedback specific? Does it possess informational value? Comments such as "nice lesson" or "poor classroom management" do little to help a teacher understand exactly what about these areas of instruction were done well, giving teachers no means for improvement (Brinko, 1990).
- **Models.** Can the feedback provider model appropriate behavior for the teacher? The power of models has been known for some time (Bandura, Ross, & Ross, 1961). It is helpful if the feedback provider is skilled enough to model these behaviors, and if not, is able to suggest colleagues who can.
- **Task and Feedback Properties.** Teaching is complex and some practices are inherently easier than others. But it is easier to use feedback for improvement when tasks are perceived as simple (or actually are simple). And feedback that is simple is easier to process and act upon rather than complex feedback (Hattie & Timperly, 2007). This is a particularly important practice to enact with beginning or struggling teachers, who may be more likely to perceive tasks as complex (Kluger & DeNisi, 1996).
- **Focus.** Does the feedback address individual improvement or comparative data? Performance data on individual past performance demonstrating growth over time is motivating and likely to increase performance, whereas comparative data decreases performance (DeNisi & Kluger, 2000).
- **Timing.** Most feedback should be provided as soon as possible after performance, particularly if the feedback is positive (Brinko, 1990). Negative feedback is more effective when provided with a slight delay and when opportunity to demonstrate improvement is on the horizon (a second observation soon follows).
- **Feed-forward.** Hattie and Timperley (2007) and Kluger and DeNisi (1998) suggest that there will be limited performance gains if feedback does not provide a means for improvement. Good feedback provides information about *how* to improve instruction.
- **Direction and Amount of Negative/Positive Feedback.** Negative feedback is more potent than positive feedback (Baumeister, Bratslavsky, Finkenauer, & Vohs, 2001; Hattie & Timperly, 2007). That is not to say that principals can get a bigger bang for their buck using negative feedback. Instead, principals should look to achieve an appropriate balance with the following points in mind:
  - Even a small amount of negative feedback may swamp positive feedback.
  - Negative feedback is more likely to be rejected as individuals seek to protect their egos and confirm their self-efficacy beliefs.
  - Negative feedback is more likely to be recalled inaccurately.
  - Administrators should be careful about how much negative feedback is provided in one feedback session.

Characteristics of the feedback recipient. We highlight three considerations when planning for the individual who will receive the feedback. As noted earlier, in best conditions, teachers want feedback. But teacher evaluation is not voluntary, so we should assume that not all teachers care about what a principal, peer, or coach have to say about their instruction (Brinko, 1990). The ability for feedback to motivate change may be determined, in part, by the teacher's *receptiveness*. Second, much research has shown how teachers move through *stages of development* and gain *experience* as they move through their careers. Understanding where the teacher is in his or her career trajectory may help situate the feedback effectively (Brinko, 1990). Lastly is the consideration of *self-efficacy*. Teachers with low self-efficacy may wonder if they can do what is requested. Low self-efficacious teachers often respond to negative feedback with negative affect and reduced motivation, and see the negative feedback as a reflection of ability (e.g., they cannot teach well) (Hattie & Timperly, 2007). High self-efficacious teachers respond well to most feedback because they believe they *can* improve.

Thus when providing feedback to teachers you need to consider both the feedback mechanisms you control (e.g., timing, mode, direction, content) and the recipient's personal attributes (e.g., self-efficacy, goals, developmental stage) in order to create good conditions for effective feedback—feedback that can improve teaching and learning.

Making feedback relate to the big picture as well as specific lesson details. Although feedback about the observed lesson is critically important, feedback conversations with teachers need to involve more than just a discussion of the observed lesson. Conversations about what preceded and will follow are often good places to ensure that balance, coherence, and a range of student outcomes are being addressed. How will tomorrow's lesson differ from today's and why? What is the most important content that students were expected to learn in this unit? To what extent did students understand the content and how do you know? Will you review today's material in upcoming lessons? Often several students do not understand a lesson, but whether teachers understand this varies widely. It is not necessarily a problem if several students are confused when the lesson ends, but it is a major problem if the teacher does not know this. In a sense, as a teacher of teachers, you are reminding teachers that learning is not always linear or successful and that some lessons go better than others. However, it is critical to understand when concepts need to be retaught.

Conclusion

Considering the busy lives of principals, in this chapter we provided principals with strategies about how to manage and protect their time for supervision. Like teachers, principals make hundreds of decisions every day—some more difficult than others. We provided a number of considerations that principals can use when making decisions related to supervision: Who should I observe first? Should I use additional observers? We then offered specific guidelines to assist principals in conducting pre- and postobservation conferences and observations, with a focus on beginning teachers and those who teach ELLs. We chose these two groups of teachers because they could benefit enormously from additional support because in some cases they may lack experience or adequate preparation, or be underserved by commonly used observation instruments. Our overarching goal was to provide helpful information given that observation instruments often fail to provide important means for improving instruction.

We want to end with noting that we sympathize with those who are assigned the task of observing and providing teachers with feedback as it is a daunting task and even more daunting if one wants to do the task well. We hope that this book offers strategies and tools to help administrators and others to manage the tasks of observing and providing feedback to teachers as well as encourages all to engage in continued research on these topics, so that we can offer even more support for an administrative practice that will likely stick around regardless of reforms that continue to come and go.

References

Bandura, A., Ross, D., & Ross, S.A. (1961). Transmission of aggression through the imitation of aggressive models. *Journal of Abnormal and Social Psychology, 63*, 575–502.

Baumeister, R.F., Bratslavsky, E., Finkenauer, C., & Vohs, K.D. (2001). Bad is stronger than good. *Review of General Psychology, 5*(4), 323–370.

Bell, C.A., Q, Y., Croft, A.J., Leusner, D., McCaffrey, D.F., Gitomer, D.H., & Pianta, R.C. (2014). Improving observational score quality: Challenges in observer thinking. In T.J. Kane, K.A. Kerr, & R.C. Pianta (Eds.), *Designing teacher evaluation systems: New7 guidance from the Measures of Effective Teaching Project* (pp. 50–97). San Francisco, CA: Jossey-Bass.

Bill & Melinda Gates Foundation. (2013). *Ensuring fair and reliable measures of effective teaching: Culminating findings from the MET project's three-year study*. Retrieved from www.metproject.org/downloads/MET_Ensuring_Fair_and_Reliable_Measures_Practitioner_Brief.pdf

Brinko, K.T. (1990). *Optimal conditions for effective feedback*. Paper presented at the Annual Meeting of the American Educational Research Association. Boston, MA.

Britton, E., Paine, L., & Raizen, S. (1999). *Middle grades mathematics and science teacher induction in selected countries: Preliminary findings*. Washington, DC: National Center for Improving Science Education. WestEd.

DeNisi, A.S., & Kluger, A.N. (2000). Feedback effectiveness: Can 360-degree appraisals be improved? *Academy of Management Executive, 14*, 129–139.

Friedkin, N.E., & Slater, M.R. (1994). School leadership and performance: A social network approach. *Sociology of Education, 67*, 139–157.

Fuller, F. (1969). Concerns of teachers: A developmental conceptualization. *American Educational Research Journal, 6*, 207–226.

Goldenberg, C., Haertel, E., Coleman, R., Reese, L., & Rodriguez-Mojica, C. (2013). *Classroom qualities for English Language Learners in language arts instruction: Technical report*. Retrieved from https://people.stanford.edu/claudeg/cqell/about

Hattie, J. (1999). *Influences on student learning*. University of Auckland. Retrieved from https://cdn.auckland.ac.nz/assets/education/about/research/documents/influences-on-student-learning.pdf

Hattie, J., & Timperly, H. (2007). The power of feedback. *Review of Educational Research, 77*, 81–112.

Holdheide, L.R., Goe, L., Croft, A., & Reschly, D.J. (2010). *Challenges in evaluating special education teachers and English Language Learner specialists*. Research and policy brief prepared for the National Comprehensive Center for Teacher Quality. Retrieved from www.gtlcenter.org/sites/default/files/docs/July2010Brief.pdf

Huling-Austin, L. (1986). What can and cannot reasonably be expected from teacher induction programs? *Journal of Teacher Education, 27*, 2–5.

Johnson, S. (2004). *Finders and keepers: Helping new teachers survive and thrive in our schools.* San Francisco: Jossey-Bass.

Kluger, A. N., & DeNisi, A. (1996). The effects of feedback interventions on performance: A historical review, a meta-analysis, and a preliminary feedback intervention theory. *Psychological Bulletin, 119,* 254–284.

Kluger, A. N., & DeNisi, A. (1998). Feedback interventions: Toward the understanding of a double-edged sword. *Current Directions in Psychological Science, 7,* 67–72.

Lavigne, A. L., & Chamberlain, R. (2014, January). *Coping with increased demands for teacher evaluation: School leaders' perceptions of problems and possibility.* Invited paper presented at Using Observational and Student Achievement Data to Improve Teaching. Tucson, AZ.

Lavigne, A., & Good, T. (2014). *Teacher and student evaluation: Moving beyond the failure of school reform.* New York: Routledge.

Lavigne, A.L., & Oberg De La Garza, T. (forthcoming). The practice and evaluation of culturally responsive literacy for English Language Learners in the 21st century. Invited chapter in R. Allington and R. Gabriel (Eds.), *Evaluating literacy instruction: Principles and promising practices.*

López, F. (2014, April). *Addressing the need for explicit evidence on the role of culturally responsive teaching and achievement among Latino youth: Preliminary findings for the Spencer/National Academy of Education Postdoctoral Fellowship.* Poster presented at the 2014 annual meeting of the American Educational Research Association. Philadelphia, PA.

McCaffrey, D.F., & Buzick, H. (2014, January 14). Is value-added accurate for teachers of students with disabilities? Carnegie Knowledge Network. Retrieved from www.carnegieknowledgenetwork.org/briefs/teacher_disabilities/#footnote-15

Veenman, S. (1984). Perceived problems of beginning teachers. *Review of Educational Research, 54*(2), 143–178.

Whitehurst, G., Chingos, M., & Lindquist, K. (2014). *Evaluating teachers with classroom observations: Lessons learned in four districts.* Brown Center on Education Policy at the Brookings Institution. Retrieved from www.brookings.edu/research/reports/2014/05/13-teacher-evaluation-whitehurst-chingos

APPENDIX A

Principals' Time Use Categories

Administration	Organizational management	Day-to-day instruction	Instructional program	Internal relations	External relations
Fulfilling compliance	Managing budgets, resources	Informally coaching teachers to improve instruction	Developing an educational program across the school	Developing relationships with students	Working with local community members or organizations
Managing school schedules	Dealing with concerns from teachers	Formally evaluating teachers	Evaluating curriculum	Interacting socially with staff about school-related topic	Fundraising
Preparing and implementing standardized tests	Maintaining campus facilities	Conducting classroom observations	Planning professional development for teachers	Attending school activities	Communicating with the district office to obtain resources (initiated by principal)
Supervising students	Developing and monitoring a safe school environment	Using data to inform instruction	Planning or directing additional or after school instruction	Counseling students and/or parents	Utilizing district office communication (initiated by district)

Source: Adapted from Horng et al. (2010).

APPENDIX B

What Is an Effect Size?

As noted, we want to avoid as much technical detail as possible in the text. But we want to underscore the value of effect sizes as these are noted in several chapters. In implementing a reading intervention, for example, calculating both significance and effect sizes can help practitioners decide both if the intervention worked and how well. Significance helps determine if the intervention worked and is determined by the probability that the finding is due to chance (and not a real difference). If we use the common alpha level of .05, a significant finding essentially means there is a 5% or less chance that the differences in the reading intervention and control group were due to chance and not the intervention. An effect size tells us how well the intervention worked—the magnitude of the difference. A reading intervention with a large effect size would suggest a stark difference between a student who participated in an intervention and one who did not. Although an intervention could result in significant differences, the size of the effect on reading achievement might not warrant allocating significant funds to school-wide implementation. This is precisely why effect sizes are so important to calculate and use. But we should caution readers. Effect sizes should be considered in context—sometimes effect sizes that would be considered small (.2 or .3) may equate to a difference that might push a school from an average category to distinguished. In short, a small effect may be very meaningful for one school and not so much for another.

APPENDIX C
Students' Perceptions of Teacher Care

Garza (2009) found that students' perceptions yielded five themes. The first and most frequently mentioned was the teacher provision of **scaffolding** instruction. Garza noted, "The scaffolding practices ensure a process to assist students who might be timid or embarrassed to ask for help during instruction" (p. 312). Second, teachers exhibited a **kind disposition**. Students made comments like "She jokes around with us," "She is always nice to me," and "She teaches you like if she were your friend." Third, the teacher was always **available** to students. Fourth, teachers showed a **personal interest** in students with questions like "How's your day been?" and "Where have you been—we've missed you," and general questions about hobbies. Fifth, teachers provided **affective academic support**. This theme included teacher actions that express concerns when students have academic difficulty, but also convey to students that they will do whatever is necessary to help them. Students reported teachers indicated academic support through responses such as "She talks to me about how I can get a good grade in her class," "Whenever I forget an assignment, she gives me a chance to bring it in."

APPENDIX D

Description of the Tripod Survey Components (7 C's)

Construct	Examples
Captivate	Schoolwork is interesting; homework is interesting.
Care	I like the way my teacher treats me when I need help; the teacher encourages me to do my best.
Challenge	My teacher pushes everybody to work hard; in this class, we have to think hard about the writing we do.
Clarify	My teacher explains difficult things clearly; in class, we learn to correct our mistakes.
Confer	My teacher tells us what we are learning and why; my teacher wants us to share our thoughts.
Consolidate	My teacher takes time to summarize what we learn; when my teacher marks my work, he/she writes on my papers to help me understand.
Control	My classmates behave the way my teacher wants them to; our class stays busy and does not waste time.

Source: Adapted from Raudenbush and Jean (2014).

APPENDIX E

Research-Based Principal Practices and Characteristics Related to Student Achievement Outcomes

---

1. Defines and communicates mission and vision (Witziers et al., 2003)
2. Is visible (Waters et al., 2004; Witziers et al., 2003)
3. Monitors (Waters et al., 2004; Witziers et al., 2003)
4. Supervises, evaluates, and coaches (Grissom et al., 2013; Waters et al., 2004; Witziers et al. 2003)
5. Meets with teachers to discuss students' needs (Shatzer et al., 2013)
6. Discusses performance results with teachers and students (Shatzer et al., 2013)
7. Limits possible interruptions on classroom instruction (Waters et al., 2004; Shatzer et al., 2013)
8. Encourages teachers to use classroom time effectively (Shatzer et al., 2013)
9. Establishes clear expectations, recognitions, and awards for teachers and students (Waters et al., 2004; Shatzer et al., 2013)
10. Plays a strong role in developing the school's educational program (Grissom et al., 2013)
11. Maintains campus facilities, manages budget, and develops a safe school environment (Grissom & Loeb, 2011)
12. Inspires and leads innovation (Kythreotis et al., 2010; Waters et al., 2004)
13. Is committed (Kythreotis et al., 2010)
14. Is aware of school functions and issues, and anticipates problems (Waters et al., 2004)
15. Keeps faculty up-to-date with current effective practices (Waters et al., 2004)
16. Challenges the status quo and engages in systematic improvement and reflection on ways of doing (Waters et al., 2004)
17. Involves teachers and staff in school decisions and policies (Waters et al., 2004)
18. Builds shared beliefs and sense of community, and supports cooperation (Waters et al., 2004)
17. Advocates for the school (Waters et al., 2004)
18. Maintains consistent operations and routines related to structure, rules, faculty, staff, and students (Waters et al., 2004)
19. Provides teachers with resources (Waters et al., 2004)

(Continued)

20. Recognizes school accomplishments and failures (Waters et al., 2004)
21. Holds strong ideals and beliefs about schooling (Waters et al., 2004)
22. Possesses clear goals for student, faculty, and staff school operations and instruction (Waters et al., 2004)
23. Stays up-to-date with recent curriculum, instruction, and assessment practices (Waters et al., 2004)
24. Maintains strong communication with teachers, students, and staff (Waters et al., 2004)
25. Adapts leadership (Waters et al., 2004)
26. Develops personal relationships with faculty and staff (Waters et al., 2004)
27. Involved in curriculum, instruction, and assessment design and implementation (Waters et al., 2004)

APPENDIX F

Findings from Waters et al. (2004): Effective Principal Practices

Responsibility	*Description*	*Average r*
Situational awareness	Aware of school functions, issues, anticipates problems	0.33
Intellectual stimulation	Keeps faculty and staff up-to-date with current effective practices	0.32
Change agent	Challenges the status quo, systematic improvement and reflection on ways of doing	0.30
Input	Involves teachers and staff in school decisions and policies	0.30
Culture	Shared beliefs (e.g., school vision), sense of community, cooperation	0.29
Monitors/evaluates	Monitors effectiveness	0.28
Outreach	Advocates for school	0.28
Order	Consistent operations and routines (e.g., structure, rules, and procedures)	0.26
Resource	Provides teachers with resources (e.g., equipment, professional development)	0.26
Affirmation	Recognizes school accomplishments and failures	0.25
Ideals/beliefs	Holds strong ideals and beliefs about schooling	0.25
Discipline	Protects teachers from instructional distractions	0.24
Focus	Clear goals for student, faculty, staff, and school operations and instruction	0.24
Knowledge of curriculum, instruction, and assessment	Up-to-date with recent curriculum, instruction, and assessment practices	0.24
Communication	Strong communication with teachers, students, and staff	0.23

(Continued)

Responsibility	Description	Average r
Flexibility	Adapts leadership	0.22
Optimizer	Inspires and leads innovation	0.20
Relationship	Develops personal relationships with faculty and staff	0.19
Curriculum, instruction, and assessment	Involved in curriculum, instruction, and assessment design and implementation	0.16
Visibility	Frequent contact with teachers and students	0.16
Contingent rewards	Recognizes and rewards accomplishments	0.15

APPENDIX G

Using Data to Make Instructional Decisions

The biggest problem with using results from standardized achievement tests to improve instruction is the lack of specificity that these tests provide about concepts that students have and have not mastered. Consider that a student or a class receives a score of minimally sufficient in mathematics. The teacher knows that the student or class has not mastered all content and concepts in order to be proficient. Unfortunately, the test score does not tell us if students are deficient in doing problems involving division with remainders, multiplying fractions, converting decimals to percent, or understanding proportional reasoning.

Test report data vary by specificity, but most of them are fairly general. For example, the math achievement test used by the State of Arizona at the seventh-grade reports data at a very general level, such as number sense, numerical operations, estimation, data analysis (statistics), probability, discrete mathematics, and so forth. However, the content topics within a category are wide. For example, number sense includes ways of representing numbers, the relationships among numbers and different number systems, and the concept of understanding and applying numbers. Thus, data reports do not provide clear, specific information to teachers about the content that students have and have not learned.

In contrast, tests used to gauge student progress during the school year can yield decision-making information about content and concepts that need more work. The rub is that in high-stakes teacher evaluations policy makers do not accept progress on these tests as legitimate evidence that students are proficient, even though these tests provide evidence about how students have performed on particular content items. Clearly, with a lot of work, some usable information can be obtained, but we feel that this is not an area of high productivity for most principals—it is probably better to delegate this task to others.

INDEX

Note: Page numbers with *f* indicate figures; those with *t* indicate tables.

academic support, teachers and 148
adaption activities, as school function 9, 10–11*t*
alignment, effective teaching and 51–2
Allensworth, E. 105
American Federation of Teachers (AFT) 52
American Statistical Association (ASA) 53
Anh Le, P.T. 113
antecedent effects model, on student learning 106
antecedent plus mediated variables effects model, principal leadership 104
anti-value-added measures (VAM) 52–3
Apfel, N. 81
appropriate expectations, expressing 68–9
Ashton, P. 69
Au, K. 82
availability, of teachers 148

Banks, J. 82
Barton, P.E. 80
basic antecedent effects model, principal leadership 104
basic direct effects model, principal leadership 104
Beckerman, T. 89
beginning teachers: audit of 130–1; principal's help for 131–2
behavior and teacher expectations, changing 70

belonging, students' need for 79
Biddle, B. 63
Bill & Melinda Gates Foundation 93
Blase, J. 116–17, 117*t*, 118
Bocian, K. 85, 86
Borman, G. 81
Bowling Alone (Putnam) 76
Brattesani, K. 70
Brophy, J. 7, 64, 66–7, 70–1, 75–6, 77, 78, 92, 93
Burch, S. 81

Camburn, E.M. 15
capacity, reforms and 48–9
Cardullo, R. 85, 86
Carnegie Foundation for the Advancement of Teaching 55
Causal Teacher Evaluation Model 39
Cazden, C. 82
Chamberlain, R. 44
Chetty, R. 36
Chingos, M. 72
clarity, good teaching and 65*t*, 92–3
Classroom Assessment Scoring System (CLASS) 39, 84–5
classroom management 94
Classroom Qualities for English Language Leaners in Language Arts Instruction 138–9

Cohen, G. 81
Coley, R.J. 80
Common Core 21
complexity, principalship and 20–1
Comprehensive School Reform (CSR) Act 7–8
conceptual knowledge, good teaching and 65t, 90–1
constructive evaluation 52
content integration 82
Conto, H. 114
Corno, L. 78, 79
Crawford, G. 9
Croft, A. 137
Cruickshank, D. 92
culturally relevant teaching (CRT) 82–4
curriculum pace, good teaching and 65t, 89

Danielson, C. 94
Darling-Hammond, L. 64
Dee, T. 45–7
Delpit, L. 73
direct effects, principals, on student achievement 104–5
Duffet, A. 108
Duffy, G. 112
Dumler, C. 40
Duncan, A. 34
Dunkin, M. 63

Ebmeier, H. 9
Eccles, J. 70
Edmonds, R. 7
education reform: history of 31–3; math-science crisis and 32; *A Nation at Risk* and 32; No Child Left Behind (NCLB) and 32; overview 31; *Prisoners of Time* and 32; similarities of 32–3; trends that characterize 33; *see also* Race to the Top (RttT)
effect size 64, 68, 147
Emmer, E. 91
emotional support, for students 84–6, 148
empowering school/societal cultures 82
English Language Learners (ELL) 47, 84; instruction for, improving 138–9; test scores, improving 137
enthusiasm, good teaching and 65t, 92–3
equity pedagogy 82
evaluators, teacher 42–3
Evertson, C. 91
expectancy effects 48

Farkas, S. 108
feedback: conversations, content of 141; effective, characteristics of 112–13, 139, 140t; in-service 114–15; postobservation conference and teacher 139–41; preservice 113–14; principal 115–18, 117t; recipient, characteristics of 140–1
Ferguson, R. 94
Firestone, W. 7
formal observation cycle 134–41: appropriate expectations 135; balanced curriculum 135–6; beginning teachers, observing 136–7; English Language Learners and 138–9; general suggestions 135; postobservation conference 139–41; preobservation conference 134–5; reviews 136; student groups, unique 137–8; supportive classrooms 135; time use 135; *see also* feedback
formal type of observation 40
Framework for Teaching, Danielson's 39, 94, 125
Freiberg, H. 91, 113
Frey, W. 82
Friedman, J.N. 36
Fuller, F. 133

Gamoran, A. 81
Garcia, J. 81
Garet, M.S. 111
Garza, R. 85, 86, 148
Georgia's Department of Education 44
goal attainment, as school function 9, 10–11t
Goe, L. 137
Good, T. 7, 25, 50, 64, 66–7, 68, 70–1, 75–6, 77, 78, 89, 90, 92
good teaching 63–95: active teaching and 65t; clarity/enthusiasm and, teacher 65t, 92–3; coherent curriculum in sequence and 65t; instructional curriculum pace and 65t, 89; knowledge and, balance procedural and conceptual 65t, 90–1; literature on, teacher expectation 87–8; Measures of Effective Teaching (MET) Project and 93–4; opportunity to learn and 65t, 89–90; proactive management and 65t, 91–2; research-based considerations for 65–6, 65t; research on 63–4; review

and 65t, 93; student learning effects of 64; students as social beings and 65t, 76–86; subject matter knowledge and 65t, 92; teacher expectations and 65t, 66–76; teaching to mastery and 65t; time use and 65t, 88–9
Great Teachers and Leaders 34, 36–7, 37t
"greening" of teacher workforce 26–7, 28, 47
Grissom, J.A. 17–18, 18t, 19
Grouws, D. 89, 90
Guskey, T.R. 110–11, 120

Hallinger, P. 106
halo effects 128
Hammond, K. 85, 86
Hamre, B. 84
Hanselman, P. 81
Harris, A.H. 113
Hart, A.W. 104, 105
Hattie, J. 139
Hawthorne effects 48
Hernandez, R. 109
Hess, F.M. 108
Hiebert, J. 90
high expectations 68
Hill, H.C. 35, 50–1
Hines, C. 92
Holdheide, L. R. 137
Horng, E. 15, 16, 16t, 17, 107
Houston, W.R. 113
Huling-Austin, L. 131
Hutchinson, L. 78
Huzinec, C. 91

indirect effects, principals, on student learning 105
Ingersoll, R. 26
instructional behavior, teacher expectations and 66–8, 67t
instructional conferences, improving instruction with 118–20; issues with 120; overview of 118–19; responding to poor performance 119
instructional pace, good teaching and 65t, 89
instructional support, for students 84
instruction time use, principal 18t
integration, as school function 9, 10–11t

Jackson, P. 77
Jean, M. 94
Jensen, B. 85
job satisfaction, principals and 21
Johnson, J. 108

Johnson, S. 130
Jordan, C. 82
Journal of Curriculum and Supervision 115
Jussim, L. 70

Kafka, J. 19
Kapitula, L. R. 35
Kelly, A.P. 108
Kennedy, J. 92
Kennedy, M.M. 120
kind disposition, teachers and 148
Klasik, D. 15, 107
Kleinfeld, J. 77
Kmetz, J. 13–15, 14t, 19
knowledge, good teaching and 65t, 90–1
knowledge construction 82
Konstantopoulos, S. 36, 54, 64
Kounin, J.S. 77, 91
Kyriakides, L. 105
Kythreotis, A. 105

Ladson-Billings, G. 82, 83
La Paro, K. 84
Lavigne, A. L. 27, 44, 50, 79–80, 138
Leach, D.J. 114
Leadership Standards, Denver Public Schools 5–6t
leadership style, principal effects and 7–8, 106–9
Lee, M. 106
Le Fevre, M. 119
Leggett, E. 82
LeMire, S.D. 109
Levine, A. 108
Lewis, J. 85, 86
Life in Classrooms (Jackson) 77
Lindquist, K. 72
Litke, E. 35
Lloyd, C.A. 106–7
Loeb, S. 15, 17–18, 18t, 19, 107
López, F. 83, 138
low-achieving students, teachers' attitudes toward 74–6
low-income schools: principalship and 23–6, 24t; teacher ratings and 24t

Madon, S. 70
maintenance activities, as school function 9, 10–11t
Marana Unified School District (MUSD) teacher effectiveness example 40–1
Marshall, H. 70
Martin, W.J. 12–13, 19

Martinez, C. 7
Marx, R. 26–7
Marzano, R.J. 107
Master, A. 81
Master, B. 17–18, 18*t*, 19
math-science crisis, education reform and 32
McCaslin, M. 25, 79
McNulty, B. 107
Measures of Effective Teaching (MET) Project 23, 35, 51; good teaching findings of 93–4
Meckler, L. 82
Menchaca, V. 109
Merrill, L. 26
MetLife Foundation survey 20; *see also* principalship, issues characterizing
Model of Teacher Change 110–11
multicultural education, characteristics of 82

National Center for Education Statistics, Schools and Staffing Survey 4
National Commission on Excellence in Education 32
National Education Association 52, 53
National Education Commission on Time and Learning 32
A Nation at Risk (National Commission on Excellence in Education) 32
Nichols, S. 76
No Child Left Behind (NCLB) 32
Noddings, N. 79

Oberg De La Garza, T. 79–80, 83, 138
observation instruments: formal type of 40; as measure of teacher effectiveness 39–40; principalship and 22–3; problems of 22–3; walk-throughs as 39–40
observers, teacher 42–3, 128–30
Ogawa, R.T. 104, 105
Oliver, W.T. 116
Osterman, K. 79
overlapping behavior 13

Padilla, M.J. 114
Pareja, A.S. 15
Parsons, T. 9
Pashiardis, P. 105
peer review and assistance (PAR) 42–3
Perry, N.E. 78
personal interest, teachers and 148
Peterson, E. 68, 71–2
Phillips, L. 78
Pianta, R. 84
placebo effects 48

polychronics 13
poor performance, responding to 119
postobservation conference, teacher 139–41
poverty *see* low-income schools
prejudice reduction 82
preobservation conference, teacher 134–5
preparation programs, principal 108–9
principal effects, on student learning 103–9; antecedent 106; context and 105; direct 104–5; indirect 105; leadership style and 106–9; overview of 103–4; practices and 107–8, 152–3; preparation programs and 108–9
principal practice, school achievement and 107–8
principal preparation programs 108–9
principals: characteristics of 2–4, 3*t* (*see also* principalship, issues characterizing); classroom observation questions for 74; influence of job conditions by 4*t*; instruction time use 18*t*; job satisfaction and 21; overview of 1–2; proscribed activities for 7; roles of 5–6*t*, 5–8; salaries of 3, 4*t*; tasks of 8–9, 10–11*t*, 12, 16*t*; teacher expectation literature and 87–8; time allocation for 12–19; time use categories 15, 146; *see also* student achievement, improving teaching and
principals, considerations for: additional observers and 128–30; context/resources for teacher supervision 127–8, 127*t*; overview of 125–6; role expectations, clarifying 133–4; supportive observation/feedback environments, creating 132–4; teacher observation, order of 130–2; time management and 126–8; *see also* feedback; formal observation cycle
principalship, issues characterizing 19–27; complexity 20–1; greening of teacher workforce 26–7; job satisfaction 21; in low-income schools 23–6, 24*t*; observation instruments 22–3; overview of 19; stress 20–1; student diversity 21–2
Prisoners of Time (National Education Commission on Time and Learning) 32
proactive management, good teaching and 65*t*, 91–2
problem conceptualization, poor 44–5
procedural knowledge, good teaching and 65*t*, 90–1

process of teacher change 110–11, 110f
professional development (PD), teacher change and 104, 111–12
Project STAR 36
Purkey, S.C. 7
Putnam, R.D. 76

Race to the Top (RttT) 8, 21; capacity issues with 48–9; evaluation and, teacher 34; higher stakes and 45–8; identifying teacher and leader effectiveness 36–7, 37t; improvement, measuring 55; lessons learned from 43–52; measures of teacher effectiveness in 38–43; opposition toward 52–5; overview of 33–4; principals as observers and 49–51; problem conceptualization and 44–5; quality and, teacher 34–5; teacher effects and, capturing 35–6; Tucson Unified School District example 38–9, 39f; see also teacher effectiveness, measures of
Ramirez, D. 85
Raudenbush, S. 53, 94
Ream, R. 85, 86
Reese, L. 85
Reschly, D.J. 137
research on effective teaching 63–95; instructional behaviors 65t; overview of 63–4; student learning and 64; students, as social beings and 76–86; teacher expectations and 66–76; see also good teaching
review frequently, as good teaching 65t, 93
Reyes, M. 84, 85–6
rigor, RttT interpretation of 38
Roberts, M. 109
Robinson, V. 119
Robinson, V. M.J. 106–7
Rochler, L. 112
Rockoff, J.E. 36
Rohrkemper, M. 78, 79
Rosenholtz, S. 35
Rosenshine, B. 93
Rosenthal, R. 68, 71–2
Ross, L. 81
Rowe, K.J. 106–7
Rubie-Davies, C.M. 68, 71–2
Ruzek, E.A. 23

Sass, T. 25
scaffolding practices 85, 148
schools: effective 7, 8–9; functions of 9
Sebastian, J. 105

self-regulated learning (SRL) 78
7 C's survey instrument 94, 149
Sherman, L. 1–2
Short, E.C. 115
Sibley, C. 68, 71–2
simple indirect model, principal leadership 104
Smith, B. 88–9
Smith, M.S. 7
social beings, students as see students, as social beings
Spillane, J.P. 15
Stallings Observation System (SOS) 113
Steele, C. 80–1
Stein, M.K. 110
stress, principalship and 20–1
Strong, M. 49, 50, 85
student achievement: data, as teacher evaluation component 41; instructional behaviors associated with 65t; outcomes, characteristics related to 150–1; teacher expectations and 70
student achievement, improving teaching and: instructional conferences 118–20; principals role 103–9; teacher change 109–18, 120; see also principal effects, on student learning
student diversity, principalship and 21–2
student groups, teacher communication with 68
student learning: teacher effects on 64; teacher expectations for 65t, 66–76
student progress, teachers and 75
students, as social beings 65t, 76–86; belonging needs and 79; culturally relevant teaching (CRT) and 82–4; described 76; emotional teacher support for 84–6; history of research on 76–8; instructional/emotional teacher support for 84; recognizing 78–9; students of color and 80–2; teacher caring and 79–80
students of color, as social beings 80–2
study of teaching 63
Styron, R.A. 109
subject matter knowledge, good teaching and 65t, 92
Sun, M. 36
Survey of American Teachers: Challenges for School Leadership (MetLife Foundation) 20

Taylor, E.S. 47, 48
Taylor, M. 53

teacher caring, students and 79–80
teacher change: feedback and 112–13; improving instruction and 109–18, 120; in-service feedback and 114–15; models of 109–10; preservice feedback and 113–14; principal feedback and 115–18, 117t; process of 110–11, 110f; professional development (PD) and 111–12
teacher clarity 65t, 92–3
teacher communication, assessing 75–6
teacher effectiveness, measures of 38–43; alignment between multiple 51–2; classroom observations as 39–41; described 38; evaluators/observers and 42–3; Marana Unified School District example 40–1; student achievement data 41; Tucson Unified School District example 38–9, 39f; value-added (VA) scores and 33, 35–6, 41–2, 50–1; see also research on effective teaching
teacher effects, capturing 35–6; see also research on effective teaching
teacher efficacy 69
teacher enthusiasm 65t, 92–3
teacher evaluation, problems with 34
teacher expectation literature 87–8; principals use of 87–8; summary of 87
teacher expectations: administrator considerations for improving 72–3; appropriate, expressing 68–9; behavior and, changing 70; collaboration of, changing 71; described 66; improving, for entire class 71–2; increasing 73–4; individual, changing 70–1; instructional behavior and 66–8, 67t; literature 87–8; low-achieving students and 74–6; research summary of 87; student achievement and 70; student groups and 68; for student learning 65t, 66–76; students' group placement, changing 71; teacher efficacy and 69
teacher observation, order of 130–2; beginning teacher audit and 130–1; described 130; principals help for new teachers 131–2
teacher quality, redefining 34–5
Teachers College Record 45

teacher types 130
teacher workforce, greening of 26–7, 28
teaching, effective see good teaching; research on effective teaching
teaching, improving see student achievement, improving teaching and
Templeton, S. 91
time allocation, for principals 12–19; across school level 16t; observational studies of 14t, 16t, 18t; overview of 12, 19; percentage of 16t
time use: categories, principals 15, 146; good teaching and 65t, 88–9; management of, principals 126–8; proactive 126–7, 154
Timperly, H. 139
Tuckman, B.W. 116
Tucson Unified School District (TUSD) RttT example 38–9, 39f
Tyler, J.H. 47, 48
Tyler, R.W. 31

Umland, K. 35
U.S. Department of Education 126
Using Student Achievement Data to Support Instructional Decision-Making (U.S. Department of Education) 126

value-added (VA) scores 33, 50–1; opposition toward 52–4; student achievement and 41–2; teacher effects measurement and 35–6
Vásquez, C. 113
Veenman, S. 132

walk-throughs, as observation method 39–40
Wallace Foundation 5, 9
Wang, M.C. 110
Waters, T. 107, 152–3
Waxman, H.C. 113
Webb, R. 69
Weingarten, R. 52–3
Weinstein, R. 67, 68, 70, 71
Whitehurst, G. 72
Widget Effect, The 34
Wiley, C.R.H. 25
Willower, D. 12–15, 14t, 19
Witziers, B. 104
Wyckoff, J. 45–7

Yeany, R.H. 114

An environmentally friendly book printed and bound in England by www.printondemand-worldwide.com

This book is made entirely of sustainable materials; FSC paper for the cover and PEFC paper for the text pages.